MW00778228

RISK-RETURN ANALYSIS

The Theory and Practice of Rational Investing

Volume II

HARRY M. MARKOWITZ

New York   Chicago   San Francisco   Athens   London
Madrid   Mexico City   Milan   New Delhi   Singapore
Sydney   Toronto

1 2 3 4 5 6 7 8 9 0   DOC/DOC   1 2 1 0 9 8 7 6

ISBN: 978-0-07-183009-6
MHID: 0-07-183009-X

e-ISBN: 978-0-07-183010-2
e-MHID: 0-07-183010-3

Library of Congress Cataloging-in-Publication Data

Markowitz, H. (Harry), 1927-
  Risk-return analysis : the theory and practice of rational investing vol. 2 / by Harry Markowitz.
    pages cm
  Includes bibliographical references.
  ISBN-13: 978-0-07-183009-6 (alk. paper)
  ISBN-10: 0-07-183009-X (alk. paper)
  1. Investment analysis. 2. Investments—Mathematical models. 3. Portfolio management. II. Title.
  HG4529.M3755 2014
  332.6—dc23   2013018660

McGraw-Hill Education books are available at special quantity discounts to use as premiums and sales promotions, or for use in corporate training programs. To contact a representative, please visit the Contact Us page at www .mhprofessional.com.

Ode to Rationality

There once was a Rational Man,
Who loved his Rational Wife,
They had four Rational Children,
And lived a Rational Life.

They had a Rational Dog,
That chased their Rational Cat,
Who tried as it would,
Never quite could,
Catch the Irrational Rat.

—Harry M. Markowitz

"The Moving Finger writes; and, having writ,
Moves on: nor all your Piety nor Wit
    Shall lure it back to cancel half a Line,
Nor all your Tears wash out a Word of it."
—*From* The Rubaiyat of Omar Khayyam
Translated by Edward Fitzgerald

ADDENDUM TO VOLUME I

On Page 45 of Volume I, copy reads as follows:

> . . . , if two utility functions U and V are related linearly,
>
> $$V = a + bU \qquad b > 0 \qquad\qquad (11)$$
>
> the probability distribution that maximizes EU also maximizes expected variance (EV).

Copy should read as follows:

> . . . , if two utility functions U and V are related linearly,
>
> $$V = a + bU \qquad b > 0 \qquad\qquad (11)$$
>
> **The probability distribution that maximizes EU also maximizes EV.**

The "expected variance" error was mistakenly inserted during the editing process. I regret that I did not catch it in the proofs.

CONTENTS

PREFACE

This is the second volume of a four-volume book on *Risk-Return Analysis: The Theory and Practice of Rational Investing.* The *theory* upon which this book is based is the "theory of rational choice" of von Neumann and Morgenstern (1944) and L. J. Savage (1954). While this theory applies to rational choice in general, rather than to rational investing specifically, for the most part the *practice* discussed in this book involves investing. In particular, a central theme throughout the volumes of this book is that risk-return analysis—and especially mean-variance analysis—is a practical way for an investor to approximate the actions of a von Neumann and Morgenstern or L. J. Savage rational decision maker (RDM).

Volume I was concerned with *single-period* choice in risky situations with known odds. The present volume is concerned with *many-period* analyses, still assuming known odds. Volume III will be concerned with single- or many-period analyses, but with unknown odds, i.e., the case of choice under uncertainty. Volume IV will deal with items of importance to financial theory and practice that do not fit neatly into the exposition of the first three volumes.

Volume I repeatedly deplored what I refer to as the "Great Confusion" in our field, namely the confusion between necessary and sufficient conditions for the beneficial use of

mean-variance analysis. Normal (Gaussian) return distributions are a sufficient but not a necessary condition. If one
believes (as I do) that rational choice among different probability distributions requires maximizing expected utility, then
the necessary and sufficient condition for the practical applicability of mean-variance analysis is that a carefully selected
mean-variance combination from the MV efficient frontier
will approximately maximize expected utility for a wide variety
of concave (risk-averse) utility functions. A central purpose of
Volume I was to dispel the Great Confusion—by showing that,
indeed, typically the "right choice" (for the particular investor)
from an MV frontier will approximately maximize expected
utility *even when the return on the associated portfolio is* not
normally distributed.

A central purpose of the present volume concerns
the relationship between single-period choice—now—and
longer-run goals. In particular, the volume deals with issues
like investment for the long run, the asset allocation "glide-
path" that the investor should use when approaching retirement, the balancing of intergenerational investment needs
and, generally, the decision rules that should be incorporated
into financial decision support systems. In particular, the last
chapter of this volume asks what such financial decision support systems will be like a few decades from now.

WARNING: SOME MATH REQUIRED

It has come to my attention that some buyers of Volume I
expected *nonmathematical* investment advice. In fact, except for
an occasional technical endnote, the present volume assumes

as prerequisite the same level of math used in Markowitz (1959), except that the reader is assumed to know how a summation sign $\left(\sum_{i=1}^{n} \right)$ works, and will be willing and able to learn (if he or she doesn't already know) how a product sign $\left(\prod_{i=1}^{n} \right)$ works. (The rare use of a first derivative can be ignored by the reader with no calculus.) As in Markowitz (1959), the present volume contains a sequence of concepts that are well known to many, but will be a struggle for others. For example, as crucial as the concept "covariance" was to Markowitz (1959), and von Neumann and Morgenstern's "expected utility" was to Volume I of this book, so is the concept of "conditional expected value" to the present volume. It is not sufficient to "sort of get the general idea" of what conditional expected value is in order to understand many-period rational choice. One must understand the concept's formal definition, and how this relates to the "general idea"; otherwise it is impossible to follow any formal analysis. In that case, you must rely on my (or someone else's) authority rather than seeing for yourself what logic implies about the concept.

Chapter 3 of Markowitz (1959), where the math stuff starts, begins with a section titled "Mathematics and You" that offers advice like "don't try to speed-read this volume" and "do try to understand proofs." I have one more word of advice: Do not be discouraged if you don't understand a concept the first time you read it. Think about it; perhaps read on a bit to see how the concept is used, and then return to the definition of the concept.

A few "hard" proofs are segregated into one or more paragraphs headed **PROOF** and ending **QED**. These may be skipped or skimmed by "nonmathematicians." Otherwise, "proofs" are part of the text, as explanations as to what implies what, and why.

As to those who are already quite familiar with such things as conditional expected value, "strategy" as defined by von Neumann and Morgenstern, and the dynamic programming principle, I hope that Markowitz (1959) is a sufficient demonstration that it is possible for a book to take the time to bring a dedicated newcomer up to speed on requisite basic principles, and then go on to present novel ideas that are worth the attention of thought leaders in several fields of both theory and practice.

TIME MARCHES ON

The following true—but misleading—story appears in print now and then, including once in the *Wall Street Journal* by a well-known financial columnist. When I worked at the RAND Corporation, circa 1952, I was offered the choice of a stock/bond portfolio in the form of CREF versus TIAA. I chose a 50-50 mix. My reasoning was that if the stock market rose a great deal, I would regret it if I was completely out of the market. Conversely, if stocks fell a great deal and I had nothing in bonds, I would also have regrets. My 50-50 split minimized maximum regret. The conclusion that some commentators draw from this story is that even Markowitz, creator of MPT, does not use MPT in his own choice of portfolio.

The 50-50 split was my choice at age 25 in 1952. *But* it would *not* be my recommendation for a 25-year-old *now*. My recommendation now would be much more heavily weighted toward equities, perhaps as much as 100 percent equities, depending on the individual's willingness to put up with fluctuations in portfolio value in the short run. Between 1952 and now a vast MPT infrastructure has been built. In 1952 there was the Markowitz (1952a) article, but no optimizers had been programmed, and no return-series data (such as that of Ibbotson 2014, or Dimson, Marsh, and Staunton 2002) were readily available. Nor had there been decades of discussion on how to use the MPT apparatus, as I have since enjoyed with the friends and colleagues I thanked in the acknowledgments in Volume I.

As to how I invest now, I have participated in the generation and use of efficient frontiers by many of my clients (such as 1st Global of Dallas, Texas, sponsor of this book, and GuidedChoice, described in Chapter 7) using forward-looking estimates of the means, variances, and covariances for the now commonly used asset classes. I know from repeated exposure the approximate asset class mix that I prefer, and I invest in that mix, roughly. I implement my choice with ETFs for equities, and with individual bonds for fixed income.

My theoretical views have also evolved over time. For example, the focal subject of Volume I of the present book— namely, the efficacy of mean-variance approximations to expected utility—was not in my 1952 paper: It made its first appearance in my 1959 book. The relationships presented in 1952—between the mean and variance of a portfolio and the means, variances, and covariances of securities—did not change. These are mathematical relationships. But *how* the relationships are to be applied, and the justification for their use, has evolved over time, with the largest change in my views occurring between 1952 and 1959. (Markowitz 2010a contains a detailed comparison of the views I held in 1959 versus those I held in 1952.)

A more immediate example of the evolution of my views is the fact that the present volume is not exactly as forecasted in Volume I. The basic topic is still rational investment for the many-period game with known odds, but the precise contents evolved in some unanticipated directions as I reexamined the subject in greater detail. In particular, as my exposition in Chapter 6 (the first chapter of this volume) unfolded, it became clear that the traditional portrayal of "The Investor" as a lone wolf, and the portfolio selection process as having only one stakeholder, was wide of the mark. This led to the exploration and inclusion of paths that I had not anticipated originally.

Nevertheless, Volume II as forecast is still here, including the dynamic programming principle, the Mossin-Samuelson model, the Markowitz–van Dijk quadratic approximation to the dynamic programming "derived utility function," and the Blay-Markowitz tax-cognizant portfolio analysis.

FRIENDLY DISPUTANTS

The *theory* we present in this volume consists of what Hume refers to as logical or mathematical *relationships between ideas.* Unless I have a bug in a proof somewhere, these relationships are beyond dispute. What is disputable—and disputed!—is how the principles encapsulated in these relationships are to be applied to practical issues. I have not been shy about forcefully arguing my own views on such issues. Inevitably I have disagreed with colleagues for whom I have the highest respect. Paul Samuelson is the most outstanding example. Other examples include Chhabra, Evensky, Ibbotson, Merton, Shefrin, Statman, and others. My friends know that I get great joy and much value from the give-and-take dialectic process that characterizes a living, growing field of knowledge. I take no offense when a colleague proposes to take investors "Beyond Markowitz," and expect none to be taken when I, in turn, offer to take investors "Beyond 'Beyond Markowitz.'"

As I said, all this is known to my friends. I just want to assure third-party readers that—almost tautologically—I have the highest respect for those whose views I consider worth reproducing here, whether or not I agree with those views.

AUTHORSHIP

The section in Chapter 11 on the Blay-Markowitz TCPA (tax-cognizant portfolio analysis) is the joint work of Ken Blay and me. Other than that, all words penned, as well as the views expressed, are mine. In the preface to Volume I, after thanking 1st Global in general and Tony Batman in particular for sponsoring this book, I noted that "Kenneth Blay has been my chief contact with 1st Global on this and other matters. . . . Given our close and continuing relationship in the production of this book, it seemed to me that the appropriate acknowledgment for Ken Blay was to list him as a joint author. This relationship continued until recently, but now Ken is no longer a 1st Global employee. (This too has changed.) I have not taken the trouble to change "we" to "I" for most of this volume, except for Chapter 12 which is listed as an essay by me. This is because Chapter 12 contains recommendations for the building of real-time decision support systems that are contrary to the currently accepted doctrine by the leaders in this field. A crucial piece of my argument is based on personal experience with an alternative approach: I have been there; done that; it really works a lot better than the way things are done currently. By writing in the first person singular, I could say "I" instead of "Markowitz says."

ACKNOWLEDGMENTS

The writing of this volume gave me the opportunity to reexamine my positions on many aspects of the portfolio selection context, temporal and otherwise, and to write out my current views on these matters, including both longstanding views and those developed concurrently with writing. As in Volume I, I wish to express my indebtedness to Stephen A. (Tony) Batman for making this all possible. I also want to thank Mary Margaret (Midge) McDonald for patiently deciphering and typing countless drafts in which I moved great batches of heavily edited material from here to there; Lilli Therese Alexander, who tracked down and processed reference information along with her other duties at Harry Markowitz Company; GanLin Xu, who read this entire volume and made invaluable observations and suggestions; and Barbara Markowitz for her unfailing interest and encouragement.

Harry M. Markowitz

San Diego, CA

March 2016

6

THE PORTFOLIO SELECTION CONTEXT

INTRODUCTION

The four volumes of this book are concerned with the theory and practice of rational investing and, in particular, how risk-return analysis can help human decision makers (HDMs) approximate such investing. As in Volume I of this book, and in Markowitz (1959), we postulate rational decision makers (RDMs) who are like HDMs in their institutions, motivations, and limited information, but who differ from HDMs in having faultless logic, unlimited instantaneous computing capacity and, as we saw in Chapter 1, the ability to accurately perceive their own preferences.

We view the RDM as a platonic ideal that we seek to emulate. The basic assumption of such an approach is that *if we do it right*, such emulation will improve our own human investment process. Obviously, "doing it right" does *not* mean attempting calculations that are assumed to be trivial for the RDM but are impractical for the HDM. It means, rather, finding economical methods by which the HDM can approximate the actions—and results—of the RDM. Hence the focus throughout much of Volume I was on risk-return approximations to expected utility, after having established in Chapter 1 the role of expected utility maximization in RDM choice.

Volume I was concerned with single-period decision making with known odds, and especially with how to choose between alternative portfolio return distributions. The present volume places such decisions into their *context*. This context has two major aspects: One aspect has to do with time and the other aspect has to do with the overall opportunities, constraints, and goals of the investor. We will view the choice of portfolio "today" as a "move" in a many-period game. The proper choice of move depends in part on how today's returns are related to opportunities that might be available "tomorrow." It also depends on the other aspect of context, namely the investor's degrees of freedom and objectives for its "game-as-a-whole."

The Mossin (1968) and Samuelson (1969) game, presented in Chapter 9, considers an investor who starts with initial wealth W_0, reinvests it without further deposits or withdrawals until some predetermined end time, and whose utility depends only on his or her final wealth W_T. Even with these very restrictive assumptions, the investor's actions *now* are highly dependent on the Pratt (1964) and Arrow (1965) *risk aversion* characteristics of the utility function $U(W_T)$. A seemingly minor change in the form of $U(\ )$ may lead to major changes in the implied optimal investment behavior.

When we move from highly stylized to real-world investors, additional opportunities, constraints, and objectives must be taken into account, either formally by our analyses or intuitively by the investor. For example, perhaps "the investor" is a couple investing both for their retirement and for other major expenditures such as a larger house or their children's college. How should their choice of portfolio today, including the location of assets in accounts with varying liquidity and tax treatments, be made in light of their multiple objectives? Alternatively, the portfolio to be selected could support a corporation's DB (defined benefit) pension plan. In that case "the investor" is the corporation that supplies these benefits. This raises questions such as: Is it sufficient to seek to stabilize the value of assets minus liabilities as proposed by Sharpe and Tint (1990)? Or need one take into account the correlation between these funding needs and the profitability of the corporation's principal business? If so, should these be taken into account formally in our models or intuitively by the model user?

TEMPORAL STRUCTURE AND TODAY'S CHOICE

A simple example will illustrate how the *joint distribution* of

1. return "this period" and
2. opportunities in later periods

affect portfolio choice today. Consider a game with three points in time—labeled 0, 1, and 2—that are the start and/or end points of two intervals (or periods) labeled 1 and 2, as follows:

Time intervals |____1____|____2____|

Time points   0   1   2

Beginning with wealth W_0 at time zero, the investor chooses a probability distribution of return, R_1, for period 1. After R_1 is generated, the investor reinvests (with no transaction costs) his or her wealth, now equal to

$$W_1 = W_0(1 + R_1)$$

and receives return R_2, ending with wealth

$$W_2 = W_0(1 + R_1)(1 + R_2)$$

The investor seeks a mean-variance efficient distribution of W_2 that approximately maximizes the expected value of a concave utility function $U(W_2)$.

Two portfolios are available at time point 0. The investor must choose one or the other and cannot split its funds between them. The values of the two portfolios at time point 1 (at the end of time interval 1) depend on the outcome (A or B) of some event, as follows:

	A	B
Portfolio One	$a + b$	$a - b$
Portfolio Two	$a - b$	$a + b$

where a and b are dollar amounts and $b \neq 0$. At time point 1 only one portfolio will be available. This will have a sure return of

$(a + b)$ if A occurred during the first time interval and

$(a - b)$ if B occurred

Thus if Portfolio One is chosen at time point 0, there is a 50-50 chance that final wealth will equal

$$W_2 = \begin{cases} (a+b)^2 \\ (a-b)^2 \end{cases} \text{ or}$$

whereas if Portfolio Two is chosen, final wealth will, for sure, be

$$W_2 = (a + b)(a - b)$$
$$= a^2 - b^2$$

Portfolio One has the higher expected value of W_2, since

$$\frac{1}{2}\left((a + b)^2 + (a - b)^2\right) > \frac{1}{2}\left(2(a + b)(a - b)\right)$$

On the other hand, if Portfolio Two is chosen, W_2 has zero variance. The choice between the two portfolios at time point 0 depends on the investor's tradeoff between risk and return on W_2, which, in turn, depends on the investor's utility function, $U(W_2)$.

The preceding is a hypothetical example of how the returns this year for different portfolios may be related differently to the investment opportunities in the following year (or years). The balance of this section notes two such situations that arose in practice.

Chapter 11 includes sections on the Markowitz and van Dijk (2003) (MvD) heuristic for approximately maximizing the expected utility of an investment-consumption game with a changing forecasted return distribution. This arose out of a situation in which Markowitz (who has an optimization specialty) consulted for Erik van Dijk, who has a forecasting specialty. A hypothetical example reported in Markowitz and van Dijk (2003) and recounted in Chapter 11 contains two assets, a "stock" and cash, and includes a stock forecasting model that can be in five states: from very pessimistic to very optimistic. The mean and variance of the stock depend on the predictive state of the forecasting model. The model includes transition probabilities from one predictive state to each of the other predictive states, and transaction costs for changing one's portfolio. The discussion in Chapter 11 also reports the Kritzman, Myrgren, and Page (2009) application of the MvD algorithm, in fact, to the rebalancing of portfolios managed by State Street Bank, and others.

The number of possible system states is small enough in the MvD experiments, and in some reported in Kritzman et al., to compute the optimum move in every possible state. MvD and Kritzman et al. compare expected utility for the game-as-a-whole of (1) the optimum solution, (2) the MvD heuristic, and (3) heuristics other than that of MvD. The MvD heuristic compares favorably with the optimum strategy, and does substantially better than commonly used alternative heuristics.

Thus the MvD heuristic, like the optimum strategy, *better accounts for the intertemporal context* than do other heuristics.

In a different area, Macaulay (1938) and Fisher and Weil (1971) each consider a situation in which an investor would like a bond that makes a single payment in $\tilde{T}$ years, but no such bond is available. Macaulay defines what is now called "Macaulay duration" as

$$T_M = \sum_{i=1}^{T_{MAX}} \frac{PV_i}{V}\, t_i$$

where T_M is the Macaulay duration; T_{MAX} is the number of time units (e.g., months) until the furthest out payment; t_i is the number of time units until the ith payment; PV_i is the present value of the amount of the payment, and V is the total of such present values. Macaulay shows for a flat yield curve (whereas Fisher and Weil shows for a sloped yield curve) that if the yield curve shifts parallel to itself, the bond portfolio is sure to be worth at least V at time $\tilde{T}$ provided that $T_M = \tilde{T}$.

Thus even if no one has any predictive ability for equities, fixed-income instruments have important intertemporal relationships for mathematical rather than empirical reasons.

STAKEHOLDERS VERSUS "THE INVESTOR"

A many-period analysis involving investment is usually modeled as a single-person consumption-investment game whose sole player is referred to as "the investor." Such was the case, for example, in the Markowitz (1959) Chapter 11 discussion of many-period rational decision making with known odds.

Actual consumption-investment choice, however, usually involves more than one utility-seeking entity. In particular, the so-called individual investor is often a household consisting traditionally of a couple who make consumption-investment decisions on behalf of a family. Even if minor children including infants play no role in the decision-making process, decisions are made in part on their behalf. The tradeoff between now and later is typically different for parents (or a single parent) than for unmarried persons.

Institutional portfolio selection also typically involves choices that mediate the interests of many parties. The interested parties in the portfolio of a municipal DB plan, for example, include the taxpayers whose taxes might be increased if the pension plan portfolio sustains large losses; the investors whose bonds might default or, at least, have their ratings lowered; the persons or organizations who run the portfolio; and, of course, the employees whose benefits might be cut if the municipality defaults—in part because of the burden of its pension plan.

The choice of portfolio of a large private university endowment, for another example, must balance the present and future needs of students, faculty, administration, and university benefactors. Present versus future interests are obviously at stake with respect to decisions concerning the rate of spending from the portfolio, but also with respect to the rate of substitution between long-run growth versus short-run stability which, in turn, has implications for the limits that should be placed on the holding of illiquid assets including real estate and private equity.

One person may be a stakeholder in many portfolios. For example, a professor in the university in the preceding paragraph may be a taxpayer in the paragraph before that, and have a fiduciary role, jointly with his wife, regarding his family's retirement portfolio.

The von Neumann and Morgenstern (1944) game-theory solutions, on the one hand, and that of John Nash (1950b and 1951), on the other, are described as "cooperative" in the former case and "noncooperative" in the latter. But a "cooperative solution" in the von Neumann and Morgenstern sense does not mean that everyone pulls together for the common good. Rather, in the three-person zero-sum game, for example, it means that two players form a coalition to their advantage and to the disadvantage of the third. While such games are often played in fact by potential heirs to large fortunes, we will seek solutions that promote the interests of all appropriate parties. Such solutions are the subject of the theory of *social choice* as pioneered by Kenneth Arrow (1951). Arrow's grand theorem and subsequent reactions to it are the topic of our Chapter 10.

INVESTOR ROLES

"The investor" in a stylized consumption-investment model combines several investor roles. These are best seen in situations where different roles are assumed by different entities. For example, suppose that a wealthy father sets up a revocable trust for a single-parent daughter and her two children.

The trust instructions specify that the earnings from the trust are to be used for the support of the daughter while she lives, whereas the remainder is to be split between the two grandchildren. The trust is put into the hands of a trust company, which assigns it to one of its trust officers. In this situation who is the investor, who are the stakeholders, and who is the decision maker?

If we define the investor to be the legal owner of the trust with power to change it, then the father is the investor since the trust is revocable. Stakeholders in the portfolio-choice decision include the father, his daughter, her two children, the trust officer, the trust company, and, therefore, all the trust company's stakeholders. Each of these would be disadvantaged by a disastrous loss in the trust portfolio. The decision makers in this situation are the trust officer who selects the securities that constitute the portfolio, the management of the trust company which can replace the trust officer, and the trustor who can withdraw the trust from the trust company. If each of these were an RDM, then each would seek or encourage action to maximize the expected values of the utilities of their respective games-as-a-whole.

DIVERSIFICATION NEEDS AND OPPORTUNITIES: RECOGNIZED AND UNRECOGNIZED

Central concerns of portfolio theory are the benefits of diversification and the role of correlated risks in the efficient allocation of resources. The usual applications of MPT (Modern Portfolio Theory) concern the allocation of the financial assets of households or of institutions such as endowments and pension funds. There are however other risk-return aspects of business that are essentially portfolio selection situations. Sometimes these are recognized as such; sometimes they are not.

In agriculture Reid and Tew (1987) show that the crop selection problem fits naturally into the general portfolio selection framework. Sam Savage (2009) shows that the locations of oil well drilling projects are also a classical portfolio selection problem. Jagpal (1999) added risk analysis to a marketing analysis literature that traditionally ignored risk. Texts on corporate finance, such as Brealey, Myers, and Allen (2008) and Bierman and Smidt (2007), routinely discuss MPT and CAPM (the capital asset pricing model) in connection with capital budgeting and project selection.

On the other hand the following are two examples of portfolio selection situations that are not recognized as such: Valentas, Levine, and Clark (1991), *Food Processing Operations and Scale-Up*, explains the economics of building large-scale facilities to process foods at an industrial level. A principal concern of the authors is the calculation of the net present value of the investments and rewards from a particular product line. The authors' analysis is fine as far as it goes, but it neglects the uncertainties in these present values and the correlations between them.

Towler and Sinnott (2013), in *Chemical Engineering Design: Principles, Practice and Economics of Plant and Process Design*, include a chapter (its Chapter 9) titled "Economic Evaluation of Projects," including a section titled "Project Portfolio Selection." But diversification and correlation are nowhere mentioned.

In each of the preceding cases some kind of portfolio needs to be chosen in light of the benefits of diversification, with a mind to the tradeoff between portfolio risk and return. But the context is the needs of a business and its stakeholders rather than, e.g., a family with its own multiple needs.

AGENDA: ANALYSIS, JUDGMENT, AND DECISION SUPPORT SYSTEMS

Portfolio theory draws from two traditions:

1. The theory of rational behavior under risk and uncertainty
2. Operations research (OR)

The first provides us goals to be sought by ourselves as investors or on behalf of the investors we advise. The second provides us techniques by which to achieve—or at least move investment choice in the direction of—these goals. Both traditions play an essential role. A goal that cannot be approached is useless. Efficiently achieving the wrong goal can be worse.

OR uses either optimization or simulation models, or both combined, to seek better decisions. Frequently optimization finds the precisely right answer to a highly simplified (perhaps too simplified) representation of the real problems, whereas simulation techniques test heuristic solutions to a more detailed model of the world. In particular, optimum solutions to simplified models is one kind of heuristic that can be tested in more complex simulation models.

This volume offers theorems, techniques, and advice with respect to both optimization and simulation. In particular, Chapter 7 offers advice as to how to plan, implement, and document a nontrivial simulation analysis. Central to this advice is the EAS-E (Entity, Attribute, Set, and Event) view of simulation programming. This view of a system to be simulated is part of the various SIMSCRIPT programming languages (described in Chapter 7), but it can be used independently of them. In particular, Chapter 7 illustrates EAS-E concepts with the JLMSim stock market simulator that was planned using the EAS-E worldview and programmed in C++.

Chapter 7 also discusses the Markowitz (1991) proposed "game-of-life" simulator. This simulator would model the financial planning process of which portfolio selection is a piece. The ultimate goal of this model would be to help develop better procedures for financial planning generally, including the portfolio selection process as one kind of "move" in the financial planning "game." One recurring theme in the following chapters concerns issues that need to be resolved to produce a game-of-life simulator whose results would be worth heeding.

Finally Chapter 7 discusses financial decision support systems (DSSs) using the GuidedChoice (GC) DSS as an example. A DSS has a boundary—with the computer's optimizers, simulators, heuristics, and required bookkeeping inside—and human decision makers on the outside. The latter may include financial advisors as well as "the client." The boundary provides for communication between the two sides. A principal objective of the game-of-life simulator is to move the boundary of rational financial DSSs out beyond portfolio selection to include financial planning more generally. We have located the discussion of DSS development in Chapter 7 because we recommend the use of the EAS-E view in the planning, implementation, and documentation of DSSs as well as simulators. We illustrate this with an extensive extract from the EAS (Entity, Attribute, and Set) table used to plan and document the GC DSS database.

Much of the remainder of this volume is devoted to optimization, both exact and approximate. In particular, Chapter 8 includes (1) concepts from von Neumann and Morgenstern (1944), *Theory of Games and Economic Behavior*, including the notion of the utility of the game as a whole; and (2) Bellman's (1957) *dynamic programming (DP) principle*. The latter asserts that the solution to the problem of maximizing the expected utility of a many-period game can be reduced to a sequence of single-period expected utility maximizations. This in turn is an application of a fundamental theorem concerning *conditional expected value*. Chapter 8 treats conditional probability and conditional expected value at length, including their interpretation as information and their relationship to the DP solution of the many-period game.

Chapter 9 presents the Mossin (1968) and Samuelson (1969) model and its optimum solutions found using DP. Its solution implies that its single player does *not* become more cautious as it approaches retirement. This has generated considerable discussion concerning (a) what it means to invest for the long run, and (b) how to modify the model so that plausible "glide paths" are optimal. These spin-offs from the Mossin-Samuelson work are also discussed in Chapter 9.

Chapter 10 considers the social choice aspect of portfolio selection, in light of a portfolio's multiple stakeholders. The chapter reviews Arrow's (1951) "impossibility theorem" and the responses to it by Goodman and Markowitz (1952), Hildreth (1953), and Luce and Raiffa (1957). It also proposes a social choice rule of our own.

Chapter 11, titled "Judgment and Approximation," addresses the gap between the optimization computations that an RDM is assumed to be capable of and the limited capabilities of HDMs and their computers.[1] In particular, the chapter includes (i) a review of the Markowitz (1959) proposals in this area; (ii) the Markowitz and van Dijk algorithm for approximately solving dynamic games; (iii) the Blay and Markowitz TCPA (tax-cognizant portfolio analysis); and (iv) our views on "buckets" heuristics.

Chapter 12 presents experts' views on the future of computing, and Markowitz's views as to how to best use future computing capabilities to build financial (and other) decision support systems.

We will not cover stochastic linear programming (SLP) models in this volume for reasons that we explain in Endnote 4 of Chapter 8. Also we will not cover continuous-time models in this volume because

1. The level of math they require far exceeds that assumed here.[2]

2. Security prices do not evolve continuously in time, markets are not perfectly liquid, and investors cannot alter portfolio holdings continuously in time, as

typically assumed in continuous-time models. This can be of great practical importance.[3]

3. Additional counterfactual assumptions are typically made in order to produce much-prized explicit solutions. For example, the Black and Scholes (1973) option-pricing model assumes that the log of the price of the underlying stock or index is a Brownian motion, whereas Markowitz and Usmen (1996) show that, in the case of daily moves in the log of the S&P 500, a Bayesian would shift belief *against* the Black-Scholes hypothesis, in favor of a student's *t* distribution with between 4 and 5 degrees of freedom, by a factor of roughly 10^{70}.

Financial products that use leverage and assume a geometric Brownian motion for an underlying return distribution have often crashed spectacularly during financial crises.

Every model that an OR specialist builds to meet some practical need involves hypotheses about what aspects of an enormously complex reality need to be represented in the model, and how "unseen forces," like a return generation process, are to be modeled. As with any hypothesis about the real world, the grand hypothesis—namely "the model" including what was incorporated and what was assumed—needs to be tested. In the first instance such testing may be done by back-testing or Monte Carlo; but the ultimate test is experience in practice. The modeler should be prepared to modify the model based on such experience. Explicitly optimizable models are fragile in the sense that slight changes in a model can move it from solved to unsolved. "Unsolved" may mean anything from "easily solved again" to "unsolvable." Between these two extremes is, "The solution would earn a PhD degree."

*The practical model builder cannot afford to rely **solely** on a methodology as fragile as explicitly solvable models.* It must be conceded, however, that continuous-time models may suggest heuristics that can be tested in more detailed, discrete-event models. See Merton (1990) for a survey of his and his followers' work on continuous-time models.

Our views on the relative merits of simulation versus analytically solvable models in the analysis of market dynamics and portfolio choice are not unique to us (see Levy, Levy, and Solomon 2000 for a survey), but they are far from the generally accepted approach today. For example, a PhD candidate asked Markowitz's advice on a computation by the student that had not converged despite dozens of hours of supercomputer time. The computation sought the solution to equations that took into account certain illiquidities that were central to the problem posed, but that are typically ignored in the economic literature. Markowitz noted that if the student simulated rather than seeking a numerical solution to his equations, his model could be more realistic—taking into account whatever seemed essential to the problem rather than being just one step beyond the current literature. Further, with a fraction of the computer time he had already spent, he could sample so intensively that he would have approximately the same accuracy as the numeric solution he sought. Finally, his numeric solution would only make intuitive sense if he used it to answer specific questions, or varied parameters to show tradeoff curves. The same questions could be answered and tradeoff curves generated for a more credible model using simulation.

The student said he would think about it. A week or two later he reported that he had spoken with one of the senior professors on his campus, that the professor agreed that the model could be made much more realistic—and useful—if simulation were used. But the problem, according to the professor, was that the results would never get published. Since the student intended to seek a job in the publish-or-perish business, he continued his search for a numeric solution to his equations. (Eventually the computation converged, and he did get a PhD degree and a job.)

It is not true that outside-the-box papers do not get published. Eventually they do, and they are the ones that have broad impact, win prizes, and are widely cited. As Max Planck famously said, "Science advances one funeral at a time." Those who defend the old are replaced by those who are ready to move on to the new. (It remains to be seen, of course, whether the views presented herein are the wave of the future, or a blind alley, as some may contend.)

7

MODELING DYNAMIC SYSTEMS

INTRODUCTION

As noted in the previous chapter, operations research (OR) techniques used to assist investment decisions need to include simulation as well as optimization procedures. For example, a half-dozen uses of financial simulation to be found in this volume are:

1. The GuidedChoice (GC) decision support system (DSS) includes simulation analysis to estimate the likely consequences of decisions by the investor being served.

2. Endnote 3 of Chapter 6 refers to the Kim and Markowitz (1989) simulator. This is a market simulator consisting of two types of investors: rebalancers and portfolio insurers. The purpose of this simulator, and the analyses performed with it, was to help settle a dispute between Harry Markowitz and Fischer Black as to the consequences of having

different proportions of the market following one strategy versus the other.

3. The Markowitz and van Dijk algorithm for approximating the dynamic programming solution to many-period games with large "state spaces," described in Chapter 11, uses a combination of simulation and search techniques.

4. The Blay and Markowitz TCPA (tax-cognizant portfolio analysis), also described in Chapter 11, uses the "TSim" simulator to transform an output stream of security or asset class returns:

   • *from* an institution's non-tax-cognizant simulator

   • *to* present values of an investor's after-tax consumption

5. The present chapter illustrates simulator concepts with examples drawn from JLMSim of Jacobs, Levy, and Markowitz (2004). This simulator includes investors who reoptimize periodically, generating orders that they pass to traders. Prices are endogenous, resulting from reoptimization and trading actions.

6. The Markowitz (1991) proposed "game-of-life" simulator, also described later in this chapter, seeks to help financial planning generally, of which portfolio selection is a part.

Clearly financial OR individuals and teams should be facile with both simulation and optimization.

The remainder of this chapter begins with some definitions concerning simulation analysis generally, introduces the

EAS-E (Entity, Attribute, Set, and Event) worldview that has been used for simulation analysis for more than half a century, and then proceeds as outlined at the end of Chapter 6.

DEFINITIONS

A *simulation model* refers to logical relationships independently of how these are programmed. In particular, two programs (perhaps programmed in two different programming languages) that implement the same model should produce the same output from a given input.

A *simulator* (a.k.a. simulation program) is a computer program that implements a simulation model. It typically has a few or many parameters that must be specified for any specific *simulation run*. For example, the market simulator that is the principal example in this chapter allows its user to specify the number of investors of various types to be represented in a particular simulation run.

There are two ways in which two simulation runs with the same simulator may differ from each other:

1. All input parameters are the same in the two runs except for the starting *random number seed or seeds* used by one or more random number generators. Two such runs are viewed as different *random draws* from the same *specific model*, or *special case* of a general model.

   In the case of *backtests*, as opposed to *Monte Carlo analysis*, historical data are used in place of randomly generated inputs. Two backtests of the same specific model would differ only with respect to the historical data used.

2. A *different case* of the same general model results if parameters other than random seeds or historical data are changed.

A *simulation analysis* is typically based on a large number of simulation runs, some of which (for a Monte Carlo analysis) randomly replicate a particular special case of the general model. Other runs (for either a Monte Carlo analysis or a backtest) explore other special cases. These special cases are usually chosen to test one or more hypotheses, or to test the sensitivity of the results to variations in certain parameters, or to search for optimal parameter settings for some problem.

Financial simulators can be classified as representing either (A) single-player games or (B) many-player games. Of the six simulation analyses listed in the preceding section, the simulators in applications 1, 3, and 4 are single-player. Those in 2, 5, and 6 are many-player. In the three single-player games and in the many-player game-of-life simulator, security or asset class returns are independent of the investor's actions. In the other two many-player simulation analyses, returns are the results of player interactions.

THE EAS-E WORLDVIEW

The EAS-E (Entity, Attribute, Set, and Event) view of dynamic systems was first presented in *SIMSCRIPT: A Simulation Programming Language* by Markowitz, Hausner, and Karr (1963). We will refer to the original SIMSCRIPT as SIMSCRIPT (I), to distinguish it from subsequent versions titled SIMSCRIPT I.5, II, II.5, and III. These various versions of SIMSCRIPT will be discussed later in this chapter.

The most obvious difference between SIMSCRIPT (I) and the "standard" programming languages of that day was the central role that the EAS-E worldview played in SIMSCRIPT (I). But more fundamental than that was a difference in the objectives of SIMSCRIPT (I) as compared to those of conventional programming languages. The latter sought to tell the computer what actions it (the computer) should take. In particular, assembly language provided its programmer with the capability of specifying specific registers and storage locations to use in taking elementary machine actions. A higher-level language, such as FORTRAN, required the programmer to think and code in terms of variables and arrays, leaving a program "compiler" to figure out where and how these variables and arrays would be stored and accessed.

SIMSCRIPT (I) was a preprocessor into FORTRAN II, and therefore used precisely the same variables and arrays as did FORTRAN II. But SIMSCRIPT (I) programmers were not supposed to *think* in terms of variables and arrays. Rather, they were supposed to think in terms of the world *as they wanted to portray it*: what *types of entities* would populate their simulations, what *attributes and set relationships* would characterize the *status* of these entities at any instant of time, what kinds of *events* would alter status, and what caused these events to occur. It was up to the SIMSCRIPT (I) preprocessor to figure how these modeling specifications would be represented in variables, arrays, and FORTRAN II routines.

Thus the principal objective of SIMSCRIPT (I)—and of each of the SIMSCRIPTs that followed—was not to be a programming language, but essentially to be an "executable modeling language." It sought to allow the modeler to conveniently specify the world to be simulated, the analyses to be performed on this world, and how the results of these analyses were to be displayed—hence, for example, commands in all SIMSCRIPTs to process entities and sets, the WYSIWYG (What You See Is What You Get) report generation facilities of all SIMSCRIPTs, and SIMSCRIPTs II.5 and III's 2D and 3D graphical facilities.

The SIMSCRIPTs have been used commercially for decades to build simulators for a great variety of real-world dynamic systems. See Markowitz (1979) for examples, or the CACI website for examples and testimonials. In particular, the CACI website reports that "SIMSCRIPT III™ . . . [is used] world-wide by US Military, FAA, NASA, NATO, Lockheed Martin, JSF [Joint Strike Fighter], Canadian National Railways, Telecom France, Space Research Institute Brazil, etc." Exhibit 7.1 contains an e-mail forwarded to us by Ana Marjanski (Head, Technical Department, CACI Advanced Simulation Lab) in response to our request for an example we could quote. It describes a SIMSCRIPT simulator "extensively used by the United States, NATO, and over 20 countries for decision analyses, contingency/management plan evaluation, experimentation, emergency preparedness training, command post exercise support, and the creation of a coalition coordination environment suitable for use by groups of multi-national civil and military agencies." (The emphasis in the exhibit was also in the e-mail.)

The EAS-E view of dynamic systems can also be of value even when SIMSCRIPT is not used. For example, JLMSim was conceived in EAS-E terms but programmed in C++. As sketched in the next section, the EAS-E view helps organize one's thoughts about a simulator, whatever programming language is used.

EXHIBIT 7.1 The Joint Theater Level Simulation

The **Joint Theater Level Simulation (JTLS)** is a web-enabled, interactive wargaming and Operational Plan (OPLAN) analysis system. **The core model for JTLS is written in SIMSCRIPT.** JTLS is extensively used by the United States, NATO, and over 20 countries for decision analyses, contingency/management plan evaluation, experimentation, emergency preparedness training, command post exercise support, and the creation of a coalition coordination environment suitable for use by groups of multi-national civil and military agencies.

JTLS users gain insight into the problems and importance of effective information sharing, interoperability, and coordination in response to natural disasters or military conflicts requiring either regional or worldwide response efforts. The simulation has been connected to most Common Operational Pictures and many C4ISR systems. It has been offered to the US OSD as a decision support capability for Effects-Based Fiscal Planning (EBFP). JTLS is an easily configurable, flexible system that can be used by one person conducting an analysis or by over 200 users in an exercise decision environment.

(*continued*)

EXHIBIT 7.1 (*Continued*)

JTLS started development in 1983 and is still under constant expansion and improvement in 2015. The system has grown along with the advancements in computer technology over the entire 30-year spectrum. **This was possible in part because of the ease with which a well-defined model structure can be defined using the SIMSCRIPT programming language.** It is configuration managed by the US Joint Staff/J7, Suffolk, Virginia. The simulation is developed, maintained, and distributed by ROLANDS & ASSOCIATES Corporation from Del Rey Oaks, California. Information about JTLS and its availability may be obtained by contacting Dr. R. Jay Roland at President@ROLANDS.com or reviewing more detailed information concerning the system at www.rolands.com.

THE MODELING PROCESS

Often, in the early stages of what is to become a simulator for one or more simulation analyses, a vague notion is conceived as to the desirability of a program with certain capabilities. The specifics take form as the major entities of the simulator, and some of their attributes and set relationships, are decided upon and recorded in a preliminary EAS (Entity, Attribute, and Set) table (such as is illustrated later), and the major events of the simulated world are sketched. Further reflection and discussion fills in details. It is essential that this EAS status and event description be well developed before coding starts.

The same EAS and event description tables that are used to plan the simulator, plus additions and modifications made in the course of simulator development, can be used to document the program. This gives the interested reader greater precision as to the contents of the simulator than is provided by a general verbal or graphical description.

This process, by which simulator details are crystallized, is invariably part of a broader process for which the simulator serves a need. In the six simulator examples listed in the first section of this chapter:

- Example 1 was part of the GC decision support system.
- Example 2 was in response to an assertion by Fischer Black whose accuracy Markowitz sought to test.
- Example 3 is part of a heuristic for solving large-scale dynamic programs.
- Example 4 is part of a methodology for tax-cognizant portfolio analysis.
- Example 5 was programmed to illustrate how the analysis of capital markets can transcend classical CAPM bounds.
- Example 6 is proposed for a future generation of financial DSSs.

With examples ranging from the KM model, programmed to advance an academic discussion, to the example in Exhibit 7.1, developed to assist worldwide operations, it is difficult to generalize about the context in which simulators arise. It seems safe to say, however, that an understanding of simulation modeling is useful (perhaps essential) to the producers and consumers of practical OR models in general, and financial models in particular.

AN EAS EXAMPLE

Table 7.1 (extending from below to the middle of page 34) presents part of the EAS structure of the JLMSim stock market simulator of Jacobs, Levy, and Markowitz (2004). As previously noted, this simulator was conceived in EAS-E terms and programmed in C++. After a brief description of JLMSim objectives, we use the specifics of Table 7.1 to illustrate EAS status descriptors and their documentation.

TABLE 7.1 EAS Description of JLMSim 1.0 (Extract)*

Entity Types	Attributes	Sets Owned	Member or Data Type
TheSystem			
	SimTime		Real
	RFLendRatePerDay		Real
	BrokerRatePerDay		Real
	Liquidation_trader_nr		Integer
		Securities	Security
		KeptTradingDays	Day
		KeptMonths	Month
		Statisticians	Statistician
		PortfolioAnalysts	PortfolioAnalyst
		InvestorsTemplates	Investor _template

TABLE 7.1 (*Continued*)

Entity Types	Attributes	Sets Owned	Member or Data Type
Security			
	LastTradePrice		Real
	Price		Real
	StartOfDayPrice		Real
	StartOfMonthPrice		Real
	VolumeSoFarToday		Integer
		Buy_orders	Order
		Sell_orders	Order
Security_X_Day			
	DailyReturn		Real
	DailyVolume		Integer
	DailyClosePrice		Real
Security_X_Month			
	MonthlyReturn		Real
	MonthlyVolume		Integer
	MonthlyClosePrice		Real
Statistician			
	EstMethodForMeans		Enumeration
	EstMethodForCovs		Enumeration

(*continued*)

TABLE 7.1 (*Continued*)

Entity Types	Attributes	Sets Owned	Member or Data Type
Statistician_X_ Security			
	AnnualizedMean		Real
Statistician_X_ Security_X_Security			
	AnnualizedCov		Real
PortfolioAnalyst			
	StatisticianNr		Integer
		EfficientSet	EfficientSegment
EfficientSegment			
	HighE		Real
	HighV		Real
	LowE		Real
	LowV		Real
	HighPortfolio		CornerPortfolio
	LowPortfolio		CornerPortfolio
CornerPortfolio			
	Cp_nr		Integer
	E		Real
	V		Real

TABLE 7.1 (*Continued*)

Entity Types	Attributes	Sets Owned	Member or Data Type
Corner_Portfolio_X_ Security			
	X		Real
InvestorTemplate			
	Nr_investors		Integer
	Portfolio_analyst_nr		Integer
	Trader_template_nr		Integer
	Mean_log10_init_ wealth		Real
	Sigma_log10_init_ wealth		Real
	K		Real
	Reoptimization_ frequency		Enumeration
		Investors	Investor
InvestorTemplate_X_ Security			
	Total_bought_today		Integer
	Nr_of_buyers		Integer
	Seq_nr_of_ largest_buyer		Integer

(*continued*)

TABLE 7.1 (*Continued*)

Entity Types	Attributes	Sets Owned	Member or Data Type
	Purchase_of_largest_buyer		Integer
	Total_sold_today		Integer
	Nr_of_sellers		Integer
	Seq_nr_of_largest_seller		Integer
	Sale_of_largest_seller		Integer
Investor			
	Seq_nr		Integer
	Investor_template_nr		Integer
	StartingWealth		Real
	Deposits_received		Real
	Withdrawals_paid		Real
	Withdrawals_owed		Real
	Collateral_for_short_positions		Real
	CurrentWealth		Real
Investor_X_Security			
	X_units		Real
Trader_template			
	Buy_Alpha		Real
	Buy_Beta		Real

TABLE 7.1 (*Continued*)

Entity Types	Attributes	Sets Owned	Member or Data Type
	Buy_Alpha_inc		Real
	Buy_Beta_inc		Real
	Buy_First_time_wait		Real
	Buy_Following_time_ wait		Real
	Buy_Last_time_wait		Real
	Buy_Max_nr_price_ changes		Integer
	Sell_Alpha		Real
	Sell_Beta		Real
	Sell_Alpha_inc		Real
	Sell_Beta_inc		Real
	Sell_First_time_wait		Real
	Sell_Following_time_ wait		Real
	Sell_Last_time_wait		Real
	Sell_Max_nr_price_ changes		Integer
Trader			
	Trader_template_nr		Integer
	Investor_being_served		Investor_ID

(*continued*)

TABLE 7.1 (*Continued*)

Entity Types	Attributes	Sets Owned	Member or Data Type
Trader_X_Security			
	Buy_or_sell_amount		Integer
	Amount_on_order		Integer
		Orders_against_ amount	Order_slip
Order_slip			
	Buy_or_sell		Enumeration
	Trader_placing_order		Trader_ID
	Security_ordered		Integer
	Limit_price		Real
	Amount_to_do		Integer
	Order_status		Enumeration

*Table 7.1 shows some of the types of entities represented in JLMSim. For each type of entity, the table lists some of the attributes that characterize individuals of that type and some of the sets "owned" by (associated with) each individual of that type. The final column indicates the data types of the attributes and the entity types of the members of the listed sets.

The immediate objective of JLMSim was to be able to generate observed macroeconomic phenomena from postulated investor and trader behavior. The longer-run goal was to use such a model to answer policy questions concerning investing, trading, and market structure. In the process of building JLMSim, the authors found that a trading strategy that they thought plausible would in fact lead to what are now called "fast crashes." The authors also found that expected return estimation procedures that they thought plausible would lead to extremely unstable markets. These initial hypotheses were replaced by trading and estimation rules whose simulated consequences were more plausible.

The JLMSim authors do not consider their work to be the final word in detailed market simulation, but rather a demonstration of the capabilities of such an approach and a possible starting point for further research. The world is too complex, and the problems for which market simulators are potentially applicable are much too varied, for a one-size-fits-all simulator. JLMSim was offered as a proof-of-concept project, an example of how complex market models can be conceived and then programmed. In particular, the challenge to those who believe that investors follow particular rational or irrational behavior patterns is to encode such rules in a JLMSim-like simulator and see whether observed macro market behavior emerges. Our hope is that, eventually, some organization such as the Federal Reserve or the Treasury Department's Office of Financial Research will develop models as powerful and suited to their needs as the Joint Theater Level Simulator of Exhibit 7.1 is to its users' needs.

The first column of Table 7.1 displays "Entity Types," such as Security, Statistician, PortfolioAnalyst, Investor, Trader, and Order_slip. Instances of a given entity type are referred to as "entities" or "individuals." The second column contains the names of "Attributes" of the entity type just listed. Examples of attributes include the LastTradePrice, the StartOfDayPrice, and the VolumeSoFarToday of a security. The third column of Table 7.1 lists sets "Owned By"—that is, sets *associated with*—individuals of the particular entity type. For example, each security "owns" a set called Buy_orders and a set called Sell_orders. The final column of the table indicates the "Data Type" of an attribute or the entity type of the members of a set. For example, in JLMSim prices (such as LastTradePrice) are stored as "Real" (in fact, floating-point) numbers; VolumeSoFarToday is an Integer; and members of the Buy_orders and Sell_orders sets owned by a security are individuals of entity type Order_slip.

The use of "owns" to describe a set associated with entities of a given type works well unless the system to be described contains "owners" in a legal sense. An extreme example would be a system that contained an entity type called Partnership that owned (in the EAS sense) a set called Owners (in the legal sense). In our discussions, the sense in which an A owns a B should be clear from the context.

An EAS description invariably has an entity type called "TheSystem" representing the system as a whole. The System can have attributes and own sets. The SIMSCRIPTs do not allow The System to belong to sets. In JLMSim, attributes of The System include RFLendRatePerDay (the current daily risk-free rate) and SimTime (the current simulated time). It owns (in the EAS sense, of course) sets such as the set of all Securities in the particular simulation run, the set of all Investors, the set of all Statisticians, and so on.

Dynamic models that consist of a fixed number of "state variables" may be viewed as EAS-E models whose EAS descriptions contain only The System and its attributes.

As Table 7.1 illustrates, it is often useful to include what SIMSCRIPT programming manuals call "Compound Entities" and what mathematicians call "Cartesian products." For example, JLMSim entity types include a Statistician_X_Security combination with an attribute AnnualizedMean. This is the annualized expected return of the security as estimated by the particular statistician. A covariance estimate, on the other hand, is an attribute of Statistician_X_Security_X_Security.

GRAPHICAL DEPICTION OF ATTRIBUTES

Figures 7.1a through 7.1d (from Markowitz 1979) portray the nature of attributes. In Figure 7.1a, the Xs within the area on the left represent entities of the entity type Worker, whereas those on the right represent entities of the entity type Department. An arrow from a worker to a department represents the attribute ASSIGNED.TO. We represent a worker with no department, such as the general manager and each person on his or her staff, by an arrow to U, representing "undefined." Since many arrows may point to the same department, an attribute may represent a many-one relationship between entities of one type and entities of another type. As a special case, exactly one arrow could point from an entity of one type to any given entity of another type, representing a one-one relationship between the two entity types. An attribute—such

FIGURE 7.1 Attributes.

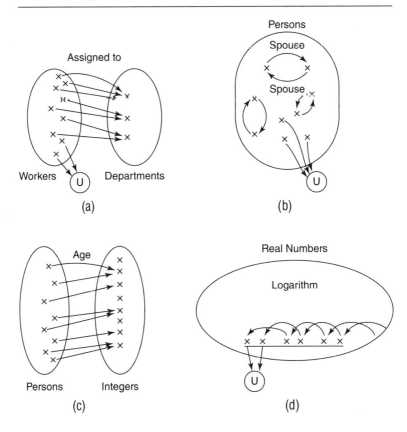

as *spouse* in Figure 7.1b—may also point from an entity of one entity type to an entity of the same entity type. Unmarried people point to U. In monogamous societies, this is a one-one relationship among a subset of the population.

In Figure 7.1c, an arrow representing the attribute AGE(PERSON) (read "Age of Person") points from a person to an integer. As discussed in Markowitz (1979) in the section on

"Entities of Logic and Mathematics," "Integer" may be thought of as an entity type whose individuals include 1, 2, 3, ...

Figure 7.1d is similar to Figures 7.1a through 7.1c except that each arrow points from a real number to a real number, associating a number with its logarithm. Such a relationship— between one of the entities of mathematics and another entity of mathematics—is usually called a *function*, but depending on the specific mathematical objects involved, it may instead be referred to as a *sequence, mapping, transformation,* or *operator.* The principal difference between the relationships portrayed in Figure 7.1d and those in Figures 7.1a through 7.1c is that the arrows in Figure 7.1d do not change with time, whereas those in Figures 7.1a through 7.1c change as workers change departments, get married, and grow older.

As illustrated in Figures 7.1a through 7.1d, *the value of an attribute is an entity (individual) or is null (undefined).* The type of the value entity may be *predefined,* like Integer, or *user-defined,* like Person. To a certain extent, what is predefined and what is user-defined depends on the programming language used to implement the EAS-E model. For example, a simulator may include an entity type Date whose attributes are Day, Month, and Year. This can be defined by the modeler if it is not predefined in the programming language.

GRAPHICAL DEPICTION OF SETS

Sets are collections of entities. In Figure 7.2a a set named Queue has machine groups (MG) as owners and Jobs as members. In the figure the members of the set are in a rectangle pointed to by

FIGURE 7.2 Sets.

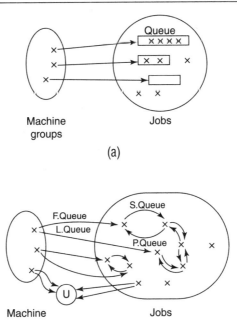

Machine groups   Jobs

(a)

Machine groups   Jobs

(b)

the owner. Figure 7.2b shows the same information in another way. The owner of the set points (by means of its F.QUEUE attribute) to the first in its set, and each member of the set points to its successor in the set by means of the S.QUEUE attribute.

Sets represent one-many relationships, as compared to the many-one and one-one relationships represented by attributes. (See Markowitz, Malhotra, and Pazel 1983 concerning how to translate back and forth between the EAS view and Peter Chen's ER, Entity Relationship, view.)

Since a given entity may have many attributes, own many sets, and belong to many sets, any attempt to portray all the entity, attribute, and set relationships of a system graphically, as in Figures 7.1 and 7.2, would lead to a hopeless mess in all but the simplest systems. On the other hand, Table 7.1 illustrates how the EAS structure of complex systems can be documented neatly.

FURTHER SPECIFICATIONS

An EAS table such as that in Table 7.1 presents an overall view of the status description of a simulation model. To avoid clutter, it omits other status descriptors such as:

> 1. *Set organization.* EAS sets are either FIFO (First In, First Out), LIFO (Last In, First Out), or Ranked (ordered by one or more attributes of its member entities).

For example, the Buy_orders and Sell_orders sets owned by a Security have their members ranked by the Limit_price attribute of Order_slip. In particular, the Limit_price on the Order_slip at the high end of the Buy_orders set is the current bid price for the security, and that on the low end of the Sell_ orders set is its asked price. As with any sets, the Buy_orders and/or Sell_orders sets owned by a particular security may be empty.

> 2. *Permanence of entities.* Simulated entities are either *temporary* or *permanent.*

In the case of permanent entities all individuals of the type are created at the start of a simulation run and persist throughout the run. The values of their attributes, the members of the sets they own, and their own set memberships may change, but the individuals persist. Temporary entities in contrast are created and destroyed during the course of the simulation run. In JLMSim, for example, Securities are permanent, whereas Order_slips are temporary.

As discussed later in this chapter and at length in Chapter 12, it was intended for SIMSCRIPT II to include *database entities* as well as main-storage entities. A program written in a system allowing database as well as main-storage entities would have to distinguish between entities that are to be stored in the database as compared to the temporary and so-called permanent main-storage entities that disappear when a program ends execution.

Additional specifications, actual and proposed, are discussed later in this chapter in sections following the section titled "Issues and Alternatives."

DESCRIBING TIME

Three ways in which time is typically represented in dynamic models are:[1]

A. Continuously
B1. Synchronously discrete
B2. Asynchronously discrete

A. In a continuous-time model, not only is time represented as a continuous variable, but the state of the system typically changes continuously. Examples include (a) Newton's model of the solar system and (b) financial models in which stock prices move as continuous functions of Brownian motions. The first is an example of the kinds of systems subject to ordinary or partial differential equations (ODEs and PDEs), which are widely used in classical physics but rarely if ever used in OR models of, e.g., factories or investment policies. The second is a system that evolves according to "stochastic differential equations" (SDEs). These are widely used in the design and pricing of financial instruments and in the exploration of highly stylized financial worlds. Endnotes 2 and 3 of Chapter 6 present the principal reasons why they are not discussed in this volume.

B. In a discrete-time model, changes in status are separated by nonnegative increments of time. Starting with initial conditions at time $t = t_0$, status changes at time points $t_1 = t_0 + \Delta t_1$, $t_2 = t_1 + \Delta t_2$, etc., where $\Delta t_i \geq 0$ for $i = 1, 2, \ldots$. As in the single-period models of Volume I, the change in status between time t_i and t_{i+1} may be due to some random or deterministic process that occurs during the interval between the two time points, and that is not modeled explicitly.

In a synchronous discrete-time model (B1), the time increments are equal:

$$0 < \Delta t_1 = \Delta t_2 = \ldots$$

In an asynchronous model (B2) the time increments may be of unequal length, perhaps determined by player decisions or random variables, provided only that $\Delta t_i \geq 0$. In some applications, a synchronous model is natural; for others, asynchronous simulation is more convenient. For example, a Monte Carlo evaluation of investment policies in which status is updated monthly, quarterly, or annually is an example of a synchronous simulation. JLMSim (whose EAS status structure is described above and whose events are described below) is an asynchronous simulator.

The chief difference between a synchronous and an asynchronous simulator is how time is advanced. In effect, a synchronous simulation program consists of a large loop whose head increments time by Δt, whose body takes actions, and whose end tests to see if a specified end-of-simulated time or condition has been reached. If not, it sends control back to the top of the loop.

In an asynchronous simulation, on the other hand, a *timing routine* keeps a list of forthcoming events, ordered by imminence of occurrence. The timing routine's main loop identifies the most imminent event and its event type. It then transfers control to applicable instructions, referred to in the SIMSCRIPTs as an *event routine*. The event routine may change system status and/or schedule future events, perhaps with the aid of subroutines, perhaps conditionally depending on existing status. When the event routine finishes its actions, it returns control to the timing routine, which selects the then most imminent event. This process is repeated until an end-of-simulation event is the most imminent.

SIMULTANEITY

It is *not* typically true that all state variables are updated at the same time in synchronous simulations. For example, a synchronous single-person consumption-investment model may update security prices once a month, then rebalance or reoptimize the investor's portfolio based on these new prices. In this case, while time is held constant at some value, $t = t_i$, the actions that take place during the event are not in fact simultaneous: prices are updated first, *then* the portfolio is rebalanced or reoptimized. It is as if time $t = t_i$ is not a single instant but a sequence of instances. A number of simultaneous actions may be taken at one instant, like the updating of all security prices, then a different batch of simultaneous actions is taken at the next instant. What characterizes a batch of actions as simultaneous is that the updating of one does not depend on the updated value of the other; they may be done in any order. Conversely, two actions whose execution must take place in a particular order are not simultaneous, whatever the simulated clock says.

An asynchronous simulation may also include periodic events with many synchronized updates. An example would be a shift change in a simulated manufacturing or retail enterprise. The many shift-change actions of both include those that end one shift followed by those that start another.[2]

ENDOGENOUS EVENTS VERSUS ENDOGENOUS PHENOMENA

The SIMSCRIPTs distinguish between *endogenous* and *exogenous* events (a.k.a. "internal" and "external" events). Exogenous event occurrences are triggered from outside the simulation run. Specifically, one or more exogenous event input files contain, in order of event occurrence:

1. The event name
2. The time of the particular event occurrence
3. Perhaps data to be read by the event routine with the specified name
4. A termination mark, usually an asterisk (*), but this can be changed.

When the particular exogenous event occurrence is more imminent than any other (exogenous or endogenous) event occurrence, the SIMSCRIPT timing routine calls on the event routine specified in the exogenous event input stream.

Endogenous event occurrences are scheduled by the execution of CAUSE or SCHEDULE statements. (CAUSE and SCHEDULE are synonyms in SIMSCRIPTs II and later.) Endogenous event occurrences can be put on the calendar before the START SIMULATION command is executed, so that the simulated system is already "in progress" when the simulation run begins.

One must distinguish between two senses in which the term *endogenous* is used, as in the following two statements:

1. The review_order event (described later) is triggered *endogenously* in JLMSim and
2. Security return distributions are *endogenous* in JLMSim, the result of the investment and trading rules of the simulated players, rather than being assumed *a priori*.

A simulator might have all event occurrences endogenous in Sense 1, but not have endogenous price formation in Sense 2. Specifically each price change could schedule the next price change for a given security, but the amount of the price change could be generated randomly from a given distribution.

JLMSIM EVENTS

JLMSim is an asynchronous simulator. It has a timing routine that was programmed in C++, building on routines for efficiently storing into and retrieving from large ranked sets, available (as this is written) at the website EAS-E.org. Also available (as this is written) is the JLMSim program itself at www.jacobslevy.com.

Table 7.2 lists the principal event routines of JLMSim. The first column of the table lists event names; the second column describes some of their actions. As noted in the table, when the *reoptimize event* occurs on behalf of a particular investor, the associated event routine randomly generates a deposit or withdrawal amount, and then has the investor's portfolio analyst compute an ideal portfolio using the estimates of some statistician. The investor next decides how far to try to move from its current portfolio toward its ideal portfolio, and places orders with its trader accordingly. Each reoptimization event schedules the next reoptimization occurrence for the given investor.

The trader's initial actions with these orders happen as part of the reoptimize event rather than as part of a separate order-placement event. This then is an example in which

TABLE 7.2 JLMSim Events

Event	
Initialize	Creates and initializes status in accord with the JLMSim user's instructions.
Reoptimize	May randomly generate deposits and withdrawals for the particular investor. Has investor's portfolio analyst compute the investor's "ideal" portfolio, using estimates supplied by its statistician. Investor computes how far it should move from its current portfolio toward the ideal portfolio, and places orders with trader. Trader executes orders if there are matching orders on the other side, and places the balance of the order on the books. If trades are executed, the trader for the other party may take further actions.
Review_order	Changes the limit price or cancels the order. If limit price is changed, actions may occur similar to those when an order is placed during the Reoptimize event.
End_of_day	Updates daily and perhaps monthly statistics. Mark-to-market accounts with leveraged or short positions. Accounts that violate maintenance margin requirements are turned over to a "liquidation trader."

In an asynchronous simulation, events change status and cause future events. This table lists the principal types of events in JLMSim, and describes some of the actions they take.

necessarily *successive* actions—optimize first, place orders second—are executed with the simulated clock stopped.

As already noted, prices and volumes in JLMSim are *endogenous* (i.e., they are determined within the system by the actions of its interacting agents) rather than being assumed *a priori*. Specifically, if one of the orders generated by a reoptimization can be filled at least partly from "the book"—that is, from the set of the security's Buy_orders in case of a sale or its Sell_orders in case of a purchase—then a transaction takes place at the limit price on the existing order slip for a quantity that is the smaller of what one side wants to buy and the other side wants to sell. If the new order is not completed, the unfilled balance of the order is put on the books, and a Review_order is scheduled. When the Review_order event happens, it considers the possibility of relaxing the Limit_price attribute of the Order_slip. See Jacobs, Levy, and Markowitz (2004) for details as to how the simulated trader decides on bid or asked prices.

JLMSim also includes an End_of_day event. Here again time stands still while the simulator takes a series of simultaneous and nonsimultaneous actions, such as (1) the accumulation of daily, and perhaps monthly, statistics, (2) the mark-to-market of leveraged accounts and short positions, and (3) broker-call actions for investors who do not meet margin requirements.

SIMPLICITY, COMPLEXITY, REALITY

Because of time constraints imposed by PCs at the time, the JLMSim authors kept the number of investors to a few thousand. But if JLMSim were run now on one of today's "personal supercomputers," one could run cases with millions of investors. Still even with millions of simulated investors and other parts of the market beefed up accordingly we should consider such a JLMSim run to be *detailed* rather than *realistic*.

For example, JLMSim trades pay no commissions. This is a hole in the model that is relatively easy to fill.

A more serious simplification is that JLMSim has no corporations standing behind its securities. Therefore, it has no corporate news, such as earnings and dividend reports. The only news is the prices themselves, determined endogenously by traders trying to execute orders generated by periodic investor reoptimizations with random deposits and withdrawals. A "realistic" market model would, of course, model real corporations. But any corporate model would surely be highly simplified as compared with reality.

Finally, the investors in JLMSim are no more than periodic reoptimizers. They show none of the structure that we analyze in various places elsewhere in this book. Thus while JLMSim is orders of magnitude more complex than models that assume that a security follows a specified random process, it is nevertheless a meager shadow of the real world.

For some purposes highly stylized models are best. For other purposes models of greater complexity are required. For example, as noted earlier the objective of JLMSim was to seek a combination of agent behaviors (rational or otherwise) that implied observed return behavior. As it turned out, it was found that certain (at first seemingly plausible) trading rules would destabilize the market. This is without any deliberate market manipulation. It seems to us that any academic, trader, or market supervisory agency that is seriously interested in the characteristics of markets containing careless traders and/or market manipulators should have an advanced JLMSim-like simulator at their disposal.

At the other extreme from situations that require detailed models to think through are situations in which simple deductions suffice. For example, if a government sets a price below market equilibrium, it does *not* take a complex model to predict that there will be a shortage, and therefore some form of rationing will be needed; and that a rough magnitude of the shortage in the short and long runs can be estimated from rough estimates of the short- and long-run elasticities of supply and demand. For situations such as this, relatively simple supply and demand analysis beats detailed simulation. As to what features should be included in a model to be used for some given purpose, we can do no better than repeat Einstein's advice, that a model should be "as simple as possible, but no simpler."

THE SIMSCRIPT ADVANTAGE

JLMSim was conceived in EAS-E terms and then programmed in C++. Had it been programmed in SIMSCRIPT it would have been a fraction of its current size (probably in the one-half to one-fifth range) based on prior comparisons, and would have taken correspondingly less time to code and debug. In particular the SIMSCRIPTs have commands that are tailored to create and destroy temporary entities, file or remove (temporary or permanent) entities into or from sets, compute various statistics describing the simulated system at an instant in time, accumulate simulated system performance statistics over time, and perform blocks of code for members of sets meeting specified conditions.

For example, suppose that some entity type owns a set called a QUEUE. The SIMSCRIPT II, II.5, or III description of this entity type might include the following instruction:

ACCUMULATE MQ = the Mean, SDQ = the STD DEV, and MaxQ = the maximum of N.QUEUE.

The SIMSCRIPTs are not case sensitive. Therefore this statement could have been written as all lowercase, all uppercase, or any combination thereof. The three appearances of the word *the* are optional and are there for readability. (One of the SIMSCRIPTs' objectives is to be self-documenting.) N.QUEUE is the number of members of the set QUEUE and is automatically defined as an attribute of the owner of QUEUE. MQ, SDQ, and MaxQ are names chosen by the programmer and (because of their appearance in the Accumulate statement) are automatically defined as attributes of the entity type that has N.QUEUE as one of its attributes. The previous statement, as it says, arranges to have MQ and SDQ contain the *time-weighted* mean and standard deviation, and to have MaxQ contain the maximum value of N.QUEUE, either since the start of simulation or since these statistics were last reset. The Accumulate statement can also include the minimum, sum, and sum of squares statistics. The position occupied by N.QUEUE in the example can be any function of the attributes of some (temporary, permanent, system, or compound) entity. The TALLY statement provides similar options for attributes (like mean time in shop) for which ordinary averages rather than time-weighted averages are appropriate.

SIMSCRIPT II.5 and III are extensions of SIMSCRIPT II. Hence all features of SIMSCRIPT II are also features of SIMSCRIPTs II.5 and III. The example illustrates the following SIMSCRIPT II (and later) features:

- SIMSCRIPT II automatically defines many useful variables, such as the N.QUEUE attribute of the owner of QUEUE. This requires SIMSCRIPT to make up names. The SIMSCRIPT II programmer is advised not to define his or her variables with names of the form letter-dot-name or name-dot-letter like N.QUEUE or SimTime.V. This will avoid conflicts with SIMSCRIPT II's automatically generated names.

- SIMSCRIPT II includes optional words like *the* that the programmer can include if he or she seeks readability or omit if he or she seeks compactness.

- SIMSCRIPT II is not case sensitive, as many programming languages are now. This way, the programmer does not create a bug if he or she usually writes SimTime.V but occasionally writes SimTime.v; or would like to start each statement with a capital letter, as English does; or capitalizes words that serve a particular function, such as ACCUMULATE in the example before.

- Unlike many programming languages, SIMSCRIPT does not terminate statements with semicolons, just as they are not thus terminated in English sentences. SIMSCRIPT II permits (but does not require) terminal periods.

- The ACCUMULATE and TALLY statements cause statistics to be updated whenever the executing program updates specified attributes. This saves a great deal of coding. Chapter 12 has an example of a COMPUTE statement that computes similar statistics concerning aspects of a system at a point in time; and describes the FIND statement that finds an entity with specified characteristics.

The SIMSCRIPTs also include functions to generate random variables with a variety of probability distributions, and (as already noted) WYSIWYG report generation facilities. SIMSCRIPTs II.5 and III can combine continuous-time and discrete-event simulation, and have two- and three-dimensional graphical facilities that naturally become animated when combined with simulation capabilities.

GUIDEDCHOICE AND THE GAME OF LIFE

Markowitz (1991) proposed a "game-of-life" simulator that would include a family's health and housing, its educational plans and achievements, its social security, insurance, etc., in addition to its investment opportunities and decisions. Ideally, a game-of-life simulator could serve as a guide to a family's financial planning, of which portfolio selection is but a part. Just as the various subsystems of a car (engine, transmission, brakes, etc.) all interact, so too do the various types of family decisions and events, such as the choice of a residence and its furnishings, education, career choice, job availability, retirement time, births (planned or otherwise), the luck of the draw with respect to health, natural disasters, etc. In particular, they all affect the supply of, and need for, "financial assets."[3]

Late in the 1990s Sherrie Grabot, the GuidedChoice CEO, explained to Markowitz that GuidedChoice (GC) was a 401(k) advisory service business with a different business model from that used by others in the industry, such as Bill Sharpe's Financial Engines. Markowitz gave Grabot a copy of Markowitz (1991), agreed to form a San Diego–based design and production team, and to consult for GC. GC would not try to build a complete game-of-life model, but to set it as an ideal—a North Star—toward which it would direct its model building, starting with the immediate objective of helping investors save for their retirement.

As it turned out the design team—consisting of Ming Yee Wang, Gan Lin Xu, and Markowitz, under Sherrie Grabot's guidance—designed and supervised the building of a set of interrelated programs and procedures that constitute GC's decision support system (DSS). This includes programs and procedures to:

1. make forward-looking estimates of asset-class expected returns, variances, and covariances;

2. generate a mean-variance efficient frontier at the asset-class level;

3. elicit from a new client [namely, a corporate 401(k) plan sponsor] plan specifics such as the securities in which plan participants may invest and the plan's provisions for matching participants' contributions;

4. assign a portfolio of plan-permitted investments to each mean-variance efficient asset-class portfolio;

5. elicit from a plan participant, and from the plan's record keeper on behalf of the participant, information needed for the simulation analysis in the following item;

6. inform the participant of the results of a simulation analysis concerning the probability distribution of possible post retirement consumption levels, taking into account the participant's savings rate, selected portfolio, social security payments, spouse's income (if the client so specifies), the company's matching policy, etc.;

7. instruct the plan's record keeper to execute GC's advice if the participant so elects; and

8. report the account status to the participant and the plan sponsor.

In the first instance the policies evaluated in Step 6 include (a) the participant's current allocations and savings rates, and (b) GC's "initial advice" in these areas. The participant may vary these inputs, either at the same session or in one or more following sessions.

GC's first product, GuidedSavings, evaluates the participants' savings and investment plans up to the time of their retirement. A second product, GuidedSpending, evaluates their savings, investment, annuitization, and consumption strategies, perhaps starting before retirement and continuing through retirement. See Markowitz (2015) for further details.

THE GC DSS DATABASE

The GC DSS was designed with an EAS-E viewpoint and implemented using the Oracle database system. Table 7.3 presents an extract from the EAS table used to plan, implement, and document the GC DSS database. The first column of Table 7.3 contains a three-character code ("ENT," "ATT," "SET," or "COM") indicating whether the line contains the name of an Entity type, an Attribute, or a Set, or is a Comment line. The second column of Table 7.3 indicates the entity type, such as Person, Account, Portfolio, Position, Dependent, or Planned_disbursement. The third column contains the names of the attributes of entities of a just-listed entity type. Examples of attributes include the Birth_date, Gender, and Marital_status of a person. The fourth column of the table lists sets "Owned By"—that is, sets *associated with*—individuals of the particular entity type. For example, each Person owns sets called Dependents, Portfolios, and Planned_disbursements. The fifth column of the table indicates the data type of an attribute or the entity type of the members of a set. For example, the Birth_date of a Person is in Date format, and the members of the set called Dependents are of the entity type Dependent. The sixth column is labeled Precision. It shows, for example, that 32 characters are allotted for a State's name. The final field of Table 7.3 contains comments and cross-references. The list of entity types under the comments/cross-references heading across from entity type Authorization_memo, for example, indicates that individuals of this entity type are referred to by The_SYSTEM and entities of entity type Person.

TABLE 7.3 GuidedChoice's Database EAS*

COM COM	ENT TYPE	ATTR	OWNS	Data/Memb TYPE	PREC (*)	COMMENT/Cross References (*) All "Integer"s 32 bit All "Number"s 12,3
ENT	The_SYSTEM					
SET			Sponsors	Sponsor		
SET			Record_keepers	Record_keeper		
SET			GC_AC_frontiers	GC_AC_frontier		
SET			Trust_families	Trust_family		
SET			Security_types	Security_type		
SET			Securities	Security		
SET			Asset_classes	Asset_class		
SET			Partcpnt_auth_memos	Authorization_memo		Authorization memos of participants
SET			DB_users	DB_user		Other than participants
SET			Stdd_comp_types	Compensation_type		

TABLE 7.3 (*Continued*)

COM COM ENT TYPE	ATTR	OWNS	Data/Memb TYPE	PREC (*)	COMMENT/Cross References (*) All "Integer"s 32 bit All "Number"s 12,3
SET		Stdd_plan_texts	Plan_text		
SET		Transaction_log_book	Transaction_log_entry		
SET		Event_log_book	Event_log_entry		
SET		Error_log_book	Error_log_entry		
SET		States	State		
ATT	Fed_limit_pretax_dlrs		Number		Currently $10,500
ATT	Fed_limit_pretax_pct		Number		Currently 25%
ATT	Fed_limit_total_dlrs		Number		Currently $30,000
ATT	Fed_limit_total_pct		Number		Currently 25%
SET		Fed_tax_brackets	Inc_tax_bracket		

(*continued*)

TABLE 7.3 (*Continued*)

COM COM	ENT TYPE	ATTR	OWNS	Data/Memb TYPE	PREC (*)	COMMENT/Cross References (*) All "Integer"s 32 bit All "Number"s 12,3
ENT	State					SYSTEM
ATT		State_id		ID		
ATT		State_name		Text	32	
ATT		State_code		Char	2	
SET			Inc_tax_brackets	Inc_tax_bracket		
ENT	Inc_tax_bracket					SYSTEM, State
ATT		Inc_tax_bracket_id		ID		
ATT		Taxing_government		ID		State_id or -1 for federal govt
ATT		From_income		Number		

TABLE 7.3 (*Continued*)

COM COM ENT TYPE	ATTR	OWNS	Data/Memb TYPE	PREC (*)	COMMENT/Cross References (*) All "Integer"s 32 bit All "Number"s 12,3
ATT	To_income		Number		
ATT	Marginal_rate_pct		Number		
ENT Authorization_memo					SYSTEM, Person
ATT	Authorization_memo_id		ID		
ATT	Participant		Person_id		Person
ATT	Access_pin		Char	12	
ATT	Personal_question		Text	128	
ATT	Secret_answer		Text	128	
ATT	Pin_change_allowed		Char	1	
ATT	Pin_change_date		Date		<=Tocay

(continued)

TABLE 7.3 (*Continued*)

COM	COM ENT TYPE	ATTR	OWNS	Data/Memb TYPE	PREC (*)	COMMENT/Cross References (*) All "Integer"s 32 bit All "Number"s 12,3
ENT	Person					||Person, Authorization_memo, GC_case, Session,
ATT		Person_id		ID		>Transaction_log_entry, Event_log_entry
ATT		First_name		Text	32	>Error_log_entry, Expenses_worksheet
ATT		Last_name		Text	32	
ATT		Middle_initial		Char	1	
ATT		Birth_date		Date		<Today
ATT		Gender		Char	1	=MF
ATT		Contact_info		Contact_info_id		
ATT		Country_of_legal_residence		Text	32	

TABLE 7.3 (*Continued*)

COM COM ENT TYPE	ATTR	OWNS	Data/Memb TYPE	PREC (*)	COMMENT/Cross References (*) All "Integer"s 32 bit All "Number"s 12,3
ATT	Marital_status		Char	1	YN
ATT	Why_in_DB		Char	1	=PSB Partcpnt, Spouse, both)
ATT	Other_income		Number		Not in Account's Persor_comps
ATT	Total_income		Number		
ATT	Retirement_age		Integer		
ATT	Ret_income_goal_DorP		Char	1	D|P
ATT	AT_ret_income_goal		Number		
ATT	Spouse		Person_id		Perso1
ATT	Expenses_worksheet		Expenses_ worksheet_id		

(*continued*)

TABLE 7.3 (*Continued*)

COM ENT TYPE	ATTR	OWNS	Data/Memb TYPE	PREC (*)	COMMENT/Cross References (*) All "Integer"'s 32 bit All "Number"'s 12,3
ATT	Nr_dependents		Integer	2	
SET		Sign_ons	Authorization_memo		>=1 source doc says this is set?
SET		Dependents	Dependent		?should this be hooked ontc marriage?
SET		GC_accounts	Account		
SET		Portfolios	Portfolio		
SET		Positions	Position		= positions in all of Person's portfolios
SET		Pensions	Pension		

TABLE 7.3 (*Continued*)

COM COM ENT TYPE	ATTR	OWNS	Data/Memb TYPE	PREC (*)	COMMENT/Cross References (*) All "Integer"'s 32 bit All "Number"'s 12,3
SET		Planned_ disbursements	Planned_ disbursement		
SET		Non_GC_plans	Non_GC_plan		Plans of Person rprsntng spouse go here
ENT Dependent					||Planned_disbursement
ATT	Dependent_id		ID		
ATT	Participant		Person_id		
ATT	Dependent_name		Text	32	
ATT	Dependent_birthdate		Date		>=Tocay
ATT	Dependent_gender		Char	1	=M|F

(continued)

TABLE 7.3 (*Continued*)

COM COM ENT TYPE	ATTR	OWNS	Data/Memb TYPE	PREC (*)	COMMENT/Cross References (*) All "Integer"'s 32 bit All "Number"'s 12,3
ENT Planned_disbursement					
ATT	Planned_disbursement_id		ID		Person
ATT	Participant		Person_id		
ATT	Dependent		Dependent_id		.=0 if not for college
ATT	Disbursement_period		Char		=M|Q|S|Y
ATT	Disbursement_amt		Number		
ATT	Inflation_adjust_amt		Char	1	YN
ATT	Start_date		Date		
ATT	End_date		Date		>=Start_date

TABLE 7.3 (*Continued*)

COM	COM ENT TYPE	ATTR	OWNS	Data/Memb TYPE	PREC (*)	COMMENT/Cross References (*) All "Integer"'s 32 bit All "Number"'s 12,3
ATT		Disbursement_type		Integer		
ATT		Disbursement_name		Text	128	
ENT	Account					Plan, Person || Pension, Session
ATT		Account_id		ID		>Transaction_log_entry,
ATT		Participant		Person_id		
ATT		Plan		Plan_id		
ATT		Sponsor		Sponsor_id		
ATT		Contact_info		Contact_info_id		
ATT		Tax_state		Text	32	1 of 2 |=""

(*continued*)

TABLE 7.3 (*Continued*)

COM COM ENT TYPE	ATTR	OWNS	Data/Memb TYPE	PREC (*)	COMMENT/Cross References (*) All "Integer"s 32 bit All "Number"s 12,3
ATT	Spouse		Spouse_id		
ATT	Employee_status		Enum		1 Active 2 Hardship 3 Terminated
ATT	Eligibility_date		Date		
ATT	Eligibility_match		Char	1	YN
ATT	Eligibility_pension		Char	1	YN
ATT	Years_service		Integer		
ATT	Highly_compensated		Char	1	YN
ATT	Hire_date		Date		<=Today
ATT	GC_advice_accepted		Char	1	YN
ATT	Start_advice_date		Date		
ATT	End_advice_date		Date		

TABLE 7.3 (*Continued*)

COM COM ENT TYPE	ATTR	OWNS	Data/Memb TYPE	PREC (*)	COMMENT/Cross References (*) All "Integer"s 32 bit All "Number"s 12,3
ATT	Eligibility_profit_share		Char	1	YN
ATT	Phone_access		Char	1	YN
ATT	Annual_salary		Number		
ATT	Pretax_earnings		Number		
ATT	Posttax_earnings		Number		
ATT	Last_use		Date		<=Today
ATT	RK_update_date		Date		
ATT	Accepted_case		GC_case_id		
ATT	Date_case_accepted		Date		
ATT	Base_case		GC_case_id		
ATT	Initial_advice		GC_case_id		

(*continued*)

69

TABLE 7.3 (*Continued*)

COM COM ENT TYPE	ATTR	OWNS	Data/Memb TYPE	PREC (*)	COMMENT/Cross References (*) All "Integer"s 32 bit All "Number"s 12,3
ATT	Modified_advice		GC_case_id		
ATT	Next_case		GC_case_id		
ATT	Last_session		Session_id		
ATT	OK_rcvd_prime_bnf_NE_spouse		Char	1	YN OK received for prime beneficiary not spouse
SET		Beneficiaries	Beneficiary		
SET		Portfolios	Portfolio		
SET		Person_Comp_types	Person_Comp_type		
ATT	Contrib_spec_PorD		Char	1	P|D If Plan permits either P (%) or D ($)
SET		Current_contribs	Contrib_instruction		

TABLE 7.3 (*Continued*)

COM COM ENT TYPE	ATTR	OWNS	Data/Memb TYPE	PREC (*)	COMMENT/Cross References (*) All "Integer"s 32 bit All "Number"s 12,3
SET		BT_contrib_allocs	Contrib_allocation		
SET		AT_contrib_allocs	Contrib_allocation		
SET		PS_contrib_allocs	Contrib_allocation		
SET		Archived_cases	GC_case		
ENT Portfolio					Person, Account||Contrib_instrucion
ATT	Portfolio_id		ID		
ATT	Participant		Person_id		

(*continued*)

TABLE 7.3 (*Continued*)

COM COM ENT TYPE	ATTR	OWNS	Data/Memb TYPE	PREC (*)	COMMENT/Cross References (*) All "Integer"s 32 bit All "Number"s 12,3
ATT	Account		Account_id		NULL if not owned by GC_Account
ATT	Tax_type		Investment_tax_ type_id		Enum in EJB; Entity in Administrator
ATT	Portfolio_name		Text	128	
ATT	Accum_AT_contrib		Number		
ATT	Monthly_planned_con- trib_dlrs		Number		
ATT	Inflation_adjust_contrib		Char	1	YN
SET		Positions	Position		
SET		AC_exposures	Exposure		

TABLE 7.3 (*Continued*)

COM COM	ENT TYPE	ATTR	OWNS	Data/Memb TYPE	PREC (*)	COMMENT/Cross References (*) All "Integer"s 32 bit All "Number"s 12,3
ENT	Position					Person, Portfolio||Kept_investment
ATT		Position_id		ID		
ATT		Security		Security_id		
ATT		Portfolio		Portfolio_id		
ATT		Person		Person_id		
ATT		Security_type		Security_type_id	32	Must be on security type list
ATT		Tax_type		Enum		
ATT		Quantity		Number		Shares or face value

(*continued*)

TABLE 7.3 (*Continued*)

COM COM ENT TYPE	ATTR	OWNS	Data/Memb TYPE	PREC (*)	COMMENT/Cross References (*) All "Integer"s 32 bit All "Number"s 12,3
ATT	Valuation_method		Enum		Mkt price, user price, user total
ATT	User_supplied_price		Number		
ATT	Date_of_user_info		Date		
ATT	Total_value		Number		
ATT	Restricted_for_partici-pant		Char	1	YN Company requirement
ATT	Date_unrestricted		Date		
ATT	Total_cost_basis		Number		

TABLE 7.3 (*Continued*)

COM COM ENT TYPE	ATTR	OWNS	Data/Memb TYPE	PREC (*)	COMMENT/Cross References (*) All "Integer"s 32 bit All "Number"s 12,3
ENT Person_Comp_type					Person, Compensation type Combo
ATT	Person_Comp_type_id		ID		
ATT	Account		Account_id		
ATT	Compensation_type		Compensation_type_id		
ATT	Compensation_type_name		Text	128	

(continued)

75

TABLE 7.3 (*Continued*)

COM COM ENT TYPE	ATTR	OWNS	Data/Memb TYPE	PREC (*)	COMMENT/Cross References (*) All "Integer"s 32 bit All "Number"s 12,3
ATT	Pay_periods_per_year		Integer		
ATT	Amount_per_pay_period		Number		
ENT Compensation_type					SYSTEM, Plan, Eligible_comp_type ||
ATT	Compensation_type_id		ID		>Person_Comp_type, Contrib_instruction
ATT	Plan		Plan_id		
ATT	Compensation_type_name		Text	32	

76

TABLE 7.3 (*Continued*)

COM COM ENT TYPE	ATTR	OWNS	Data/Memb TYPE	PREC (*)	COMMENT/Cross References (*) All "Integer"s 32 bit All "Number"s 12,3
ENT Eligible_comp_type					Plan(2) || PCH_ECT, Contrib_instruction
ATT	Eligible_comp_type_id		ID		
ATT	Plan		Plan_id		>Savings_rate_spec
ATT	Eligible_comp_type_ name		Text	32	
SET		Compensation_types	Compensation_type		Overlaping sets

*An extract from the EAS (Entity, Attribute, and Set) table for GuidedChoice's database.

Such cross-references are not usually part of an EAS table, but they proved quite useful in implementing this complex system relatively quickly with minimal resources.

As we saw in the JLMSim example, an EAS description invariably has an entity type called The System representing the system-as-a-whole. Table 7.3 shows that the GC System owns various sets of "top-level" entity types. Entities of other entity types are accessed through these top-level entities. Top-level entity types include everything from Sponsors [of 401(k) plans], Record_keepers, Securities, and so on down to entries in the Transaction_log_book, the Event_log_book, and the Error_log_book. Attributes of The System include federal limits on the dollars and percents that may be contributed to a 401(k) plan. (The amounts listed in the comments are obsolete, but the amounts in the database are current of course.)

The only compound entity included in this extract from the full GC EAS table is the Person_X_Comp_type combination. (Comp_type is short for "compensation type" such as full-time as opposed to overtime salary.) The full GC EAS documentation has many more compound entities, as does Table 7.1.

For the most part the contents of Table 7.3 should be self-explanatory. In part they reflect the context of the portfolio selection decision including income tax rates for various income brackets, both federal and state, with the latter varying from state to state; regulations and company policies with respect to how much income the participant can shelter in his or her 401(k) plan; the company's matching policy; the participant's birth date and intended retirement age; perhaps the participant's spouse; the participant's dependents and planned disbursements to them; the participant's other accounts such as 401(k) plans with prior employers, etc.

Other data in the database are oriented toward reporting status information to the participant and the plan sponsor, and the running of the DSS itself. The database must remember, for example, the set of accounts to be reviewed at a particular time for possible rebalancing transactions, and for collecting GC's fee.

The events of a decision support system are the points in time at which system status is updated, reported, or called upon to take actions. For example, a participant calling the system at some unscheduled moment is an exogenous event, whereas a periodic rebalancing is an example of an endogenous event. Thus a complete EAS-E summary of the GC DSS would spell out in greater detail items 1 through 8 listed in the preceding section.

SIMULATOR VERSUS DSS MODELING

A major difference between a simulation aimed at developing policies and a DSS that implements such policies is a matter of *The General* versus *The Particular*. For example, the GuidedChoice DSS keeps track of the name, address, and telephone number of each investor it guides, whereas JLMSim does *not* do so for the investors it simulates.

Another major difference has to do with the need for hypotheses about how the world works. For example, a job shop simulator must model the job arrival-time process. In a job shop DSS, arrivals just happen, perhaps as predicted, perhaps not. Similarly, one of the major problems in building a consumption-investment simulation model is how to model return distributions. In the real time of a DSS, returns just happen—again, perhaps as predicted, perhaps not.

On the other hand one thing in common between the building of a simulator and a DSS database is the modeling process: deciding what types of entities need to be tracked, what attributes and set relationships are needed to characterize their status, what kinds of endogenous events need to be caused in the simulator or scheduled in the DSS, and what kinds of exogenous events affect the system. Furthermore many of the entity types in the simulator are (or will be) in the DSS and, ideally, the decision rules tested in the simulator will be transferred, essentially "as is," to the DSS. It seems to us axiomatic that it is advantageous for the specifications and programs of the simulator and the DSS to speak the same language.

ISSUES AND ALTERNATIVES

The remaining sections of this chapter are directed toward a limited audience, such as simulator or DSS builders who are thinking about programming in some EAS-E-oriented way, or computer language developers who are interested in borrowing from SIMSCRIPT or who would like to see what SIMSCRIPT has borrowed from them. We begin with some details on the members of the SIMSCRIPT family of languages, including a version developed at IBM Research that we will refer to as IBM EAS-E. Other topics include the process view, subsystems, polymorphism and strong data typing, subsidiary entities, and inheritance. We discuss how these things are currently done (in SIMSCRIPT III and IBM EAS-E) and, in some instances, how we believe they could be done better. We begin with a brief description of the various versions of SIMSCRIPT.

THE SIMSCRIPTS

SIMSCRIPT (I) was a preprocessor into FORTRAN II, developed at the RAND Corporation and put into the public domain via SHARE. SIMSCRIPT I.5 could be described as a smoother version of SIMSCRIPT (I) that removed certain language restrictions imposed by it being a FORTRAN II preprocessor. SIMSCRIPT I.5 was developed at CACI at the same time that RAND was developing SIMSCRIPT II. The SIMSCRIPT II compiler used an EAS view of the compilation process. Specifically, SIMSCRIPT II was programmed in SIMSCRIPT II (after a "kernel" of the language programmed in SIMSCRIPT (I) was bootstrapped to the same kernel programmed in SIMSCRIPT II). The same basic idea was used to write SIMSCRIPT I.5 in SIMSCRIPT I.5.

As described in Markowitz (1979), SIMSCRIPT II was to be implemented—and documented—in seven levels. Specifically,

- Level 1 is a simple "teaching language."
- Level 2 is a full-fledged programming language with capabilities comparable to those of FORTRAN II.

- Level 3 is a more advanced general-purpose programming language.
- Level 4 introduces Entities, Attributes, and Sets, and commands to process them.
- Level 5 presents the SIMSCRIPT II simulation capabilities.
- Level 6 was to introduce database entities and sets.
- Level 7 was to make available to systems programmers the LWL (Language Writing Language) with which SIMSCRIPT II was built.

The basic plan for SIMSCRIPT II, including its LWL, was designed by Markowitz while Hausner and Karr completed the SIMSCRIPT (I) preprocessor and programming manual. Sometime after SIMSCRIPT (I) was completed, released through SHARE, and used by the RAND Logistics Department for at least one large logistics simulation project, RAND began the building of SIMSCRIPT II. Bernie Hausner programmed the kernel of the SIMSCRIPT II compiler; in other words, he brought the SIMSCRIPT II compiler to the point where SIMSCRIPT II was capable of compiling itself. He then recruited Richard Villanueva to continue adding planned SIMSCRIPT II features to the compiler and library routines. Markowitz recruited Phil Kiviat to write the SIMSCRIPT II programming manual (Kiviat, Villanueva, and Markowitz, 1968). Kiviat and Villanueva completed SIMSCRIPT II through Level 5 with Markowitz as a consultant—after Karr and Markowitz left RAND to form CACI, to give SIMSCRIPT (I) courses, do simulation consulting, and, later, rebuild SIMSCRIPT (I) as CACI's SIMSCRIPT I.5.

On March 15 (the Ides of March), 1968, Herb Karr, with $47\frac{1}{2}$ percent of CACI stock, and James Berkson, with 5 percent of CACI stock, fired Markowitz, who had $47\frac{1}{2}$ percent of the stock, thus settling the question of how CACI would make major decisions when its founders disagreed. This ended Markowitz's control of the content of CACI's proprietary products. Markowitz no longer owns CACI stock: He sold much of his stock after the Karr and Markowitz split, partly in the CACI IPO and partly in the aftermarket, and divested the remainder at the request of an IBM lawyer when he joined IBM Research. Nevertheless he retains a strong paternal affection for all things SIMSCRIPT.

SIMSCRIPT II.5, CACI's proprietary version of SIMSCRIPT II, was developed after the Karr and Markowitz split. It includes all of the RAND SIMSCRIPT II (i.e., SIMSCRIPT II, as planned, through Level 5) plus neat features such as two- and three-dimensional graphic output, mixed continuous and discrete-event simulation, and the process view discussed later. Unless otherwise specified, "SIMSCRIPT II" refers to the RAND SIMSCRIPT II. Any capability of SIMSCRIPT II is also a capability of SIMSCRIPT II.5.

SIMSCRIPT III added to SIMSCRIPT II.5 features that will be discussed later, such as subsystems, polymorphism, and inheritance. Thus any capability of SIMSCRIPT II.5 is also a capability of SIMSCRIPT III. Steve Rice was the project leader and principal designer of the SIMSCRIPT III additions to SIMSCRIPT II.5. Steve Bailey programmed the additions, and Markowitz served as consultant, all under the supervision of Ana Marjanski. See Rice, Markowitz, Marjanski, and Bailey (2005).

Any reference to SIMSCRIPT without specification of *which* SIMSCRIPT refers to *all* SIMSCRIPTs.

After Karr and Berkson fired Markowitz, Markowitz taught (at UCLA) and consulted, with the Planning Research Corporation (PRC) being one of his first clients. After a few months with PRC, Markowitz was told that PRC's own internal information system, programmed in COBOL, was obsolete and hard to update. Markowitz proposed an information system programmed in the then-popular PL/I with calls on subroutines that processed database entities, attributes, and sets. The resulting information system, named SIMSCRIPT$_{PDQ}$, proved as flexible as predicted, and was PRC's internal information system for many years, long after Markowitz had moved from Santa Monica to New York to run a convertible-bond hedge fund. Current efforts to find out how long SIMSCRIPT$_{PDQ}$ served PRC have been frustrated by the fact that PRC eventually merged with Litton Industries, and PRC Litton eventually was absorbed into Northrup Grumman. Apparently any institutional memory of SIMSCRIPT$_{PDQ}$ has disappeared.

IBM EAS-E is the RAND SIMSCRIPT II with Level 5 removed and with the Markowitz, Malhotra, and Pazel (1983) implementation of Level 6 added. The IBM EAS-E implementation of Level 6 was completed about the time that IBM finished converting from IMS to System R—including software development, manual writing, and staff training. IBM management was not about to be persuaded to convert again in the then-foreseeable future.

THE PROCESS VIEW

Russell (1975) introduced the *process view* into CACI's SIMSCRIPT II.5. A process consists of a series of steps, like a subroutine. The difference is that a process routine can include simulated time delays between the execution of successive steps, either because the process routine encounters a WAIT command that instructs the simulator to wait a specified amount of simulated time before executing the next statement, or because the process encounters a SUSPEND command, in which case the process does not proceed until some other routine ACTIVATEs it.

To better understand the relationship between the process view and the event view, we must consider in greater detail how a timing routine keeps track of forthcoming events. Glossing over some efficiency-oriented implementation details, when a future event is scheduled in an asynchronous simulation by a CAUSE or SCHEDULE statement, an *event notice* entity is (essentially) placed in a *set* called the *calendar*. When this particular event occurrence is the most imminent one on the calendar, the timing routine removes the event notice from the calendar and passes it to the appropriate event routine. The event routine can do anything with the event notice that it could do with any other temporary entity whose ID it knows. Specifically, it can "destroy" (delete from the simulation) the specific event notice. This happens so routinely that SIMSCRIPT II destroys the event notice automatically unless it is instructed otherwise with a "SAVING THE EVENT NOTICE" phrase. In the latter case, the event routine can either immediately schedule another occurrence of itself using the given event notice, or save the event notice for possible future use.

The SIMSCRIPT II CANCEL statement removes a specified coming event notice from the calendar without destroying it. Again, this event notice can be destroyed, reused immediately, or saved for possible use later.

Process control actions are implemented using the coming event mechanisms of the event view. Each process-instance has an associated coming event notice. The WAIT statement places the particular process-instance coming event notice on the calendar, as would a CAUSE or SCHEDULE command. The SUSPEND pauses in its execution of the process routine by returning control to the timing routine *without* placing its coming event notice on the calendar. There is also an INTERRUPT command that removes a WAITing process, just as a CANCEL statement would. The ACTIVATE statement places a SUSPENDed or INTERRUPTed process back on the calendar, again as would a new CAUSE or SCHEDULE statement. (The CAUSE statement has two versions: one creates a new coming event notice and places it on the calendar; the other does so with a specified existing coming event notice.)

Thus the process view—with its WAIT, SUSPEND, INTERRUPT, and ACTIVATE commands—adds a layer on top of the event view of dynamic systems description. SIMSCRIPTs II.5 and III retain event routines and commands to CAUSE and CANCEL events, as well as offering process routines. CACI recommends the process view. Markowitz still programs using the event view, perhaps because of habit, since he never programmed a major project using the process view. Since JLMSim was implemented in C++ using a made-for-the-occasion timing routine, it was easiest (at least for Markowitz) to think in terms of programming event routines rather than adding a process layer.

SUBSIDIARY ENTITIES

Experience with IBM EAS-E suggested that the following feature would be useful both for database entities and for EAS-E-oriented simulation programming. Conceptually, if entity E_1 has an attribute A whose value is entity E_2,

$$E_2 = A(E_1)$$

then E_2 may be either part of E_1 or referenced by E_1. At a modeling level, the difference is that when E_1 is deleted from a simulation, E_2 should also be deleted if it is part of E_1 and not if it is referenced by E_1. Similarly the entities of a set owned by E_1 may be *internal* (or *subsidiary*) and should disappear when its owner (E_1) disappears, or *external*, just referenced by E_1 and should not disappear with E_1.

At present, when a temporary entity, T, is destroyed in a SIMSCRIPT program, it is up to the programmer to also destroy any internal entities pointed at or owned by *T*. This internal information could be cleaned up automatically if the compiler knew which attribute values and sets are internal. We consider this a better solution than Java's "garbage collection" procedure of destroying objects that no one references, since the failure to reference some external entity may be a bug that should be warned against rather than "fixed" without question.

SIMSCRIPT III FEATURES

SIMSCRIPT III added certain desirable modern computer programming features to SIMSCRIPT II.5, such as *subsystems* and *polymorphism*. It also added inheritance in a way that Markowitz finds disturbing. The various subsections of this section discuss the desirability of some SIMSCRIPT III features.

Polymorphism, Reference Variables, and Strong Data Typing

All SIMSCRIPTs through II.5 refer to attributes of a temporary entity (such as the due date of a job) by expressions such as

Due.date (J)

Due.date (JOB)

where J and JOB are integer variables containing the location in memory of the job's information. SIMSCRIPT compilers check that J and JOB are integer variables, but not that they point to jobs. This can lead to a hard-to-find bug when a reference to job attributes by J or JOB points to some irrelevant place in memory—especially when data are written to an irrelevant location, clobbering who-knows-what.

In SIMSCRIPT III, J would be user-defined as a job *reference variable*. This is referred to as *strong data typing*. As in SIMSCRIPT II, SIMSCRIPT III automatically defines a global variable called "JOB" when a temporary entity type with that name is declared. The difference is that SIMSCRIPT III automatically defines JOB as a job reference variable rather than as an integer.

Polymorphism refers, generally, to the use of a word in two or more ways. An example would be two or more entity types with attributes that have the same name. For example, a simulator or DSS might include entity types Passenger, Suitcase, and Observation (the latter being an observation of prior airline traffic on a given route). Each of these might have an attribute called "Weight," the first and second of them being a physical weight and the third a weight to be used in some kind of weighted average. The first two might be stored as an integer (pounds) and the third as a floating-point number. The values of each of these could be located in different places in the records that represent individuals of the respective entity types. This poses no problem if, when referring to an instance of "Weight" as in Weight (I), the argument "I" has been defined as a Passenger, a Suitcase, or an Observation reference variable. The compiler would then know the attribute's location and data type.

Attributes of permanent entities are stored as one-dimensional arrays. For example, if Machine.Group is a permanent entity that owns a set named QUEUE, then in the statement

$$N.QUEUE \, (MG)$$

MG must be an integer in the range

$$1 \leq MG \leq N.MACHINE.GROUP \qquad (1)$$

where N.MACHINE.GROUP is a variable (automatically defined by SIMSCRIPT II when told that MACHINE.GROUP is a permanent entity) equal to the number of machine groups in the current simulation run. SIMSCRIPT III does not provide for MG to be declared as a MACHINE.GROUP reference variable. But this would be a desirable addition. Not only could the compiler check that an attribute, such as N.QUEUE, is in fact an attribute of the entity type that MG references, but the executing program could check that Equation (1) is satisfied whenever a value is assigned to MG.

Subsystems and Data Hiding

The designers of SIMSCRIPTs (I) and II had no idea that SIMSCRIPT would be used for enormous models with thousands of lines of PREAMBLE (containing the model's global definitions) and hundreds of thousands of lines of event or process routines and their subroutines, developed by teams at various locations. The need for "Subsystems" had been clear for some time, and was finally introduced in SIMSCRIPT III. Each subsystem has its own Public and Private Preambles, the former declaring global information that is available to the Main System or other Subsystems, and the latter being known only to routines within the Subsystems. A SIMSCRIPT III simulation always has a "Main" System that can elect to import one or more Subsystems.

A useful subsystems feature that is not in SIMSCRIPT III would be to (optionally) allow instances of a subsystem to have their own calendars of coming event occurrences, with some events being public and some private to the subsystem. Only the most imminent public event occurrence need be posted to the Main System's calendar. This feature would facilitate the running of separate subsystems on separate ("parallel") processors.

Inheritance

The EAS view of status description was first published in Markowitz, Hausner, and Karr (1963), whereas the currently fashionable object-oriented (OO) view is based on SIMULA, first published in Dahl and Nygaard (1966). The OO view may be characterized as an enhanced EA view. In particular, an OO "object" corresponds to an EAS "entity," an OO "property" corresponds to an EAS "attribute," and an OO "class" corresponds to an EAS "entity type." Further details vary from one

OO implementation to another. In particular, we will consider two such implementations, namely

1. C++, the first of the Microsoft OO languages, and the one in which JLMSim is programmed
2. The SIMSCRIPT III version of the OO view

The concept of a set is not intrinsic to the OO view, as it is to the EAS-E view. Microsoft's Foundation Classes (MFC) provide assistance to C++ programmers in the use of certain kinds of sets. The MFC rules for interfacing sets stored one way differ from those for interfacing sets stored a different way, and all of these MFC interface rules are awkward as compared to the SIMSCRIPT command

File J in QUEUE (MG)

The latter, as it says, directs the computer to file job J into the queue of the machine group MG. The same command is used to file into LIFO, FIFO, or Ranked sets, whether the entities involved are "permanent," temporary, or database entities. To change the set discipline of QUEUE, one changes the set specification in the program's PREAMBLE and recompiles the program.

Inheritance is a feature that plays a prominent role in OO languages, was not a formal part of the SIMSCRIPTs through II.5, and was introduced in SIMSCRIPT III. For example, in SIMSCRIPT III, one can now declare that

Every Human *is a* Mammal.

In this case, all Humans *inherit* (that is, they also have) all the attributes of Mammals. Since SIMSCRIPT III is an EAS-oriented language, Humans also inherit the set ownership and membership capabilities of Mammals. In this respect, the effect is as if one copied and pasted the attribute and set definitions of Mammal into those of Human.

Ideally SIMSCRIPT III should have added inheritance capabilities to SIMSCRIPT II's temporary and permanent entities, and used SIMSCRIPT II's synonym capabilities to make "Object" and "Entity" synonyms. In fact, it was decided not to touch existing temporary or permanent entity capabilities. Thus, SIMSCRIPT III has "objects" with inheritance and "entities" without.

Markowitz objects to SIMSCRIPT III's bifurcation of the things of the world into Entities or Objects. The whole purpose of the SIMSCRIPT exercise, starting with SIMSCRIPT (I) onward, was to provide a seamless path from a vision of a world to be simulated to an executing program. When one looks at the things about one—such as bookcases, shelves, and books—one cannot **see** any difference between things that are entities and things that are objects. Things are things.

It was a business decision to add OO-style programming to SIMSCRIPT, to accommodate new or potential users who were accustomed to an OO point of view. It was not immediately obvious how to seamlessly merge OO conventions with EAS conventions, so in the interest of getting the job done,

SIMSCRIPT III allows the programmer to draw on many of SIMSCRIPT II's facilities (including sets) either from an OO view or from an EAS view. At the time, Markowitz concurred, since SIMSCRIPT III introduced highly desirable features like subsystems and strong data typing, and one could always program with an EAS viewpoint rather than an OO viewpoint. This was an OK temporary solution, but less than ideal.

CONTINUED IN CHAPTER 12

Chapter 12, the last chapter in this volume, has recommendations for "the next 62 years," including suggestions for a SIMSCRIPT II-based language (perhaps to be called SIMSCRIPT M) that include database entities and exploit the parallelism of modern computers.

8

GAME THEORY AND DYNAMIC PROGRAMMING

INTRODUCTION

The previous chapter explored the use of simulation in financial analysis. The present chapter is our first on optimization. Specifically, in this chapter we seek relationships that hold generally; in the next chapter we present the optimum solution to a highly simplified but historically important model; and Chapter 11 explores the use of approximation and judgment for models beyond our optimization capabilities. But the models whose solutions we approximate in Chapter 11 are themselves enormous simplifications of the real world. The section that follows this introduction fantasizes as to what a "more realistic model" might contain.

PRWSim (A POSSIBLE REAL-WORLD SIMULATOR)

To visualize "a more realistic model" into which we could place an RDM (Rational Decision-Making) family, consider what a possible real-world simulator (PRWSim) would be like. Start with the JLMSim model. Add firms in a multitude of industries, issuing all sorts of corporate news. Add a stream of major new products, both on the consumer side and on the production side of the market. Add macroeconomic considerations such as Fed policies and their consequences. For the stylized investors of JLMSim substitute game-of-life families at various stages of their life cycle. Add other kinds of investors sketched in Chapter 6, including various kinds of institutional investors and investors with stock trading programs whose programs are not known publicly. Add news media such as the *Wall Street Journal* and TV pundits. Include crooks, scoundrels, and political risk, such as politicians who believe (or say they believe) that profit seeking is evil. Last, but definitely not least, include HDM financial advisors and their decision support systems that the RDM family can call upon if it so desires.

Into this circus add an RDM family, perhaps consisting of a father, a mother, four children, and pets. Recall that an RDM is assumed to make no errors in logic or arithmetic, and suffers no fuzziness in its perception of its own preferences. But it has only such information as would also be available to a similarly situated HDM. For example, suppose that an RDM is in a poker game. Since the present volume assumes known odds, assume that the RDM knows the betting rules that the other players are following. He or she also knows his or her own cards, the bets ("raise," "see," or "fold") made, and the number of cards drawn by each of the other players. But the RDM does not observe the cards that the other players hold (or held, if they have now folded). Using its logic and calculating abilities, the RDM must infer the *conditional probabilities* of alternative possible sets of hands of the other players, *given* the information that the RDM has. Similarly, mom and pop RDMs do not have special information about companies or industries. They have to decide, for example, from information available to the general public, whether to choose their own portfolio or to seek outside advice and, in the latter case, which advisor to use.

Of course the number of possible states of a poker game is minuscule as compared to that of a possible real-world game. *Nevertheless,* there are useful concepts and relationships that are applicable to all such games, as we will review in the remainder of this chapter.

CONCEPTS FROM GAME THEORY

As defined by von Neumann and Morgenstern (1944) (vNM), the word *game* refers to a set of rules. It is to be distinguished from a specific *play* of the game. For example, the rules that define the game "chess" include the setup of the chessboard, who moves first, what moves are permitted in a particular situation, how long a player may take to make a move, and the like. In this strict sense a rule that allows players to e-mail moves the next day defines a different game from one that allows each player only a certain number of minutes to complete a specified number of moves.

The distinction between a game as a set of rules and a particular play of that game is not commonly made in day-to-day
speech. One asks, "How about playing a game of chess?" But
vNM needed to distinguish between the two, and chose the word
game to represent the set of rules, as opposed to a specific *play*
of the game. We will abide by this distinction when the distinction is important. But often, when the meaning is clear from the
context, we find it harmless and extremely convenient to ignore
the distinction and say, for example, that a particular event "ends
the game," rather than say the perhaps puzzling "ends the play"
or the verbose "ends the particular play of the game."

A many-period game consists of a series of *moves* by each
player. VNM assumes that these are made sequentially, even
when it is natural to think of them as simultaneous. For example,
in a two-person game of "paper, rock, and scissors" each player
chooses one of these, and the two decisions are revealed simultaneously. But one may regard even these moves as happening
sequentially, since a game's rules may specify that the information
available to the second player to move does not necessarily include
decisions already made by the first player. *Our formal analyses
will adopt the convention that moves are made sequentially.*

A *strategy* is defined by vNM to be a set of rules that specify
a player's choice of move at any time as a function of the opportunities and information available to the player at that time.
Thus a deterministic two-person zero-sum game with complete
information (namely one in which there are no random elements, each player's prior moves are known to the other player,
and one player's loss is the other's gain) is described by a single
(perhaps very large) *payoff* matrix $\Pi = (\pi_{ij})$. The entry in the

*i*th row and *j*th column of Π specifies the positive or negative payoff to Player 1 from Player 2 if Player 1 chooses the *i*th of its possible strategies and Player 2 chooses its *j*th.

When the outcome of a two-person game with complete information depends on random elements as well as players' choices of strategies, the payoff matrix shows the *expected* gain or loss to each player. This assumes that each possible outcome is zero-sum. The situation changes when each player is maximizing the expected value of a nonlinear utility function. For example, if the game consists of one flip of a coin, say for $100, and each of two players has a strictly concave utility function, then both players have a negative expected return from playing the game, and should decline to play it if that is an option. Generally, if the game is not zero-sum or there are $n > 2$ players in the game, then each player has its own payoff array showing the expected utility, $EU^I(i_1, i_2, \ldots, i_n)$, of the Ith player as a function of the strategy number chosen by each of the n players.

Von Neumann and Morgenstern distinguish between the *normal* form of a game and what they called the *extensive form* and we will call the *extended form* of a game.[1] The extended form of a specific play of the game of chess, for example, is traditionally described as

WHITE	BLACK
P-KP4	P-KP4
N-KB3	N-KB3
...	...

The normal form would use the fact that there is an enormous—*but finite*—number, N_W, of strategies (as defined earlier) that White can adopt, and a (perhaps different) finite number, N_B, that Black can adopt. (The fact that there are only a finite number of possible board configurations, and that the game is declared a draw if the same configuration occurs a third time, assures that games end in a finite number of moves, and that consequently there is only a finite number of possible strategies.) If a pair of rational opponents played a game of chess in normal form, White would choose a number between 1 and N_W, and Black would choose a number between 1 and N_B. They would hand their strategy-numbers to a referee, who would consult the payoff matrix (Π) and announce that either White won, Black won, or the game was a draw. As we will show in our discussion of how (in principle) to solve such a game using the dynamic programming principle, each RDM would know the outcome of the game before it started. Therefore RDMs would not play chess.

NON-"THEORY OF GAMES" GAMES

There are at least two ways in which some of the games we consider, or that appear in the financial literature, differ from those of vNM. One difference concerns a fixed versus a variable number of players. VNM discusses two-person games, three-person games, n-person games, and even briefly one-person games. It does not discuss games in which players drop in and out, as happens now, for example, in some Internet games. The simple stylized consumption-investment games we discuss in the next chapter are one-person games. But a game-of-life simulator, for example, would allow for births and deaths and therefore would have a varying number of players.

A second way in which some games in the financial literature differ from those of vNM is that they may not be *time-bounded*. A game such as chess, which has a maximum number of moves, is time-bounded. But many stylized financial games are *time-unbounded*. Some run forever and seek to maximize the present value of future expected utilities. Others terminate almost surely in a finite number of moves, but there is no upper bound as to when this will happen. An example of the latter is Bernoulli's (1738, 1954) "St. Petersburg Paradox" game which ends when the first tail appears in a sequence of coin flips.

For the most part, we will confine ourselves to time-bounded games, since, for example, a game that automatically terminates when the sun is expected to implode is the same as an infinite game *for all practical purposes* and, as usual, finite math is much easier to explain rigorously than nonfinite math.

(*Note*: We say "time-bounded," but we really mean "maximum-number-of-moves-bounded." For example if, like the arrow in Zeno's paradox, the first move happens at $t = 1/2$; the second at $t = 3/4$; the third at $t = 7/8$, etc., the game would be time-bounded but not maximum-number-of-moves-bounded. In particular, it would *not* have a *last move* whose existence is assumed in most of our analyses.)

RANDOMIZED STRATEGIES

VNM permits *mixed* strategies in which a player chooses randomly among *pure* strategies. For example, a player in a two-person rock-scissors-paper game can assure itself a 50-50 chance of winning by choosing its moves randomly. This avoids the possibility that, in trying to outguess its opponent's next move, the opponent outguesses the player's.

Large institutional investors are rarely secretive about their portfolios, but they often need to be secretive about intended changes in their portfolios. They hope thereby to avoid front-running, in which traders take positions in the direction in which the institution is headed. Perhaps the general theory of games, including randomized strategies, would be of practical use to traders on either side of large institutional trades. But (except for a brief mention of Nash equilibria toward the end of this chapter) general game theory including randomized strategies is beyond the scope of this volume. In particular, we typically assume that, while an RDM individual or family may live in a complex world, no one in this complex world will take action that will affect the RDM adversely because he or she anticipates the strategy of the specific RDM.

THE UTILITY OF A MANY-PERIOD GAME

Our Chapter 1 defined the expected utility maxim for single-period situations as that of acting as if one assigns a number, called its utility, to each possible outcome of a chance situation, and then chooses among alternative probability distributions of outcomes so as to maximize the expected value of utility. The definition of the expected utility maxim for many-period risk situations is the same—except that utility U^I to Player I may depend on the entire *trajectory* of the game, namely the sequence of *states* $s_1, \ldots, s_T$ through which the game passes. I.e.,

$$U^I = U^I (s_1, s_2, \ldots, s_T) \tag{1a}$$

The states $s_1, s_2, \ldots, s_T$ of a trajectory may be thought of as the status descriptions (describable in terms of Entities, Attributes, and Sets, of course) generated by a run of a synchronous or asynchronous discrete event simulator.

Chapter 11 of Markowitz (1959) argues, axiom by axiom, that the three axioms of its Chapter 10 (and of our Chapter 1)—which imply the desirability of the expected utility maxim for single-period situations—also apply to probability distributions of trajectories. Such an argument is not really needed, since the vNM concept of a strategy in normal form converts any many-period game into a single-period game. Either way, we conclude that the same set of axioms that implied the maximization of EU for choosing among probability distributions of outcomes, as defined in our Chapter 1, apply equally to choosing among probability distributions of trajectories here.

Specifically, as in Volume I, an *outcome* is *that of which an RDM seeks a good probability distribution*. Or, to put it the other way around, the basic assumption of any particular utility analysis (here, as in Chapter 1) is that the situation has been analyzed such that it is a good probability distribution of outcomes—*thus defined*—that the RDM seeks.

Our discussion of dynamic programming, starting in the section after this, assumes that status s_t, $t = 1, \ldots, T$, includes enough information to compute the utility U^I to the Ith player of a play of the game. Usually a small subset of the trajectory of a play of a game will suffice for computing its utility to each player. For example, the next chapter presents the single-player many-period investment model analyzed by Mossin (1968) and Samuelson (1969) in which the utility of a play of the game is a function of final wealth only. In this case nothing would need to be remembered at each point in time in a simulated play of the game other than the player's current wealth. More generally, the utility to the player in a single-player, many-period consumption-investment game is typically assumed to be a function of a sequence of consumption expenditures plus, perhaps, final wealth as a bequest:

$$U = U\,(C_1, C_2, \ldots, C_T, W_T) \tag{1b}$$

(We omit the Player I superscript in analyses of single-player games.) It is often assumed that the utility function is a discounted present value:

$$U = \sum_{t=1}^{T} \frac{u(C_t)}{(1 + d)^t} + v(W_T)/(1 + d)^T \tag{2}$$

where d is a discount factor, $u(C_t)$ is the utility at time t of consumption level C_t, and $v(W_T)$ is the utility of the bequest W_T.

In this case, in order to compute final utility, one need only remember the partial sums

$$\sum_{i=1}^{t} \frac{u(c_i)}{(1 + d)^i}$$

Equation (2) is a convenient but not a necessary form of utility function, and is often not realistic. For example, Markowitz (1959) Chapter 13 suggests as a possible utility function (with $T = 3$)

$$U = \log C_1 + 0.9 \log C_2 + 0.81 \log C_3$$
$$- 0.5 \log[\max(1, C_1/C_2)] - 0.45 \log[\max(1, C_2/C_3)] \qquad (3)$$

If C always rises over time, then U in Equation (3) is the discounted value of the logarithms of consumption. But if C_t is lower than C_{t-1} then U reflects the discomfort of reducing consumption as compared to keeping it at a constant or rising level.

A somewhat similar utility function is used by GuidedChoice (GC) as part of its GuidedSpending product. Recall from Chapter 7 that GuidedSpending may be started before retirement but continues into retirement. GuidedSpending asks the participant for two levels of consumption, $C_U > C_L$. These two consumption levels are used in Monte Carlo simulation runs that estimate the probability distribution of possible consequences of any given consumption-investment strategy. At any point in simulated time a tentative current consumption, C, is determined by an actuarial calculation that allows for the participant living somewhat longer than expected. If C exceeds C_U the difference, $C - C_U$, is saved. If C is less than C_L then $C_L - C$ is dissaved if available. If the participant declines to supply either C_L and C_U, or a target bequest level B, then default values are computed as a function of the participant's likely retirement wealth.

To compute a utility U for a particular consumption and bequest trajectory, GuidedSpending forms a score S by combining *average* consumption level A and maximum year-to-year *decline* in consumption D:

$$S = A - \alpha D \qquad (4)$$

The idea here is similar to that behind Equation (3): Declines in consumption are unpleasant, even if the lower consumption level would have otherwise been considered ample. GuidedSpending then computes a "normalized score," NS, such that if $A = C_U$ and $D = 0$, then $U = 1$, whereas if $A = C_L$ and $D = 0$, then $U = 0$. The utility U assigned to the consumption stream is a function of NS,

$$U = f(\text{NS}) \qquad (5)$$

where f is a smooth curve with $U = 1$ as an asymptotic upper bound, and with U dropping off at an increasing rate, especially as NS drops below zero. A term reflecting W_T versus B is added for a final score.

For a utility function such as that used by GC's GuidedSpending product—which depends on A, D, and W_T—it is sufficient to save:

1. current wealth W_t

2. the partial sum $\sum_{i=1}^{t} C_i$

3. the largest (in absolute value) consumption decline so far, and

4. the current consumption level C_t in case $C_{t+1} < C_t$

In general, for a utility function like that in Equation (1b), it is sufficient to save current wealth W_t and consumption levels so far, $C_1, \ldots, C_t$.

In what follows we assume that the ending system status, s_T, includes enough information to compute the utility to each player of a play of a game. Thus without loss of generality we assume that

$$U^I = U^I(s_T) \tag{6}$$

We emphasize that this does not assume that utility is a function of final wealth only, as in the Mossin-Samuelson game, but it can be any function of the trajectory of the play of the game.

DYNAMIC PROGRAMMING

In the case of a time-bounded game, the *dynamic programming* (DP) procedure starts from the last period, $t = T$, and works backward to the first period, $t = 1$. In doing so, it reduces the T-period game in extended form to a sequence of single-period games. As we discuss later in this chapter, the DP last-to-first method of computation is of limited use as a computing procedure, because typically only the simplest games can be explicitly solved by this method. On the other hand, it is conceptually of the greatest importance. In particular, it shows the relationship between the single-period analyses discussed in Volume I and the many-period analyses covered in the present volume.

The game of tic-tac-toe can serve to illustrate the basic DP idea for deterministic games with complete information. We will drop these assumptions later in this chapter.

SOLVING TIC-TAC-TOE

As we assume most readers know, tic-tac-toe is played on a 3×3 grid such as the one in Figure 8.1 showing a possible status of the game after the fourth move. The game starts (at $t = 0$) with a blank grid. The first player places an "X" in any of the nine blank squares. This is the move labeled *Move 1* in the timeline below. It transforms the system in its initial state

FIGURE 8.1 A Tic-Tac-Toe Game After Four Moves.

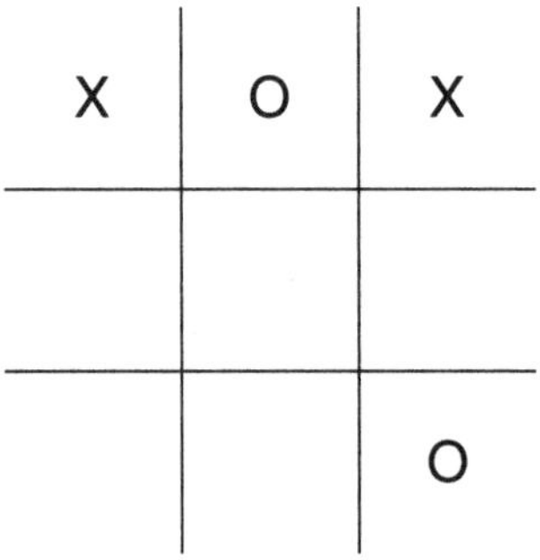

s_0 to its next state s_1. The other player then places an "O" in any of the eight squares that are still blank.

$t = 0$	1	2	3	4	5	6	7	8	9
Move	1	2	3	4	5	6	7	8	9
Player	X	O	X	O	X	O	X	O	X

This is *Move 2*, which transforms state s_1 into state s_2. The X player then places an "X" in any of the seven still-unoccupied squares, and so on. The game ends when either:

1. the X player wins by having placed three Xs in a row, or three in a column, or three in either of the two three-square diagonals; or

2. the O player does the same before the X player does (with Os instead of Xs, of course); or

3. all nine squares are filled without either player winning.

Let us assign scores +1, −1, and 0 to outcomes (1), (2), and (3) respectively. The X player tries to maximize the score; the O player tries to minimize it. Thus the score of the game is the utility of the game to the X player, and the negative of the score is the utility to the O player. (In a deterministic game, it is only the ordinal ranking of outcomes that determines choice, rather than cardinal utility.)

The optimum strategy for each player, and the score of the game if each player follows its optimum strategy, can be computed as follows. In dynamic programming (DP) fashion, start by analyzing possible states at time point $t = 9$ when the game is over. These possible states consist of grids in which one player or the other has won, or in which all cells are filled and no one has won. If a player wins before the ninth move of the game, some squares will still be blank at $t = 9$. Thus one can divide all 3×3 grids with Xs, Os, and blanks into four sets, namely those in which:

A. the X player won;

B. the O player won;

C. the grid is full and no one won; or

D. this grid could not be s_9, either because the game is still in progress or because this grid could never happen, e.g., because it has the wrong number of Xs and Os.

Store a "1" with each grid in subset A, a "−1" with each grid in subset B, a "0" with each grid in subset C, and delete (or mark appropriately) each grid in subset D.

Next process all grids with *at most* eight nonblank entries, at $t = 8$. Again divide these grids into four subsets labeled A, B, C, and D. Again subset A contains completed games in which X has won; subset B, those in which O has won; and subset D, grids that could not happen at $t = 8$.

Subset C contains the remaining grids, namely those that could occur at $t = 8$, but in which neither player has won *yet*. Specifically, they contain *exactly* one blank square, since possible grids at $t = 8$ with more than one blank square must already have a winner. As the timeline reminds us, at $t = 8$ it is X's turn to make *Move 9* by placing an X in the sole empty square. This produces a grid without blanks. In the previous step (for $t = 9$) a score was assigned to all such grids. This is also the score for each grid in subset C at $t = 8$, since this will inevitably be the score of the game if this grid is reached.

Next process grids with at most seven nonblank entries at $t = 7$. This step will more fully show what is going on in this example and, analogously, in dynamic programming calculations generally. As before divide all grids with at least two blank squares into four subsets depending on whether (A) X has won, (B) O has won, (D) this grid cannot occur at $t = 7$, or (C) the game is still in play and it is O's turn to move. In the last case, the O player makes the eighth move of the game by filling in one of the two blank squares. The way an RDM O player would decide where to place its O is as follows:

> For each grid in subset C, and for each of the two blank squares in that grid, tentatively place an O in that square. This yields a grid with only one blank square. The values of all such games have been determined. For the particular $t = 7$ grid in subset C, the RDM O player would choose the move (among the two available) that minimizes the game score (this being best for the O player). This minimizing value is the score for the particular $t = 7$ grid, since it will inevitably be the score of the game.

Similarly for the X player when $t = 6$,

> For each of the three blanks in a possible $t = 6$ grid with the game not already decided, tentatively place an X in that blank. This produces a $t = 7$ grid whose score has already been determined. Choose the move that maximizes the game score (which is X's utility). That will be the final score of the game *if each player chooses optimally for itself* in the remainder of the game.

The general case may now be stated, not only for the $t \leq 5$ move for tic-tac-toe, but for any deterministic game with complete information. In such games one starts the DP computation by considering each possible state s_{T-1} at time $T-1$, the last possible point in time when a decision can be made if the game is still in play. (At $t = T$, there is nothing to decide.) In general, though not in tic-tac-toe, the player to move at this time may be a function of the current system state, s_{T-1}. However in tic-tac-toe, as in general, there may be no "player to move" because the game is already over. The player to move (if any) considers in turn each possible move it can make in this state, and chooses the one whose resulting next (and final) state, s_T, has the highest utility for said player to move. We may assume—without loss of generality—that this utility is a function only of the final state, s_T.

In games other than two-person zero-sum games, ties for the choice of best move must be broken by some definite rule, known in advance by all players. This is because two moves that are *equally* good for the player to move may not be *equally* good or bad for all players in an n-player game, including for the other player in a two-person non-zero-sum game. In order to carry through the DP calculation in such a game, each player must know what each other player will do in each possible state that may arise subsequently.

In addition to finding the best action for a given next-to-last state, s_{T-1}, the DP calculation also determines the utility $U^I(s_{T-1})$ attached to that state for each Player I. This will be the utility of the game for Player I if state s_{T-1} is reached and the player to move makes its optimal last move. This permits the DP computation to iterate one step backward in time, to $t = T - 2$, and repeat the process used for $t = T - 1$, but now using $U^I_{T-1}(s_{T-1})$ as the *derived* utility functions for what one might call the derived game. At each time t, the player-to-move maximizes a single-period utility function $U^I_{t+1}(s_{t+1})$ by the appropriate choice of actions available to it in state s_t.

We will see that in games in which each player knows the current state but the next state is random, the DP process proceeds as just discussed, except using expected utilities rather than known, deterministic utilities. In games with incomplete information, the RDM acts to maximize its expected utility *conditional on the information it has.* To define this formally, and to prove these assertions about DP, we need to discuss *conditional expected value.*

$U^I_{t+1}(s_{t+1})$ is the *central concept we seek from dynamic programming.* It is the expected value to Player I of the game as a whole on the condition that state s_{t+1} prevails at time $t + 1$ and each player plays optimally (for him- or herself, of course) at $t + 1$ and thereafter. It is the *derived utility function.* Given its possible choices in state s_t, the player to move chooses its move at time t, in state s_t, so as to maximize the expected value of this single-period derived utility function, i.e., it maximizes $EU^I_{t+1}(s_{t+1})$.

CONDITIONAL EXPECTED VALUE: AN EXAMPLE

The DP principle is an application of a simple but powerful theorem concerning *conditional expected values.* This section illustrates the concept and theorem with an example.

The following section generalizes the discussion, restricting ourselves to *finite sample spaces*. In other words, the random variables we consider can take on only a finite number of different values. Like Reason 1 in Chapter 6 for not dealing with continuous-time models, general sample spaces can also require math levels well beyond that assumed in this book. In particular, the *definitions* of conditional probability and conditional expected value are far from elementary for finite sample spaces, and are completely incomprehensible for non-finite sample spaces for someone not initiated into the inner sanctum of modern mathematics starting with Cantor's distinction between countably and uncountably infinite sets.

Table 8.1 shows a *sample space* representing the toss of a pair of dice. The first column presents a state number, i, for $i = 1$ to $N = 36$. The second column presents the probability p_i that the ith state will occur. In the present instance, all p_i equal $1/N$. The remaining columns present *random variables* defined on this sample space.

Suppose that the two dice are tossed one at a time. The first random variable, in the third column of the table, is the value, D_1, of Die One, the first die to be tossed. The next column presents the value, D_2, of Die Two. The following column shows the sum of the two dice.

Table 8.1 divides the 36 *sample points* of this sample space into six subsets, separated by blank lines and page breaks. We will refer to this as a *partition* of the sample space. As with any partition, the subsets of this partition are disjoint (no sample point is in more than one set) and exhaustive (every point in

TABLE 8.1 A Sample Space and Some of Its Random Variables

Sample Point No.	Prob	Die One	Die Two	Sum	Cond Exp Sum	Cond Exp Win (1)	Cond Exp Win (2)	Cond Exp Win (3)
1	1/36	1	1	2	4.5	-1.0000	-0.2707	-0.1252
2	1/36	1	2	3	4.5	-1.0000	-0.2707	-0.1252
3	1/36	1	3	4	4.5	-0.3333	-0.2707	-0.1252
4	1/36	1	4	5	4.5	-0.2000	-0.2707	-0.1252
5	1/36	1	5	6	4.5	-0.0909	-0.2707	-0.1252
6	1/36	1	6	7	4.5	1.0000	-0.2707	-0.1252
7	1/36	2	1	3	5.5	-1.0000	-0.1190	-0.1252
8	1/36	2	2	4	5.5	-0.3333	-0.1190	-0.1252
9	1/36	2	3	5	5.5	-0.2000	-0.1190	-0.1252
10	1/36	2	4	6	5.5	-0.0909	-0.1190	-0.1252
11	1/36	2	5	7	5.5	1.0000	-0.1190	-0.1252
12	1/36	2	6	8	5.5	-0.0900	-0.1190	-0.1252

(continued)

115

TABLE 8.1 (*Continued*)

Sample Point No.	Prob	Die One	Die Two	Sum	Cond Exp Sum	Cond Exp Win (1)	Cond Exp Win (2)	Cond Exp Win (3)
13	1/36	3	1	4	6.5	-0.3333	0.0141	-0.1252
14	1/36	3	2	5	6.5	-0.2000	0.0141	-0.1252
15	1/36	3	3	6	6.5	-0.0909	0.0141	-0.1252
16	1/36	3	4	7	6.5	1.0000	0.0141	-0.1252
17	1/36	3	5	8	6.5	-0.0909	0.0141	-0.1252
18	1/36	3	6	9	6.5	-0.2000	0.0141	-0.1252
19	1/36	4	1	5	7.5	-0.2000	0.0141	0.0970
20	1/36	4	2	6	7.5	-0.0909	0.0141	0.0970
21	1/36	4	3	7	7.5	1.0000	0.0141	0.0970
22	1/36	4	4	8	7.5	-0.0909	0.0141	0.0970
23	1/36	4	5	9	7.5	-0.2000	0.0141	0.0970
24	1/36	4	6	10	7.5	-0.3333	0.0141	0.0970

(*continued*)

TABLE 8.1 (*Continued*)

Sample Point No.	Prob	Die One	Die Two	Sum	Cond Exp Sum	Cond Exp Win (1)	Cond Exp Win (2)	Cond Exp Win (3)
25	1/36	5	1	6	8.5	−0.0909	0.2141	0.0970
26	1/36	5	2	7	8.5	1.0000	0.2141	0.0970
27	1/36	5	3	8	8.5	−0.0909	0.2141	0.0970
28	1/36	5	4	9	8.5	−0.2000	0.2141	0.0970
29	1/36	5	5	10	8.5	−0.3333	0.2141	0.0970
30	1/36	5	6	11	8.5	1.0000	0.2141	0.0970
31	1/36	6	1	7	9.5	1.0000	0.0626	0.0970
32	1/36	6	2	8	9.5	−0.0909	0.0626	0.0970
33	1/36	6	3	9	9.5	−0.2000	0.0626	0.0970
34	1/36	6	4	10	9.5	−0.3333	0.0626	0.0970
35	1/36	6	5	11	9.5	1.0000	0.0626	0.0970
36	1/36	6	6	12	9.5	−1.0000	0.0626	0.0970

117

the sample space is in some subset). We will label the sets of the partitions as $P_1, P_2, \ldots, P_K$, with $K = 6$ here.

In the present example, each set in the partition contains sample points with the same value of Die One. For example, all sample points in P_3 have Die One equal to three. The table shows that if a randomly drawn sample point i is in P_3—in symbols, $i \in P_3$—the value of the sum, S, must be 4, 5, 6, 7, 8, or 9. The *conditional probability distribution given that $i \in P_3$* may be obtained by deleting all rows except those with Die One equal to three, then rescaling the probabilities in the second column so that they sum to one. Thus the probability that the sample point i will take on various values given that the sample point is in P_3 is

$$\text{Prob}(i|i \in P_3) = 1/6 \tag{7}$$

The sixth column of the table has the *conditional expected value of S given that i is in a particular partition*. We denote this as

$$E(S|i \in P_k)$$

This is read "*E* of *S* [or Expected *S*] given *i* is in P_3." It is computed from the sums, $S(i)$, in the fifth column of Table 8.1 using conditional probabilities. Thus,

$$E(S|i \in P_k) = \sum_{i \in P_k} \text{Prob } (i|i \in P_k) \times S(i) \tag{8}$$

In the present example, since $i \in P_3$ is equivalent to $D_1 = 3$, we could also write $E(S|i \in P_3)$ as $E(S|D_1 = 3)$.

Note that $E(S|i \in P_k)$ is a random variable defined on this 36-point sample space. In other words, each of the 36 points in the sample space has an $E(S|i \in P_k)$ value assigned to it, with all points in a given partition having the *same* value. For example, all sample points in P_1 have

$$E(S|i \in P_1) = E(S|D_1 = 1)$$
$$= 4.5 \qquad (9)$$

Table 8.2 presents a new sample space with as many sample points as there are partitions in Table 8.1 ($K = 6$). The probability assigned to the sample point k in Table 8.2 is the same as the probability that $i \in P_k$ in Table 8.1, namely the sum of probabilities p_i for $i \in P_k$:

$$\text{Prob}(i \in P_k) = \sum_{i \in P_k} p_i \qquad (10)$$

The random variable in the third column of Table 8.2 equals the conditional expected sum, $E(S|i \in P_k)$, that all $i \in P_k$ share in Table 8.1.

The relationship we need subsequently is that

$$E(S) = \sum_k E(S|i \in P_k) \cdot \text{Prob}(i \in P_k) \qquad (11)$$

TABLE 8.2 A Related Sample Space

Sample Point No.	Prob	Cond Exp Sum
1	1/6	4.5
2	1/6	5.5
3	1/6	6.5
4	1/6	7.5
5	1/6	8.5
6	1/6	9.5

or, more compactly,

$$E(S) = E(E(S|i \in P_k)) \qquad (12)$$

In words, the expected value of S in the original 36-point sample space is the same as the expected value of the random variable $E(S|i \in P_k)$ either in the original 36-point sample space or in its implicit six-point sample space. The reader can confirm this numerically in the present case. In the next section we will prove it for any partition and random variable defined on any finite sample space.

GENERALIZATION

Let a random variable $r(i)$ take on values $v_1, v_2, \ldots, v_N$ on the N points of a finite sample space whose points have probabilities $p_1, p_2, \ldots, p_N$. Its expected value is

$$E(r) = \sum_{i=1}^{N} p_i v_i$$

Let P be a partition of the sample space into K disjoint, exhaustive sets $P_1, P_2, \ldots, P_K$. The probability, $\text{Prob}(P_k)$, that a randomly chosen i will be in P_k is given by Equation (10). The probability of i given that $i \in P_k$ is

$$\begin{aligned}\text{Prob}(i|i \in P_k) &= p_i/\text{Prob}(i \in P_k) &&\text{if } i \in P_k \\ &= 0 &&\text{otherwise}\end{aligned} \tag{13}$$

As characterized previously, the first line of Equation (13) results if one deletes all rows except those in P_k, and then rescales the remaining p_i so that they sum to one. As in the example in the previous section, the conditional expected value of a random variable, $r(i)$, given that the underlying sample point i is in the partition P_k, is computed using the conditional probabilities. With the current notation, this is

$$E(r(i)|i \in P_k) = \Sigma\, \text{Prob}(i|i \in P_k) \times v_i \tag{14}$$

The sum in Equation (14) can be either over only $i \in P_k$ or over all $i = 1$ to N, since $\text{Prob}(i|i \in P_k) = 0$ for i not in P_k.

Again as in the example in the preceding section, we can define a new sample space with K sample points—one for every partition in the analysis—with $\text{Prob}(i \in P_k)$ for $k = 1, \ldots, K$ as the probabilities assigned to each of the K sample points, and $E(r|i \in P_k)$ for $k = 1, \ldots, K$ as the value of a random variable defined on this sample space.

We are now prepared to prove the following:

Theorem: *Equation (11) and its Equation (12) interpretation are true.*

Proof

Except for the name of the random variable, the left-hand side (lhs) of the first line of Derivation (15) is the right-hand side (rhs) of Equation (12), and the rhs of the last line of the derivation is the lhs of Equation (12). The intervening steps show that these two are equal. Specifically, the rhs of the first line is the definition of expected value, applied to the random variable $E(r|i \in P_k)$; the rhs of the second line of the derivation substitutes Equations (10), (13), and (14) into the rhs of the first line. The next line results from canceling $\left(\Sigma_{i \in P_k} p_i \right)$ from the numerator and denominator of the prior line. The final lines result from adding the same terms in a different order and using definitions.

$$
\begin{aligned}
E(E(r|i \in P_k)) &= \sum_{k=1}^{K} \text{Prob}(i \in P_k) \times E(r|i \in P_k) \\
&= \sum_{k=1}^{K} \left(\sum_{i \in P_k} p_i \right) \times \left(\sum_{i \in P_k} p_i v_i \right) \Big/ \left(\sum_{i \in P_k} p_i \right) \\
&= \sum_{k=1}^{K} \sum_{i \in P_k} p_i v_i \\
&= \sum_{i=1}^{N} p_i v_i \\
&= E(r)
\end{aligned}
\tag{15}
$$

QED

PARTITIONS, INFORMATION, AND DP CHOICE: AN EXAMPLE

Imagine a friendly two-person game of "craps" to determine which of two players pays for their beers. The game starts with a flip of a coin to decide who will be the "shooter" today and who will be the "house." The shooter rolls a pair of dice. As usual, the shooter wins on this first roll (the *roll-out*) if the pair sums to 7 or 11; he or she loses if the sum is 2, 3, or 12. If the dice sum to any other number on this first roll, that other value—4, 5, 6, 8, 9, or 10—is now the shooter's *point*. The shooter continues to roll the dice until a follow-up roll produces a sum equal to either 7 or the shooter's point. In the former case the house wins and the shooter pays for their beers; whereas if the point is thrown before a 7, the shooter wins and the house buys the beers.

The game as just stated is time-unbounded. For example, suppose the shooter's point is eight. Since the probability of getting a seven on any roll is 6/36 and that of getting an eight is 5/36, there is a probability of 25/36 that neither a seven nor an eight will appear on any given roll. The chance that neither a seven nor an eight has appeared after a hundred rolls of the dice is $(25/36)^{100} \cong 1.5 \times 10^{-16}$. This is like owning "one and one-half" tickets for a lottery in which

$$(\text{ten million}) \times (\text{a billion}) \text{ tickets}$$

were sold. It little affects the expected outcome to each player if instead of letting the game continue indefinitely, we assume that after 100 rolls of the dice without a winner, the two players split the tab.

We will refer to the two players as Players A and B. Let us assign a score of $S = +1$ if A wins and $S = -1$ if B wins, and ignore as practically impossible the negligible fraction of plays that have not produced a winner after 100 follow-up rolls. Without loss of generality, we can assume that all games have 102 time points labeled -1 through 100. Status at $t = -1$ is "The shooter is to be determined." Status at time $t = 0$ is either "Player A is the shooter and the point is to be established" or "Player B is the shooter and the point is to be established." For $t > 0$ the status is either

Game Over. Player A won;

Game Over. Player B won;

Player A is the shooter; 4 is the point;

Player A is the shooter; 5 is the point;

etc. And similarly for Player B.

Table 8.3 calculates the expected payoff to the shooter. The first column shows the sum of the dice on the first roll. The second column shows the number of chances out of 36 of having this sum as the first roll. It equals the number of times that the sum appears in the Sum column in Table 8.1. The third column contains the expected payoff conditional on the sum on the first roll equaling the number in the first column. In the case of the sum on the first roll equaling 2, 3, 7, 11, or 12, the +1 or −1 in the third column follows immediately from craps' rules. We return shortly to the other entries in the

TABLE 8.3 Craps Probabilities

First Roll	36 X Prob	Payoff	Pay X Prob
2	1	−1.00	−0.028
3	2	−1.00	−0.056
4	3	−0.33	−0.028
5	4	−0.20	−0.022
6	5	−0.09	−0.013
7	6	1.00	0.167
8	5	−0.09	−0.013
9	4	−0.20	−0.022
10	3	−0.33	−0.028
11	2	1.00	0.056
12	1	−1.00	−0.028
Sum	36		−0.014

column. The fourth column is the product of the probability of the entry in the first column (equal to the entry in the second column divided by 36) times the conditional expected value in the third column. Equation (12) assures us that the sum of these, −0.014, is the expected payoff of the game for the shooter.

To see how the entries in the third column of Table 8.3 are calculated when the roll-out does not produce a winner, consider the entry when four is the point. This equals

$$(+1)\left(\frac{3}{3+6}\right)+(-1)\left(\frac{6}{3+6}\right)=-0.33$$

Confirm that this is the expected score if the game is settled on the first follow-up roll, namely, (+1) times the fraction of the time that the point, four, occurs plus (−1) times the fraction of those times when a seven occurs, given that one or the other occurs. But if the score is not settled on the first follow-up roll, this is also the expected score if the winner is determined on the second follow-up roll. Or on the third, or the fourth, etc., except for the ignored, negligible percent of cases that are still not settled after 100 follow-up rolls. It follows, again from Equation (12), that −0.33 is the expected win for the shooter no matter when the result is determined.

Even if a play of this game lasts the full 100 follow-up rolls, it is still a single-period game as defined in Volume I, since it involves no additional decisions other than the initial decision to play the game. In Las Vegas the shooter is allowed to increase his or her bet when the point has been established. But an RDM shooter would not accept this option (assuming that the player wants to lose as little as possible per hour while enjoying the Las Vegas ambiance), since even the most favorable point has a greater expected loss than does the game as a whole.

Now let us introduce some additional opportunities to increase the bet. These would not be offered by a Las Vegas casino, since they can be favorable to the shooter, but they could be allowed in our friendly game, since each player has an equal chance of being "the house." Specifically, we will let the shooter—at his or her option given certain information—add to the wager appetizers that cost the same as the beer.

Instead of rolling two dice, suppose the "shooter" is dealt two cards—Card One from a "red deck" and Card Two from a "blue deck"—with the same probabilities as Die One and Die Two in Table 8.1. The third from last column in Table 8.1, labeled "CondExpWin (1)," presents the conditional expected win given the *pair* of cards (or dice) as in the third column of Table 8.3. The next column, labeled CondExpWin (2), presents the conditional expected values of the game payoff given different values of Card One. We see, for example, that the expected payoff (if the bet is not increased) is −0.27 if Card One equals 1, and equals 0.21 if Card One equals 5. The final column of the table is the conditional expected win (if the bet is not increased) if the shooter is told only that "the first card is low," i.e., equals 1, 2, or 3, or "the first card is high," i.e., equals 4, 5, or 6. These conditional expected wins are computed, as previously illustrated, by applying Equation (12) to the appropriate partitions of the sample space.

We can imagine different versions of an augmented craps game, depending on what information the shooter has when he or she can increase the bet. We analyze the version wherein the only opportunity the shooter has to increase the bet is after he or she has been informed whether the first card is high or low. In this case an RDM shooter would have limited information about the current state of the system but, nevertheless, can compute the conditional expected outcome depending on this information and the action taken.

As to whether the increase should be accepted, that depends on the shooter's and the house's utility functions.

Up to this point the game has had two outcomes, which we will characterize as "win D dollars" or "lose D dollars." Since, as explained in Chapter 1, the origin and scale of a utility function are arbitrary, we may assign to each player a utility of +1 to winning D and −1 to losing D.

There is another possibility implicit in our discussion: that of not playing the game. Implicitly we have assumed that the utility of this is negative since the players *do* play the game. (Since the game is symmetric, each player must have a 50-50 chance of winning or losing the game, if it is played.) When we add the possibility of the shooter doubling the bet, the situation has five possibilities that need consideration: Win D, Win $2D$, Lose D, Lose $2D$, No Game. We will denote their respective utilities as

$$U^I(D), U^I(-D), U^I(2D), U^I(-2D), U^I(0) \text{ for } I = A \text{ or } B$$

Again we ignore as negligible the possibility that the game runs its full length without a winner. Note that $U^I(D)$ here is *not* the utility to the Ith player of having a free beer, but the utility of playing the game *and* having the beer; and, similarly, $U^I(-2D)$ is the utility of playing the game and paying a total of \$2D for both parties' beer and appetizers.

If we abide by the vNM convention that precludes simultaneous moves, we now have a three-move game embedded in four points in time, $t = 0, 1, 2, 3$. (Compare this with the tic-tac-toe timeline earlier in this chapter.) In Move 1, Player

A decides whether or not to play the game. As a consequence, status at $t = 1$ is either

1. Player A is in; Player B to decide; or
2. No game.

In the latter case, "No game" will also be the status at $t = 2$ and $t = 3$. If Player A decides to play, then Move Two is for Player B to decide whether or not it also wants to play. If it declines to play, then "No game" is the status at $t = 2$ and $t = 3$. On the other hand, if Player B decides to play, then a number of events occur before $t = 2$ is reached and a third move is to be decided. While these would be discrete points in, e.g., a computer simulation of the game, they are not time-points at which someone must choose a move, therefore they are not time-points in the *game description*. Specifically, in the game under discussion, a coin is flipped to determine the "shooter." A first card is drawn, and the "shooter" is told whether it is high or low. Based on this information the shooter decides, as the game's Move 3, whether or not to increase the bet. If increasing or not increasing the bet are equally good, the shooter breaks the tie by some definite rule, like "don't increase," so that its choice for Move 3 is a specific function of the state at $t = 2$.

Once the shooter makes its decision at $t = 2$, a good many more events may intervene until $t = 3$ is reached and the game is over: The first card is revealed, and the second card is drawn. If the roll-out does not determine the winner, pairs of cards are drawn until the winner is determined (with no more than

100 pairs being drawn, we assume). At that point, $t = 3$ and the game is over. The outcome of the game is either "No Game" or one player or the other has won $\$D$ or $\$2D$ worth of consumables.

As previously asserted, in order to solve this game, each player must know the other's utility function. This is automatically known if there are only two outcomes. It is also not needed if the game is deterministic with complete information and with each player knowing how the other player ranks outcomes (and breaks ties). Otherwise the opponent's utility function is needed in order for each player to know what the other player will do in each possible situation.

Since $t = 3$ for this game, the DP calculation starts by considering, in turn, each possible state, s_t, that can occur at $t = 2$. For some s_2 the state of the game is that there is no game and therefore there is no decision to be made. If the game is still on at $t = 2$, then the shooter computes the conditional expected utility—given the information it has in state s_2—for each of the two actions it can take. It chooses the one with the higher conditional expected utility, thereby maximizing the conditional expected utility for the game given its information, breaking ties by some rule known in advance by its opponent. This move establishes the expected utility of the game-as-a-whole for each state that can occur at time $t = 2$ and for both players. These are the "derived" utility functions $U_2^I(s_2)$, one for each player at time $t = 1$, as if the game were a one-period game with $U_2^I(s_2)$ as its payoffs. One of the results of this derived one-period game is to determine $U_1^I(s_1)$, the expected utility for the game-as-a-whole for Player I for every possible state at $t = 1$. This in turn can be used to determine the optimum first move for Player B at $t = 1$, and similarly for Player A at $t = 0$. This is analogous to moving back in tic-tac-toe from $t = 9$ to $t = 8$, and then from $t = 8$ to $t = 7$, and then to 6, 5, 4, 3, 2, 1, 0. The difference between the two games is that, since tic-tac-toe contains no random variables, the player who chooses at $t = 8$ (or $t = 7$, 6, etc.) *knows* what utility it will get given its move, assuming that everyone chooses rationally thereafter. In the craps example, the player only knows the *expected* value of the utility it will get. Each step in this backwards process is justified by Equation (12).

GENERALIZATION: TWO TYPES OF GAMES

Let D be a discrete event dynamic model. We will describe it as if it were programmed from an EAS-E (Entity, Attribute, Set, and Event) viewpoint, as described in the preceding chapter. This assumption is a convenience rather than a necessity, since anything that any digital computer can do can also be done by a primitive "Turing machine." See Kleene (1971) and Turing (1936, 1937).

D is a *specific model* rather than a generic model, i.e., all its parameters are specified—except for random seeds. Thus we can speak of multiple runs of the D special case. D's EAS (Entity, Attribute, and Set status description) includes *Player* as a permanent entity type. One attribute of Player may be its Existence, whose possible values are, for example, "Unborn," "Playing," and "Gone." Thus defining Player as a permanent entity does not limit the games described to ones in which a fixed set of players are active from the start to the end of a play of the game. For example a game-of-life simulator would include births and deaths. In certain random scenarios a potential player may never get born. As discussed previously, we assume that (1) the game is sure to be over in at most T moves and (2) the status of the system, s_T, contains enough information to compute the utility, $U^I(s_T)$, that each player derives from the particular "play of the game" (i.e., "run of the simulator"). It seems natural to assign $U^I(s_T) = 0$ if Player I is never born. If I is born and ends with $U^I(s_T) < 0$, it would have been better off never having been born.

To generalize the discussion of the previous section, we must distinguish between two types of games, namely:

A. games in which the player-to-move can always calculate the conditional probability distribution of the possible states of the world currently, given the player's information, without *guessing at* the strategies being followed by other players; and

B. games in which Assumption A is false.

All financial games analyzed in this volume will be of the first type. Specifically the Mossin-Samuelson game is a single-player game, so there are no other players whose strategies the player needs to guess. The same is true for the games being played by the investor in the various examples of the Markowitz and van Dijk heuristic in Chapter 11, the Blay and Markowitz TCPA (tax-cognizant portfolio analysis), also in Chapter 11, and the simulation analyses performed for participants in GuidedChoice's GuidedSavings and GuidedSpending products.

On the other hand a JLMSim run may include thousands—or millions—of investors. Security returns are endogenous in JLMSim, being determined by investing and trading policies. But the investors in JLMSim take the prices as given. They make their moves based on observed levels and changes in the market, not on guesses as to other investors' strategies. In a sense, the investors in the JLMSim many-player game are the same as the players in the Mossin-Samuelson, Markowitz and van Dijk, Blay and Markowitz, and GC games. The Mossin-Samuelson game-player is not to be thought of as the only investor in the world, but as one of the many that form the marketplace, and take return distributions as unaffected by their own actions.

In addition to single-player games, other Type A games include (1) games of perfect information, such as tic-tac-toe and (2) games with imperfect information but not due to other players' actions, such as the augmented craps game presented earlier in this chapter.

Poker and most other card games are examples of Type B games. (Earlier in this chapter, we assumed that an RDM knew the betting strategies of other players in a poker game, but that was to illustrate a particular point, and is not usually the case in fact.) An RDM trader of an illiquid stock should probably try to infer the intentions of the other buyers and sellers currently in the market. But such trading strategies are beyond the scope of this book.

Solution of Type A Games

Time-bounded (actually, maximum-number-of-moves-bounded) Type A games are solved as illustrated in the augmented craps game example. We may assume that each play of such a game lasts for exactly T intervals, embedded in time-points 0 through T, including the possibility that the status of the game may be "game over" for t from some $t < T$ onward. The time-points t_1, t_2, t_3, ... do not necessarily represent equal increments in clock time. For example, in a run of a synchronous simulated game, several players may take actions with the clock stopped. In accord with the vNM convention, these actions are deemed to happen sequentially. Thus some (or many or even all) so-called time-points t_1, $t_1 + 1$, $t_1 + 2$, ..., may occur at the same simulated clock time.

The DP calculation proceeds from T backward in time. At every step in the calculation,

$$U_{t+1}^I(s_{t+1})$$

has already been established for every state that can occur at time-point $t + 1$. The calculation considers in turn every state, s_t, that can occur at time-point t. Given state s_t there is either zero or one player to move. One reason for there to be no player to move is because the game is over.

The player-to-move (if any) does not necessarily know the current state s_t, but may have information about it, like the craps player who knows whether the first card is high or low. This information implies a conditional probability distribution of possible states,

$$\text{Prob}(\tilde{s}_t \,|\, \text{Infor}^I(s_t))$$

The player-to-move also knows the probability distribution

$$\text{Prob}(s_{t+1} \,|\, \tilde{s}_t, \alpha)$$

of possible states at time $t + 1$ given that $\tilde{s}_t$ is the state at time t and α is the player-to-move's action. The player chooses an α that maximizes

$$U_t^I(s_t) = \Sigma(\text{Prob }(\tilde{s}_t|\text{Info}^I(s_t)) \cdot \Sigma(\text{Prob}(s_{t+1}|\tilde{s}_t,\alpha) \cdot U^I(s_{t+1}))$$

where I is the player-to-move, the first sum is over possible current states, and the second sum is over all possible states at time $t + 1$ that can follow $\tilde{s}_t$. (We assume that an EU maximizing α exists.[3]) Ties are broken by a rule known to all. The choice of move, α, determines not only the utility $U_t^I(s_t)$ but $U_t^J(s_t)$ for the other players as well. The calculation can now be repeated for $t = t - 1$ until $t = 0$ is reached. The initial calculation, at $t = T - 1$, uses $U^I(s_T)$ as specified by the rules of the game.

Solution of Type B Games

The solutions to Type B games may be mixed strategies, discussed in an earlier section of this chapter, where we already ruled out games requiring such strategies as beyond the scope of this volume. Currently, practical applications of game theory typically use Nash (1950b, 1951) equilibrium solutions. In a Nash equilibrium, each player follows a strategy that maximizes its expected utility given the strategies that the other players are using. A game may have more than one Nash equilibrium solution, and some of these may not be "Pareto optima," i.e., there may be a different Nash equilibrium in which some player has a higher EU and none has a lower EU.

The finding of Nash equilibria is way beyond the scope of this volume. We note, however, that given a particular Nash equilibrium, each player knows the strategies of the other players. They are therefore like the RDM poker player in an earlier section who was assumed to know the betting and folding strategies of the other players. Therefore the player's strategy can be computed as if it were a Type A game.

THE CURSE OF DIMENSIONALITY

By hypothesis, an RDM can perform any well-defined calculation, including the dynamic programming calculation for some huge Type A game. But HDMs are not RDMs. Clearly it would be infeasible for an HDM to perform such a calculation for a PRWSim world. But the DP process is also infeasible for HDMs for many quite small problems. For example, the DP calculation considers each possible state s_{T-1} at the last time-point at which a decision can be made. The size of a state space is usually characterized by its dimensionality, that is, the number of *state variables* used to specify a point in this space. For example, Sun, Fan, Chen, Schouwenaars, and Albota

(2006a and b) present the result of a five-security portfolio rebalancing problem. Each point, $(X_1, X_2, X_3, X_4, X_5)$, in their five-dimensional state-space represents a possible deviation of a portfolio from the target weights to which the portfolio is supposed to be rebalanced. The objective of the calculation is to minimize a sum of "costs" including (1) transaction costs for changing the X vector and (2) penalty costs for deviating from the target portfolio. Since X is continuous, the problem had to be discretized. Sun et al. approximated the state space by a grid of points permitting 15 different values for each X_i. Thus the state space had $15^5 = 759,375$ points. An optimization had to be solved at $t = T - 1$ (with $T = 24$) for each point in the state space, then the process iterated backward until $t = 0$ was reached. The problem was solved with the aid of an MIT supercomputer.

As we will recount in Chapter 11, Kritzman, Myrgren, and Page (2009) show that a fast, scalable heuristic by Markowitz and van Dijk produced a better solution, showing that the Sun et al. grid was too coarse. But a significantly finer grid—for example, one permitting 100 values for each X_i, and thus having $100^5 = 10^{10}$ states—would have been well beyond feasible HDM calculation. This illustrates what is referred to as dynamic programming's *curse of dimensionality*.

The rebalancing problem simplifies greatly if securities are perfectly liquid—i.e., if they can be bought or sold at their current price without any transaction cost. In this case, any portfolio with a given net asset value (NAV) can be converted to any other portfolio with the same NAV by selling the one and buying the other. Thus, there are high-dimensional models that can be solved relatively easily. But the example in Sun et al. illustrates how a touch of realism may destroy the possibility of such a solution.

Computability also breaks down if one or more state variables are unbounded. For example, if an investor's wealth W_t is a state variable, and W_t is unbounded, then one cannot list all possible states at time t. This constraint on problems solvable by a DP calculation is handled in various ways. For example, the Mossin-Samuelson model discussed in the next chapter can be solved analytically for all $W_T \geq 0$. In the Markowitz and van Dijk experiment described in Chapter 11, unbounded W_t is avoided by assuming that the investor withdraws any portfolio gains and covers any losses. If W_0 is given, T is small, and $\Delta W = W_{t+1} - W_t$ is tightly bounded, then the range of W_{T-1} may be manageable. Generally, designing a dynamic programming problem that is both relevant and solvable is an art.

FACTORIZATION, SIMPLIFICATION, EXPLORATION, AND APPROXIMATION

How is an HDM investor—or HDM financial DSS designer— to proceed in a PRWSim world? Necessarily, the HDM must factor the world into the part it will analyze formally and the part it will leave to judgment. Necessarily, it is left to judgment to decide this division of labor between formal analysis and judgment.

We can imagine the decisions of an HDM and its DSS to be the output of two cooperating workers: Analysis and

Judgment. Analysis may use a highly stylized model that can be solved analytically, such as the Mossin-Samuelson model, or it may use a more detailed simulation such as that used in GC's GuidedSavings or GuidedSpending. No matter how stylized or detailed the model that Analysis uses, Judgment should understand its assumptions and weigh whether—or to what extent and in what way—the model's simplifications may invalidate the practical applicability of its conclusions. This is not always easy, and may require the collective wisdom of our profession's (friendly but intense) debates. An example of this is the differing interpretations of the counterintuitive result that flows from the Mossin-Samuelson model's premises, as recounted in the next chapter.

9

THE MOSSIN-
SAMUELSON MODEL

INTRODUCTION

The Mossin (1968)-Samuelson (1969) (MS) model is a stylized
dynamic investment model of great historical importance to
financial theory and practice. Its impact is due to its clear
but counterintuitive result: that investors should not become
more cautious as they approach retirement.

Mossin extended his basic result to special cases involving
a risk-free asset with a zero or nonzero unvarying interest rate.
Hakansson (1971) reports bugs in some of Mossin's results and
provides some generalizations. We will not recount these cases
here. Our interest is in the basic result and its applications.
More generally we consider only a small fraction of the enormous literature on stylized financial models, since our own
approach lies in a quite different direction. See Campbell and
Viceira (2002) for a survey of recent literature, and Hakansson
(1971) for an early and extensive exploration of such models.
Based on Campbell and Viceira, the Hakansson results seem

to have been forgotten, perhaps having been crowded out by the continuous-time models of R. Merton and followers. (See Merton 1990.)

The present chapter deals with three related topics:

A. the Mossin-Samuelson model and its solution;

B. a once-ongoing debate between Paul Samuelson and Harry Markowitz on investment for the long run; and

C. "glide-path" or "target-date" investment strategies.

THE MS MODEL AND ITS SOLUTION

As in Mossin and Samuelson, we assume that an investor starts with initial wealth W_0. It chooses a probability distribution of return R_t at time-points $t = 0, 1, 2, \dots, T - 1$ at the start of time intervals $1, 2, \dots, T$. The investor may change its portfolio choice costlessly at any point in time. For the present, we will not specify whether or not successive R_t are independent. Unless stated otherwise our only assumption concerning R_t is that it is independent of any *previous* choice of portfolio.

The utility assigned to the play of the MS game depends only on final wealth:

$$U = U(W_T) \tag{1a}$$

Mossin and Samuelson do not so specify, but their arguments also apply if we assume that W_T is *real* wealth rather than nominal wealth, and R_t is real return. We will assume this to be the case. In particular the utility functions used by GuidedChoice, discussed later in this chapter, are functions of real wealth.

We will first assume that

$$U = \log(W_T) \qquad \textbf{(1b)}$$

and then assume that

$$U = \operatorname{sgn}(a)\, W_T^a \qquad a \neq 0 \qquad \textbf{(1c)}$$

where

$$\operatorname{sgn}(a) = \begin{cases} +1 & \text{if } a > 0 \\ 0 & \text{if } a = 0 \text{ (not used here)} \\ -1 & \text{if } a < 0 \end{cases}$$

In particular,

$$U = W_T^a \qquad \text{if } a > 0 \qquad \textbf{(1d)}$$

$$U = -W_T^{-\alpha} \qquad \text{if } a < 0$$

$$\text{and } \alpha = |a| \qquad \textbf{(1e)}$$

(An equivalent formula in place of Equation (1c) and related topics are discussed in Endnote 4 to this chapter.) Equation (1d) is linear for $a = 1$ and strictly concave for $a < 1$.

With Equation (1b) as its objective, at time-point $t = T - 1$, the expected utility of the game depends on the last-period return, R_T, as follows:

$$\text{EU} = E \log(W_T)$$
$$= E \log(W_{T-1}(1 + R_T))$$
$$= \log(W_{T-1}) + E \log(1 + R_T) \qquad (2)$$

The first term on the last line of Equation (2) is already determined by time $t = T - 1$. Thus Equation (2) implies that, at $t = T - 1$, EU is maximized by whatever distribution of R_t maximizes $E \log(1 + R)$. Therefore if the investor chooses an optimal last move, the expected value of the game-as-a-whole is

$$\text{EU} = \log(W_{T-1}) + m_T \qquad (3)$$

where m_T is *maximum $E \log(1 + R_T)$*—or *MEL* for short. This is the maximum *conditional $E \log(1 + R_T)$ given* the state s_{T-1}. If R_1, R_2, ... , R_T are generated by an arbitrary random process, then m_T as well as W_{T-1} will vary between draws from this process. We assume that such an m_T maximizing choice always exists.[1]

Next consider the options available at time $t = T - 2$, assuming that the investor will move optimally at $t = T - 1$. For any wealth level W_{T-2}, the expected utility of the game is

$$\text{EU} = E \log(W_T)$$
$$= E \log(W_{T-2}(1 + R_{T-1})(1 + R_T))$$
$$= \log(W_{T-2}) + E \log(1 + R_{T-1}) + Em_T \qquad (4)$$

We write Em_T rather than m_T since m_T is a conditional expected value dependent on the particular trajectory drawn thus far from the return generating process. At time $t = T - 2$, $\log(W_{T-2})$ is already determined. So is Em_T—but this is less obvious. The value of m_T is not necessarily independent of m_{T-1}, but it is assumed to be independent of the *choice of portfolio* at time-point $T - 1$. Therefore, the expected value of m_T—given state s_{T-2}—is determined at time-point $T - 2$. It follows that MEL is the optimum choice for the distribution of R_{T-1}, as it was for R_T. If we repeat the process for time $t = T - 3$, we find that EU given the state s_{T-3} is

$$EU = \log(W_{T-3}) + E\log(1 + R_{T-2}) + Em_{T-1} + Em_T \qquad \text{(5a)}$$

where the expected values are conditional on the state s_{T-3}, with MEL again being the optimal choice. Repeating the process T times, we find that the optimal value of the game is

$$EU = \sum_{t=1}^{T} Em_t \qquad \text{(5b)}$$

This is achieved by selecting a MEL portfolio from among the single-period return distributions available at each time t. In particular, this is true whether or not the R_t are autocorrelated, since we did not rule out autocorrelation in deriving this result. The expected values in Equation (5b) are unconditional (or, equivalently, conditional on the initial state of the game).

We conclude, therefore, that the logarithmic utility function is *myopic* in the sense that *the same decision rule is used* *to select the distribution of R_t at time t in a T-period game as would be used to select the distribution of R_1 in a one-period game. This result holds even if returns are autocorrelated.*

Next let us consider a utility function of the form in Equation (1e). An essentially identical argument with the same general conclusion applies to utility functions of the form in Equation (1d), and hence to all utility functions of the form in Equation (1c). At time $T - 1$, the expected utility of the MS game is

$$U = E\left(-W_T^{-\alpha}\right)$$
$$= -E\left(W_T^{-\alpha}\right)$$
$$= -E\left(W_{T-1}(1 + R_T)\right)^{-\alpha}$$
$$= -W_{T-1}^{-\alpha} E(1 + R_T)^{-\alpha} \tag{6}$$

Thus the expected value of the game is maximized by choosing the distribution with (equivalently)

$$\max -E(1 + R)^{-\alpha} \tag{7a}$$
$$\min E(1 + R)^{-\alpha} \tag{7b}$$

In the steps of Equations (6) we made use of the fact that W_{T-1} is already determined by $t = T - 1$. At time $T - 2$, we have

$$EU = -E\left(W_T^{-\alpha}\right)$$
$$= -E\left(W_{T-2} \cdot (1 + R_{T-1})(1 + R_T)\right)^{-\alpha}$$
$$= -W_{T-2}^{-\alpha} E\{(1 + R_{T-1})^{-\alpha}(1 + R_T)^{-\alpha}\} \tag{8a}$$

If R_{T-1} and R_T are independent, then

$$EU = -W_{T-1}^{-\alpha} E(1 + R_{T-1})^{-\alpha} E(1 + R)^{-\alpha} \qquad \textbf{(8b)}$$

The maximum value of this is

$$EU = -W_{T-2}^{-\alpha} \cdot m_{T-1} \cdot m_T \qquad \textbf{(8c)}$$

where m_{T-1} and m_T are provided by the portfolios with

$$\min E(1 + R_t)^{-\alpha} \qquad t = T - 1, T$$

In general, still assuming independence, maximum EU is

$$EU = -\prod_{t=1}^{T} m_t$$

where m_t is the minimum value of $E(1 + R_t)^{-\alpha}$. If the distributions are i.i.d. (identical as well as independent), then the same portfolio is chosen each period.

Since the expected value of a product is not in general the product of expected values, the result in Equations (8) depends on our independence assumption. (Independence is a simple sufficient condition. A more general, necessary and sufficient, condition would be messy.) No such assumption was needed for the log utility function.

In sum, "under suitable assumptions," if the utility of an investment game depends only on final wealth, with $U = U(W_T)$ given by either Equation (1b) or Equation (1c), then action is myopic. The investor would choose the same portfolio at age 24 as at age 64.

MARKOWITZ VERSUS SAMUELSON: BACKGROUND

Through the years Paul Samuelson and Harry Markowitz have had an ongoing debate on whether an investor who "invests for the long run" should choose MEL each period. Markowitz said yes; Samuelson said no. Their written works on the subject include Samuelson (1969, 1979) and Markowitz (1959, 1976, 2006). Our discussion of this topic necessarily best reflects Markowitz's views. Unfortunately, "All men are mortal," and Paul Samuelson can no longer add to this discussion. Now his already-published works must speak for him.

The MEL criterion was proposed by Kelly (1956) and embraced by Latané (1957, 1959). The Markowitz (1959) Chapter 6 position was that the cautious investor should not choose a mean-variance efficient portfolio with a higher arithmetic mean (and therefore higher variance) than that of the efficient mean-variance combination that approximately maximizes expected log. A portfolio that is higher on the frontier subjects the investor to more volatility in the short run with no greater *return in the long run*. The cautious investor, however, may choose a mean-variance combination that is lower on the frontier, giving up return in the long run for greater short-run stability of return.[2]

Breiman (1961) supplied the "strong law of large numbers" argument that we use below supporting the MEL rule. Samuelson (1969, 1979) provides an expected utility argument that contradicts MEL. Markowitz (1976) provides an alternative expected utility argument in MEL's favor.

The issues that separate the Kelly, Latané, Brieman, and the present authors' arguments *for* MEL and the Samuelson arguments *against* MEL are already present when returns are i.i.d., and the investor must always rebalance to the same (investor-chosen) portfolio. We will deal only with this special case here. See Markowitz (1976) for a more general analysis.

Argument *for* MEL

If an investor repeatedly draws from a return distribution without adding or withdrawing funds beyond the initial W_0, then at time T, the investor's wealth is

$$W_T = W_0 \prod_{t=1}^{T}(1 + R_t) \qquad (9)$$

where R_t here represents the *sample* rate of return actually achieved on the portfolio at time t. The sample *growth rate*, g, for the entire return trajectory satisfies

$$
\begin{aligned}
(1 + g) &= (W_T / W_0)^{1/T} \\
&= \left(\prod_{t=1}^{T}(1 + R_t) \right)^{1/T}
\end{aligned}
\qquad (10)
$$

Here g is the rate of return that, if earned each period, would grow wealth from W_0 to W_T in T periods. Taking the logarithm of both sides of Equation (10), we see that wealth at time T is a strictly increasing function of

$$\text{Log}(1 + g) = (1/T) \sum_{t=1}^{T} \log(1 + R_t) \qquad (11)$$

Unless otherwise stated, we assume that $R > -1$; therefore $\log(1 + g)$ in Equation (11) is always finite. We also assume that $E \log(1 + R)$ is finite. Equation (11) implies the following casually stated but crucial fact:

> **Theorem:** *If Harry repeatedly invests in a portfolio whose $E \log(1 + R)$ is greater than that of Paul, then—with probability 1.0—there will come a time (T_0) when Harry's wealth exceeds Paul's and remains so **forever** thereafter.*

Equation (11) says that the log of one plus the *sample growth rate* is the *sample average* $\log(1 + R)$. The strong law of large numbers says that—with probability 1.0—the sample average of i.i.d. random variables approaches its expected value. In particular, the average log approaches the expected log, m. In symbols,

$$\text{Prob}\left(\lim_{T \to \infty} \sum_{t=1}^{T} (\log(1 + R_t))/T \to m \right) = 1.0 \qquad (12)$$

With the R_t already assumed to be i.i.d., the only other assumption needed to assure that Equation (12) holds is that m is finite (see Cramér 1946). Recalling the calculus definition of a limit, Equation (12) tells us that, with probability one, for *every* positive number, ε, there will come a time T_ε such that the difference between m and the sample average of $\log(1 + R)$ is less than ε for *all* T greater than T_ε.

QED

Argument *Against* MEL

Again consider an investor who invests W_0 at time 0 and lets this investment ride without additional investments or withdrawals. Now pick some *fixed*, distant time T. At time T the investor, or its heirs, will "cash in" the investment. The investor must decide the portfolio to which the trustees of this investment will rebalance repeatedly. We continue to assume that successive returns are i.i.d.

Suppose that the investor seeks to maximize expected utility with Equation (1d) as its utility function. Since returns are i.i.d., expected utility equals

$$\text{EU} = E\left(\prod_{t=1}^{T} (1+R)^a \right)$$
$$= (E(1+R)^a)^T \qquad (13)$$

Thus, the expected utility maximizing portfolio is the one with the greatest *single-period* $E(1+R)^a$. This will usually *not* be the MEL portfolio.

Thus, no matter how distant the goal, MEL is not the optimum strategy for this game with Equation (1d) as the utility function. A similar argument applies with Equation (1e) instead.

*Samuelson concludes that maximizing **any** of the MS myopic utility functions should be considered investing for the long run.*

Example

An example will illustrate how the mathematical facts that Samuelson and Markowitz each use to support their respective positions can *both* be true. Consider two portfolios P and Q.

P provides 6 percent per year with certainty, whereas each year Q provides a 50-50 chance of 200 percent gain or 100 percent loss. Here we allow $R = -1.0$ and consequently will encounter calculations involving $\log(0) = -\infty$. The requisite *extended real number* calculations should be self-explanatory. (See Halmos 1974, page 1.) The expected return and expected log(1 + return) of P are 0.06 and $\log_e(1.06) = 0.058$. The expected return and expected log of Q are $\frac{1}{2}(2.00) + \frac{1}{2}(-1.00) = 0.50$ and $\frac{1}{2}\log(3.00) + \frac{1}{2}\log(0.0) = -\infty$, respectively. An investor who followed the MEL rule would prefer P. For any fixed investment horizon T, the investor who maximized expected value of an Equation (1c) utility function with $a = 1$—in other words, an investor who maximized expected final wealth—would prefer Q.

Imagine that the return on Q is determined by a toss of a fair coin, with heads being favorable. If the coin is flipped repeatedly, with probability 1.0 eventually a tail will be tossed. From that time on, $0 = W_T^Q < W_T^P = (1.06)^T$. Thus, in the particular case as in general with probability 1.0 there will come a time when the MEL portfolio pulls ahead—and stays ahead— of the alternative strategy.

On the other hand, pick some fixed point in time, such as $T = 100$. At that time, P provides $(1.06)^T$ with certainty. Q provides nothing if a tail has appeared in the first 100 tosses. If not, $W_T^Q = 3^T$. Therefore expected final wealth is

$$EW_T^Q = \left(\frac{1}{2}\right)^T 3^T = (1.50)^T > (1.06)^T = EW_T^P$$

Thus, in the example—again, as in general—the portfolio that maximizes EU for $T = 1$ also maximizes EU for arbitrarily large

T—fixed in advance—even though almost surely there will come a time T_0 when $W_T^P > W_T^Q$ for all $T > T_0$.

Another Argument *for* MEL

Markowitz (1976) argues that an assertion that something is "best in the long run" should be an asymptotic statement that some policy approaches optimality as $T \to \infty$. The Samuelson argument against MEL is presented in terms of a game of fixed length. Since this fixed length is arbitrary, the Samuelson argument can be transformed into an asymptotic argument as follows. Imagine a sequence of games G_1, G_2, G_3, ... , G_{100}, ... The first game is a single-period game; that is, it has $T = 1$. The second game G_2 is "just like" the first except that it is two periods long, $T = 2$. The third game G_3 is just like the first two except that it is three periods long, $T = 3$, and so on. Samuelson's argument against MEL is that, with a power function $U(W_T)$ as in Equations (1c) and (1d), the EU(W_T) provided by MEL does not approach that provided by the EU(W_T)-maximizing portfolio.

In general, the notion that game G_{T+1} is "just like" game G_T, only longer, assumes that

1. the same random process generates returns in each game;
2. the investor is subject to the same kinds of constraints in each G_{Ti} and
3. the same method is used to *score* a play of each game.

In effect, the way the Samuelson analysis interprets the last requirement—that each game in the sequence be scored the same way—is to score both games by the same function of *final wealth*. One could instead score the successive games by the expected value of the same function of *the sample growth rate g*. In the example in the last section, P always supplies a growth rate of 0.06. The rate of return supplied by Q is

$$
g_Q = \begin{cases}
-1.0 \text{ with probability } 1-\left(\dfrac{1}{2}\right)^T \\[2ex]
2.0 \text{ with probability } \quad \left(\dfrac{1}{2}\right)^T
\end{cases}
$$

If $H_1, H_2, \ldots, H_{100} \ldots$ are just like the Mossin-Samuelson games *except* that each is scored by the expected value of the same function of g, $V = f(g)$, then, in the above example,

$$
EV_T^P = f(0.06) \text{ for all } T
$$

$$
EV_T^Q = \left(1-\left(\frac{1}{2}\right)^T\right) f(-1.0)
$$

$$
+ \left(\frac{1}{2}\right)^T f(2.0) \tag{14a}
$$

$$
\rightarrow f(-1.0) \tag{14b}
$$

Thus if these games are scored by the same $f(g)$ as T increases,

$$
\lim EV_T^P > \lim EV_T^Q
$$

Markowitz (1976) shows that if one scores a Mossin-Samuelson-like game by the expected value of the same continuous, increasing function of growth rate g, then *quite generally* MEL *is* asymptotically optimal.

Suppose one wants to compare the performances of two investment strategies for varying horizons, such as for a decade or a century. How should we decide whether increasing time is more favorable to one than to the other? For all interesting cases, no matter how long the horizon, there is *some* chance that *one* strategy will do better and *some* chance that the *other* will do better. The question is how to choose among probability distributions of these various possibilities. One way—the unchanging utility of *final wealth* way—assumes that the tradeoffs between making a dollar grow to $3 versus $6 or $9 should be the same in 100 years as in 10 years. The unchanging utility of the *rate-of-growth* way assumes that the tradeoffs between achieving a 3 percent, 6 percent, or 9 percent *growth rate* should be the same during the 10 or 100 years. For a fixed T, any utility of final wealth, $U(W_T)$, can also be expressed as a utility of sample growth, namely

$$U(W_T) = U(W_0(1+g)^T) = f(g)$$

But, as the example in the preceding section illustrates, assuming that $U(W_T)$ remains the same versus assuming that $f(g)$ remains the same as T increases has very different implications for the asymptotic optimality of MEL.

Conclusion

If in a given context there is any doubt as to which meaning of "long run" is intended, one could refer to one as investing for the long run *in the Kelly sense*, or *in the Samuelson sense*. In fact the Kelly sense is used much more often than the Samuelson sense. (See, for example, the MacLean, Thorp, and

Ziemba 2011 volume on the subject.) This does not prove that one is right and the other wrong; only which is more likely to be meant if it is not explicitly specified.

As we noted before, Markowitz (1959) does not recommend that an investor choose the MEL portfolio. Rather, it recommends that the investor *not* select a portfolio that is *higher* on the efficient frontier, since such a portfolio has greater short-run volatility but less long-run return—in the Kelly sense—than the MEL portfolio.

GLIDE-PATH STRATEGIES AND THEIR RATIONALES

It is generally considered plausible that an investor should become more cautious as retirement approaches. Thus one practical consequence of the Mossin-Samuelson result is to warn the designers of a computer-assisted retirement plan that if one assumes an MS utility function when choosing portfolios under this plan, these portfolios will not become more cautious as the designated retirement time approaches. In the remainder of this chapter, we examine three methods for avoiding this consequence. The first is used by a leading family of "life-cycle funds" and is typical of such funds, the second is used in GC's GuidedSaving product, and the third would be part of an implementation of the Markowitz (1991) proposed game-of-life.

Chapter 7 of Ibbotson (2014) describes a family of life-cycle funds offering "glide-paths" that shift their asset allocations in a cautious direction as a target date approaches. The rationale presented there, and in works that they cite, involves the shrinkage of the value of *human capital* as retirement approaches. Ibbotson defines the value of human capital as the present value of future income from employment. This clearly shrinks as retirement nears.

Ibbotson asserts that human capital is typically more bondlike than stocklike. It notes that the human capital of some investors (such as stockbrokers) is more stocklike than bondlike, as compared to that of tenured professors whose human capital is bondlike. But, overall, Ibbotson estimates human capital to be like a portfolio containing 70 percent bonds and 30 percent stocks.[3]

Thus Ibbotson views the typical investor's total portfolio as consisting of a tradable subportfolio, including publicly traded stocks and bonds, and nontradable human capital equivalent to a 30-70 mix of stocks and bonds. The Ibbotson methodology in effect assumes that the investor seeks to maximize the expected value of a myopic utility function of target-date wealth, and therefore seeks to keep a constant proportion between stocks and bonds. But to do so requires that the portfolio of tradable assets be shifted in a cautious direction as the target date approaches.

The Ibbotson glide-path strategy has additional embellishments—the selection of equities shifts in a more cautious direction, for example, and fixed income begins to include more TIPS as the target date approaches—but the basic structure is as stated previously: the tradable subportfolio is shifted from stocks to bonds to compensate for the shrinkage of the mostly bondlike human capital subportfolio.

We question the basic premises of the Ibbotson approach (and similar approaches by others) that

a. human capital is typically bondlike, and

b. compensating for the shrinkage of a bondlike untradable asset is the principal reason behind the intuition that typically an investor should invest more cautiously as retirement approaches.

We view an investor's human capital as being bondlike if the investor's noninvestment income is reasonably *recession-proof*. Clearly this is *not* the case for most self-employed individuals or for anyone who can easily be laid off by a business in trouble.

RELATIVE RISK AVERSION

The next section presents a different view of why investors invest more cautiously as retirement approaches. But first we must discuss the widely used concept of *relative risk aversion*.

The power and logarithm utility functions of Equations (1b) and (1c) share a property called *constant relative risk aversion* (CRRA). (See Arrow 1965 and Pratt 1964.) As we have noted before, a single-period utility function of wealth, W_1,

$$U = U(W_1) \tag{15a}$$

can also be expressed as a function of return, R_1, in the forthcoming period,

$$U = U(W_0(1 + R_1)) \qquad \textbf{(15b)}$$

One implication of a CRRA utility function is that the investor's choice among probability distributions of return R does *not* depend on the investor's wealth level. We do not find this assumption plausible, nor did the GuidedChoice (GC) design team. For example, suppose that the year before their retirement—after they have made their last annual contributions to their retirement plans, so they have no more human capital in the Ibbotson sense—Investors A and B must choose a mixture of a safe and a risky investment. Investor A is a married couple, each of whom will be automatically retired from a menial job at $t = T$. Their meager savings, plus Social Security, will allow them to live frugally but tolerably. Investor B, on the other hand, is a prosperous couple. The husband is the CEO of a large company who, by company policy, must retire at $t = T$. His wife is a patron of the arts. The couple gives generously to charities. Because of health and/or job opportunity reasons, no one from either couple will work after $t = T$. Both couples will live off their respective savings.

Even though each investor couple is out of human capital, one would expect the less wealthy couple to select a more cautious portfolio than the wealthier one. If the market suffered another year like 2008, the wealthier couple would have to adjust their charitable contributions, and perhaps the lavishness of their travel and entertainment plans. But if the poorer couple suffered a similar percentage loss in their retirement portfolio value, the result would be tragic.

The GC decision support system (DSS) designers concluded, therefore, that a typical investor's utility of start-of-retirement wealth, $U(W_T)$, does not have the same relative risk aversion at all wealth levels. It is therefore not a CRRA utility function as assumed by Mossin and Samuelson.

THE GUIDEDSAVINGS UTILITY FUNCTION

Recall from Chapter 7 that GC's first product, GuidedSavings, evaluates a trajectory by a function, $U(W_T)$, of wealth at retirement time. Since the returns on asset classes in GC's return generation model may be autocorrelated, the power utility function of Equation (1c) would not necessarily be myopic. But GC's system designers felt that a utility function that would be myopic "under suitable assumptions" was undesirable, and that the fault lay in its CRRA assumption. They experimented with what they considered to be the simplest possible non-CRRA utility function and found it quite satisfactory. Specifically they used

$$U(W_T) = \begin{cases} -(W_T/\tilde{W})^{-\alpha} & \text{for } W_T \le \tilde{W} \\ \log(W_T/\tilde{W}) - 1 & \text{for } W_T > \tilde{W} \end{cases} \tag{16}$$

for some $\alpha > 0$, where W_T is *real* wealth at time T. We will refer to $\tilde{W}$ as the *breakpoint* or *target level*. Increases in wealth above $\tilde{W}$ are welcome but not essential, whereas decreases below $\tilde{W}$ hurt increasingly.[4]

THE WELL-FUNDED CASE

The downside to using the utility function in Equation (16) rather than that in Equation (1b) or (1c) to score a play of a Mossin-Samuelson-like game is that the game no longer has a neat analytic solution. We find that the following calculation provides some insight into the nature of the solution to the game with the GC utility function. We consider the case in which current wealth W_t is sufficiently large that the optimal portfolio for the GC game is presumably close to that of the Mossin-Samuelson game with the log utility of Equation (1b). Specifically—*not in fact, but for the purposes of this illustrative example*—assume that

- W_t is i.i.d. log-normally distributed.
- The investor commits to following the MEL strategy from time t to the end, T.

Then final wealth W_T is also log-normally distributed, and therefore $\log(W_T)$ is normally distributed. We ask:

- What is the level of wealth $\hat{W_t}$ at time t such that if $W_t > \hat{W_t}$, then $\log(W_T)$ is at least k standard deviations above $\log(\tilde{W})$?

Interestingly, $\hat{W_t}$ is not monotonic with time. For example, in the example below $\hat{W}$ is greatest nine years before retirement, at which point $\hat{W}$ is roughly 2.5 $\tilde{W}$. When there are fewer years until retirement, a smaller margin of safety is needed because there is less time for adverse market moves to seriously reduce capital. But a smaller safety margin is *also* needed when there are more than nine years-to-go in this example because, roughly speaking, there are more years for "investment for the long run," a.k.a. "the law of large numbers," to work. In particular, if there are 36 years until retirement, then no margin of safety is needed: $\hat{W} = \tilde{W}$ in the example. All this follows from the relationship between $\log(\hat{W})$ and $\log(\tilde{W})$ in Equation (18) in which expected log wealth scales linearly with time-remaining until retirement whereas the standard deviation of log wealth scales by the square root of time-remaining. This same interplay between the scaling of expected log wealth and the standard deviation of log wealth must be at play generally but in less obvious ways.

Let m be the mean and σ be the standard deviation of

$$y = \log(1 + R_t)$$

Then the mean and standard deviation of the sum of T i.i.d. draws from the y distribution are

$$m_T = Tm \tag{17a}$$
$$\sigma_T = \sqrt{T}\sigma \tag{17b}$$

Let $\hat{w} = \log(\hat{W})$ and $\tilde{w} = \log(\tilde{W})$. If there are T periods (say, years) until retirement, then the wealth level $\hat{w}$ that is k standard deviations above $\tilde{w}$ satisfies

$$\hat{w} = \tilde{w} + \sqrt{T} \, k\sigma - Tm \tag{18}$$

It is shown in an endnote[5] that if we let

$$K = \frac{k\sigma}{m} \tag{19}$$

then $\tilde{w} = \hat{w}$ at $T = 0$ and $T = K^2$. Also, $\hat{w} - \tilde{w}$ is greatest at

$$T = K^2/4 \tag{20a}$$

at which time

$$\hat{w} - \tilde{w} = k^2\sigma^2/(4m) \tag{20b}$$

For example, if $m = 0.1$, $\sigma = 0.2$, and $k = 3$, then $K = 6$ and $\hat{w} = \tilde{w}$ at $T = 0$ and 36 years. In other words, with these parameter values, one may reasonably expect MEL to be near optimal from now until retirement if current wealth equals breakpoint wealth, $W_t = \tilde{W}$, when there are at least 36 years left before retirement. The greatest ratio $W_T/\tilde{W}$ is required at

$$T = K^2/4$$

$$= 9 \text{ years}$$

At that time the ratio required for a MEL policy to be 3-sigma above the breakpoint is

$$\hat{W}/\tilde{W} = \exp(k^2\alpha^2/4m)$$

$$= 2.46 \tag{21}$$

Thus, in this respect at least, the glide-path associated with the utility function defined in Equation (16) is quite different from the one implied by the human capital explanation. In the latter, bond holdings increase monotonically in a manner unrelated to the investor's wealth. This is not the case for the utility function in Equation (16).

A stand-alone product based on maximizing the expected value of Equation (16) could be characterized as a "target-date/target-wealth" fund. Further results along these lines can be found in Levy (forthcoming). For example, Levy concludes that "For $T = 30$ year horizon or more [MEL] dominates other investment strategies by Almost FSD [first-order stochastic dominance]."

A GAME-OF-LIFE UTILITY FUNCTION

A DSS design must partition the world into those aspects that the DSS will take into account and those that will be ignored or left to judgment. The Markowitz (1991) game-of-life proposal seeks to move more aspects of the financial planning process from outside to inside the standard financial DSS. To do so along the lines of the GuidedSavings and GuidedSpending examples, the DSS designers must model, in their simulators and their DSS databases and decision rules,

1. the expanded state-space and how it evolves;

2. how investor action modifies this evolution; and

3. how to assign utilities to trajectories.

In the present case the last seems to us to be the most difficult. For example, in addition to "mortality tables," the existence of disability insurance has induced insurance companies to tabulate "morbidity tables" that show the probabilities of transition from health to illness and perhaps back; and the Bureau of Labor Statistics has data that would help a game-of-life design team model the transition from employed to unemployed—and possibly back again.

But assigning utilities to enhanced trajectories is more challenging. Specifically, rather than characterizing consumption at time t by a single number, C_t, the simulated family's enjoyment for the period would depend on the size of the family, whether it lives in a large house or a small apartment, whether it now has to move because someone has a new job elsewhere, etc. The approach required here should be both *behavioral* and *rational*. It should be behavioral in that it reflects plausible human choices. It should be rational, for example, in that the RDM family understands the consequences of high-interest-rate credit card debt.

In the first instance (with Items 1 and 2 in place, but without 3) one could use heuristics to model family decisions, and display various summary statistics from one or many simulation runs. We view this as implicit EU maximization. But any attempt at explicit EU maximization, or even the ranking of alternative heuristics based on backtests or Monte Carlo analysis, must wait for the development of an explicit utility function. It may take a considerable effort by many disciplines, and much debate back and forth, to produce a plausible algorithm for assigning utilities to game-of-life trajectories, but the process should produce light as well as heat concerning actual and ideal financial planning objectives. As von Neumann said,

If you think mathematics is hard, it is because you think life is easy.[6]

10

PORTFOLIO SELECTION
AS A SOCIAL CHOICE

INTRODUCTION

In Chapter 6 we saw that a portfolio typically has many stakeholders whose needs should be taken into account. This is
what Arrow (1951) refers to as a *social choice*. He shows that
there is no voting system for choosing a winner, based on voters' rankings of candidates, that can be sure to satisfy a list
of *conditions* that Arrow considers self-evidently essential.
Goodman and Markowitz (1952) and Hildreth (1953) do not
consider all of Arrow's conditions essential, or even desirable.
Instead, they each propose their own list of conditions that
can always be satisfied by a suitable voting system. In their
authoritative text, *Games and Decisions: Introduction and
Critical Survey*, Luce and Raiffa (1957) list, as the principal
replies to Arrow's impossibility theorem, the Markowitz and
Goodman paper, the Hildreth paper, and their own generalization of the Nash (1950a) paper on the *bargaining problem*.

The present chapter reviews the Arrow, Goodman and Markowitz, Hildreth, and Luce and Raiffa proposals, and adds another that we believe is worth considering.

Our objective in this chapter is normative rather than positive. We do not consider the complex issues of how joint decisions are made in fact. Our concern is with how they *should* be made. For example, how should a decision support system that recommends financial actions for a family take into account the needs and preferences of parents and children?

The prefatory material to Volume I of this book contains an outline of plans for Volumes II, III, and IV. In his plan for Volume III, Markowitz notes Hume's distinction between (1) empirical assertions (such as Newton's "law" of gravity) and (2) relationships between ideas (such as the Pythagorean theorem). Philosophers traditionally have also distinguished a third type of assertion, namely value judgments, such as it is commendable to "honor your father and mother." Most of this chapter will be concerned with relationships among ideas, particularly questions involving sets of conditions that imply certain social choice rules, and other implications of these rules. As to which rules are best, that is a value judgment. While we express some preference for our own latest idea, we do not find any argument compelling. To the DSS designer, we say, in effect, "Here are some alternatives and their consequences. You choose."

ARROW'S PARADOX

Arrow presents five conditions that he considers essential requirements for a social choice rule. These conditions are somewhat technical and the reader should see the original for their precise statement. Goodman and Markowitz paraphrase them as follows:

> *Condition 1. The social welfare function is a method for obtaining a simple social ordering . . . defined for a sufficiently wide range of individual voter orderings (rankings).*

> *Condition 2. If alternative (a) rises or remains still in the ordering of every individual, and no other change takes place in those orderings, then alternative (a) rises, or at least does not fall, in the social ordering.*

> *Condition 3. (Independence of irrelevant alternatives.) If each voter ranks each available candidate exactly the same in one situation as he does in another, then, no matter what is true about the rankings of the other (non-available) candidates who have been considered, the choice among the available candidates is the same in both situations.*

> *Condition 4. The social welfare function must not be "imposed"; i.e., it must not be given independently of individual preferences.*

> *Condition 5. The social welfare function must not be dictatorial; i.e., it must not be identical with the preferences of one individual, irrespective of all other individuals' preferences.*

In Chapter 1 we spoke of "axioms" for expected utility, as did von Neumann and Morgenstern. Goodman and Markowitz spoke of "conditions," as did Arrow. We will speak of conditions when we refer to Arrow's or Goodman and Markowitz's basic assumptions, and speak of axioms when we present basic assumptions of our own that are similar to, but differ from, those of Goodman and Markowitz.

THE GOODMAN AND MARKOWITZ (1952) (GM) THEOREMS

GM does not consider Arrow's Condition 3—the independence of irrelevant alternatives—essential, or even desirable. It argues as follows:

> *Suppose you intended to serve refreshments to two friends. You could serve them either coffee or tea but not both; A preferred coffee, B preferred tea. It seems clear that a symmetric ("democratic") welfare function would rank coffee and tea equally. Suppose you had other information concerning the preferences of A and B. While A prefers coffee to tea, he prefers tea to cocoa and cocoa to milk. B, on the other hand, not only prefers tea to coffee but prefers cocoa to coffee, milk to coffee, tomato juice to coffee; he would rather drink water than coffee; and he preferred tea to cocoa, milk, tomato juice, and water. Given this added information, it seems plausible to serve tea rather than coffee; for it does not make "much difference" to A, and it makes "quite a bit of difference" to B.*

Goodman and Markowitz's own proposal makes a major assumption and three additional conditions. The major assumption is that a given voter can only discriminate among a finite number of preference levels. In their formal discussion Goodman and Markowitz assume that

For any given state of information (given by a matrix $A = [a_{ij}]$ of orderings) the social welfare function gives a simple ordering of alternatives, independently of their availability; i.e., the social welfare function orders the vectors

$$\begin{pmatrix} a_{1j} \\ a_{2j} \\ \cdot \\ \cdot \\ \cdot \\ a_{mj} \end{pmatrix}$$

as a set in an m-dimensional Euclidean space. The social welfare function is defined for all states of information ("Universal Applicability"), i.e., the ordering is defined for all matrices (a_{ij}) of positive integers.

Element a_{ij} of the A matrix is the ranking "score" that voter i assigns to candidate j. A higher score is better than a lower score. We will consider GM's assumption of "Universal Applicability" to be its "Condition 0." GM's three numbered conditions are as follows:

Condition 1 (Pareto optimality). If nobody prefers j_2 to j_1 and somebody prefers j_1 to j_2, then j_1 is *socially preferred to j_2, i.e., if $a_{ij_2} \leq a_{ij_1}$ for all i, and $a_{ij_2} < a_{ij_1}$ for some i then $\{a_{ij_2}\} < \{a_{ij_1}\}$.*

In Condition 1, "$\{a_{ij_2}\} < \{a_{ij_1}\}$" is to be read: the (column) vector $(a_{ij_1},...,a_{nj_1})'$ is socially preferred to the vector $(a_{ij_2},..., a_{nj_2})'$. More generally, whenever a vector or its typical element is enclosed in curly brackets and compared with another such, the comparison should be interpreted as a social preference. For example, $\{u\} = \{v\}$ says that the social choice function is indifferent between the vectors u and v.

GM says that "In some cases the following condition is desirable:"

Condition 2 (Symmetry). The social ordering is unchanged if the rows of A are interchanged.

This condition holds, in particular, if the tabulation of votes is anonymous. Finally, GM assumes:

Condition 3 [Only differences count]. Suppose voter i has exhibited L levels of discretion. The social ordering among candidates 1 and 2 remains unchanged if we replace a_{i1} and a_{i2} by $a_{i1}+c$ and $a_{i2}+c$, respectively. The constant c must be an integer such that $1 \leq a_{ij} + c \leq max[L_i]$ for all j.

Since a different (positive or negative) constant c can be added for each of the n voters, Condition 3 implies:

Suppose that voter i can distinguish L_i levels. The social ordering between candidates 1 and 2 remains unchanged if we replace a_{i1} by $a_{i1} + c_i$ and a_{i2} by $a_{i2} + c_i$ for each voter i. The constants a_{ij} and c_i must be integers that satisfy

$$1 \leq a_{ij} + c_i \leq L_i$$

Goodman and Markowitz define a social welfare function as "acceptable" if it meets these four conditions. They show:

Theorem 1: *(A) The ordering relation defined by $\{a_i\} = \{b_i\}$ if $\sum a_i = \sum b_i, \{a_i\} > \{b_i\}$ if $\sum a_i > \sum b_i$ is an acceptable social welfare function. (B) It is the only acceptable social welfare function.*

We prove GM Theorem 1 in the next section.

After Theorem 1, Goodman and Markowitz relabel Condition 3 as Condition 3a, and define Condition 3b as *"Vector (a) is preferred to vector (b) if and only if (ca_i) is preferred to (cb_i)."* They then state:

Theorem 2: *(A) When (3a) is replaced by (3b), then the ordering relation is defined by $\{a_i\} = \{b_i\}$ if $\prod a_i = \prod b_i$, $\{a_i\} > \{b_i\}$ if $\prod a_i > \prod b_i$ is an acceptable social welfare function. (B) It is the only acceptable social welfare function.*

The Goodman and Markowitz proof of Theorem 2, reproduced later in the next section, assumes that every a_i and b_i is positive, as is c.

A corollary of Theorems (1) and (2) is that no choice rule is consistent with the requirement that the social ranking never be affected by changing the a_{ij} to $\alpha + \beta a_{ij}$ for any α and any $\beta > 0$.

Proofs of the GM Theorems

This section presents expanded versions of the highly compressed proofs in Goodman and Markowitz.

Proof of Theorem 1: Assertion A is trivial, since the GM conditions are easily verified. We now prove Assertion B.

We will refer to a social ranking rule as "compliant" (rather than "acceptable") if it complies with a given set of conditions or axioms such as GM Conditions 0, 1, 2, and 3. Let us first consider the case with $\sum a_i = \sum b_i$. We must show that any compliant rule prescribes $\{a_i\} = \{b_i\}$. For each voter i, Goodman and Markowitz define a constant c_i to be added to both a_i and b_i that, by their Condition 3, will not affect social choice. Specifically,

$$c_i = -a_i + \sum_{s=1}^{i-1}(b_s - a_s) \qquad \text{for } i = 1, \ldots, m \qquad \text{(1a)}$$

For $i = 1$, Equation (1a) should be read as

$$c_1 = -a_1 \qquad \text{(1b)}$$

Goodman and Markowitz then, in effect, invite us to confirm that

$$a_i + c_i = b_{i-1} + c_{i-1} \qquad \text{for } i = 2 \text{ to } m \qquad \text{(2a)}$$

and

$$a_1 + c_1 = b_m + c_m$$
$$= 0 \qquad \text{(2b)}$$

We leave this as an exercise for the reader. Thus, by GM Condition 3, the choice between the two candidates is the same as the choice between two candidates with utility vectors $(a + c)$ and $(b + c)$. But the utility scores of $b + c$ are a permutation of those of $a + c$. Thus, by Condition 2, any compliant social choice function will rank the candidates equally.

Next, suppose that $\Sigma a_i > \Sigma b_i$. We must show that any compliant social choice rule prescribes $\{a_i\} > \{b_i\}$. Goodman and Markowitz now invite us to produce a vector $(c_1, \ldots, c_m)$ such that

$$\Sigma c_i = \Sigma(a_i - b_i) \qquad \text{(3a)}$$

$$c_i = 0 \quad \text{for } a_i < b_i \qquad \text{(3b)}$$

$$c_i + b_i \leq a_i \quad \text{for } a_i \geq b_i \qquad \text{(3c)}$$

(Goodman and Markowitz implicitly assume that all the c_i are nonnegative.)

To do so, let

$$K = \left(\sum(a_i - b_i)\right) \Big/ \left(\sum_{a_i \geq b_i}(a_i - b_i)\right) \qquad \text{(4a)}$$

Since the sum in the denominator omits any negative terms that appear in the sum in the numerator, and since both sums of Equation (4a) are positive, we have

$$0 < K \leq 1 \tag{4b}$$

We now let

$$c_i = K(a_i - b_i) \tag{4c}$$

The reader can confirm that all requirements in Equations (3) are met, and that $c_i > 0$ for at least one i. The reader can also confirm that

$$\Sigma(b_i + c_i) = \Sigma a_i \tag{5a}$$

$$(b_i + c_i) \geq b_i \tag{5b}$$

with $b_i + c_i > b_i$ for at least one i. Thus, a compliant social choice function will rank the vectors (a) and $(b + c)$ equally (by the preceding result in this proof) and will prefer $(b + c)$ to (b) by GM Condition 1, and hence will prefer (a) to (b). **QED**

Proof of Theorem 2: Goodman and Markowitz assert that Theorem 2 can be proved by a "slight modification of Theorem (1)" if we replace

$$a_i \text{ by } a_i = \exp(x_i)$$

and consider ranking in x space. To carry this out, note that

$$x_i = \ln(u_i) \tag{6}$$

Then note that Conditions 1 and 2 are satisfied by vectors (a_i) if they are satisfied by $(\ln(a_i))$; and that Condition 3b is equivalent to $(\ln(a_i))$ is preferred to $(\ln(b_i))$ if and only if $(\ln(a_i) + \ln(c))$ is preferred to $(\ln(b_i) + \ln(c))$. **QED**

SOCIAL ORDERING FOR RDMS

As discussed in Chapter 1, a major distinction between an RDM and an HDM is the former's ability, and the latter's inability, to perceive its preferences with complete accuracy. The inability of a voter to discriminate more than a finite number of preference levels, postulated by Goodman and Markowitz, is an HDM characteristic. An RDM voter would assign a utility number to each candidate rather than a preference level. In what follows, we assume that the ith voter seeks to maximize the expected value of utility u_i. Specifically, we assume that the voter's preferences satisfy the three axioms in our Chapter 1, whose principal implications are: (A) choice is in accord with the expected utility maxim, and (B) each RDM's utility, u_i, is bounded

$$\underline{u}_i \leq u_i \leq \overline{u}_i \tag{7a}$$

We assume that $\underline{u}_i < \overline{u}_i$; else the ith voter is indifferent to the choice of candidate. Since, as shown in Chapter 1, we may choose any outcome to have zero utility and any preferred outcome as having the unit utility, we may assume that

$$\underline{u}_i = 0, \overline{u}_i = 1 \qquad (7\mathbf{b})$$

We define the set, S_F, of m-dimensional vectors u that satisfy Equations (7) as the *feasible set*, as distinguished from S_A, the *available set*. We will speak of any $u \in S_F$ as a *feasible vector*. We will require that a social ranking rule be able to compare any *two* feasible vectors, but we make no assumptions about the available set other than $S_A \subset S_F$, including the possibility that $S_A = S_F$.

HILDRETH'S PROPOSAL

Hildreth (1953) assumes that individuals act according to the expected utility maxim, and that social choice should be based on these utilities. However, whereas each of the two sets of GM "conditions" implies specific social choice rules, those of Hildreth are too broad to imply such. For example, as one method for satisfying the conditions he lays down in his Equation (2.11), Hildreth proposes a choice of the form

$$v = \sum_{i=1}^{n} g(u_i) = \sum_{i=1}^{n} g[f_i(X)] \qquad (8)$$

where X is a "social state," $f_i(X)$ assigns a utility to X and, according to Hildreth, "g can be chosen from a wide class of functions." This is fine as far as it goes but, like the Arrow result, it cannot guide action: in Arrow's case because *no* rule can satisfy his requirements; in Hildreth's case, because *too many* can.

MARKOWITZ AND BLAY (MB) AXIOMS

In this section we restate the GM conditions and theorems in terms of utility vectors rather than vectors of rankings. To avoid confusion, we label them MB Axioms 0 through 3 rather than GM Conditions 0 through 3, and similarly for GM's two theorems. The principal difference between the GM conditions and the MB axioms (other than the substitution of "utilities" for "rankings") is that GM Condition 0 assumes a finite available set whereas MB Axiom 0 does not.

As noted earlier, we assume that the u_i are bounded above and below, and that

$$\underline{u}_i = \mathrm{glb}(u_i) = 0$$
$$\overline{u}_i = \mathrm{lub}(u_i) = 1 \tag{9}$$

without loss of generality beyond the axioms of Chapter 1.

Let

$$\underline{u} = (0)$$
$$\overline{u} = (1) \tag{10}$$

be the vectors whose *i*th components are 0 and 1, respectively. In standard matrix notation, we define u to be *feasible* if

$$(0) \le u \le (1) \tag{11a}$$

i.e.,

$$0 \leq u_i \leq 1 \qquad \text{for } i = 1 \text{ to } m \qquad \text{(11b)}$$

- Axiom 0. *Simple ordering.*

  (A) If *u* and *v* are feasible, then either $\{u\} \geq \{v\}$ or $\{v\} \geq \{u\}$ (or both).

  (B) If $\{u\} \geq \{v\}$ and $\{v\} \geq \{w\}$, then $\{u\} \geq \{w\}$.

  $\{u\} = \{v\}$ is defined to mean $\{u\} \geq \{v\}$ *and* $\{v\} \geq \{u\}$.

  $\{u\} > \{v\}$ is defined to mean that $\{u\} \geq \{v\}$ and *not* $\{v\} \geq \{u\}$.

- Axiom 1. *Pareto optimality.* For any two feasible vectors *u* and *v*, if $u \geq v$ and $u \neq v$, then $\{u\} > \{v\}$. In this case, we say that *u dominates v*.

- *Axiom 2. Symmetry.* If the components of *v* are a permutation of those of *u*, then $\{u\} = \{v\}$.

- *Axiom 3. Only differences count.* $\{u\} \geq \{v\}$ if and only if $\{u + c\} \geq \{v + c\}$ for any constant vector *c* such that *u*, *v*, $u + c$ and $v + c$ are feasible.

With the current notation, GM Theorem 1 becomes *MB Theorem 1:*

A. *The ordering function*

$$f(u) = \sum_{i=1}^{m} u_i$$

is compliant.

B. *The ordering given by f(u) in (A) is the only compliant ordering.*

The proof of MB Theorem 1 is essentially the same as that by GM for GM Theorem 1.

GM Theorem 2 may also be transcribed into MB Theorem 2 and proven as in GM. Toward this end, MB Axiom 3 is relabeled as MB Axiom 3a, and then the translation of GM Condition 3b is labeled MB Axiom 3b.

The GM corollary—that no choice rule is consistent with the requirement that the social ranking not be affected by changing a_{ij} to $\alpha + \beta a_{ij}$ for any α and for $\beta > 0$— seems to contradict the fact, shown in Chapter 1, that linearly related utility functions

$$V = \alpha + \beta U \quad \beta > 0$$

produce identical rankings of alternative probability distributions. This apparent contradiction disappears if we interpret the MB axioms as follows: each voter assigns a utility to each candidate j—the zero and unit of the u scale having already been fixed. Therefore, if $c_i > 0$, the $u_j + c_i$ in Axiom 3 refers to a higher-ranked candidate, rather than a rescaling of a utility function. This is the proper generalization of GM Condition 3, since the latter in effect assumed that $\underline{u}_i = 1$, $\bar{u}_i = L_i$, and that (for c a positive integer) "$a_{ij} + c$" is the ranking of a higher-ranked candidate.

ARITHMETIC VERSUS GEOMETRIC MEAN UTILITY

MB Theorem 1 says that if certain axioms hold,

$\{u\} \geq \{v\}$ if and only if

$$\sum_{i=1}^{m} u_i \geq \sum_{i=1}^{m} v_i \qquad (12)$$

Dividing both sides of Equation (12) by m, we have

$$\left(\sum_{i=1}^{m} u_i\right)\bigg/ m \geq \left(\sum_{i=1}^{m} v_i\right)\bigg/ m \qquad (13)$$

In other words, the MB axioms imply that

$\{u\} \geq \{v\}$ if and only if

$$\mathrm{AM}(u) \geq \mathrm{AM}(v) \qquad (14)$$

where AM( ) stands for "arithmetic mean."

MB Theorem 2 says that if slightly different axioms hold, then

$\{u\} \geq \{v\}$ if and only if

$$\prod_{i=1}^{m} u_i \geq \prod_{i=1}^{m} v_i \qquad (15)$$

Taking the mth root of both sides of Equation (15), we find that

$\{u\} \geq \{v\}$ if and only if

$$\mathrm{GM}(u) \geq \mathrm{GM}(v) \qquad (16)$$

where GM refers to the geometric mean of u. Or, taking logs of the sides of Equation (16), we see that the substitution of MB Axiom 3b for 3a implies that

$$\{u\} \geq \{v\} \text{ if and only if}$$

$$AL(u) \geq AL(v) \qquad (17)$$

where AL stands for average logarithm.

In sum, the four MB axioms—including Axiom 3a—imply the maximization of average (a.k.a. arithmetic mean) utility; whereas the substitution of Axiom 3b for 3a implies the maximization of the geometric mean of individual utility scores, or their average logarithm (not to be confused with voters having logarithmic utility functions).

SYMMETRY REVISITED

Goodman and Markowitz say that their symmetry assumption, their Condition 2, is desirable "in some cases." But what if symmetry as specified in GM Condition 2 is not desirable, e.g., if the needs and preferences of a family's parents should have more influence on choice than those of the children and pets? An immediate answer is supplied if we consider the rows of the GM choice matrix, or the components of MB choice vectors, u and v, to be votes rather than voters. Specifically, **if we**

- permit more than one vote per voter;
- assume that all n_i votes of the ith voter are identical, since they all echo the utilities of the voter rather than

any strategic considerations that might induce the voter to vary his or her stated preferences from one vote to the next; and

- assume that GM Condition 2 and MB Axiom 2 apply to votes rather than voters

then GM and Theorems 1 imply that

$$\{u\} \geq \{v\} \text{ if and only if}$$

$$\sum_{i=1}^{m} n_i u_i \geq \sum_{i=1}^{m} n_i v_i \tag{18}$$

where n_i is the number of shares "owned by" the ith voter. If we divide both sides of Equation (18) by Σn_i then we obtain an equivalent ranking criterion of the general form of

$$\sum_{i=1}^{m} \beta_i u_i \geq \sum_{i=1}^{m} \beta_i v_i \tag{19}$$

where the β_i are positive, rational numbers that sum to 1.0. Conversely, given any set of positive rational β_i (whether or not they sum to 1.0), there is a number of shares and a distribution of these shares for which Equation (19) is the choice function. (Just express all the fractions in terms of their common denominator and multiply both sides of Equation (19) by this common denominator.) Thus there is a multiple-share voting system that implements any positive, rational coefficients in Equation (19).

We note that the preceding discussion substitutes one form of symmetry for another, namely it replaces "one man, one vote" by "one share, one vote." But the former is a special case of the latter, with each individual owning one share. Lest one think that the more general assumption here is the only form of symmetry that makes sense, we call the reader's attention to "Nash symmetry" discussed in a later section.

RESCALING PLOYS

As we saw in Chapter 1, an increasing linear transformation of a utility function produces an equivalent utility function as far as the individual's preferences are concerned. But it may affect the rankings of the individual's favorite candidates by some choice function consistent with MB axioms, such as the arithmetic or geometric mean utility. Specifically, if we express the original utility assignment u as a linear function of the new assignment $\tilde{u}$,

$$u_i = a_i + b_i \tilde{u}_i \text{ for } i = 1, \ldots, m$$

then the ranking function in Equation (19) becomes

$$f(\tilde{u}) = \sum_{i=1}^{m} \beta_i \, (a_i + b_i \tilde{u}_i)$$

$$= \sum_{i=1}^{m} \beta_i \, a_i + \sum_{i=1}^{m} \beta_i b_i \tilde{u}_i \qquad (20a)$$

as compared to

$$f(\tilde{v}) = \sum_{i=1}^{m} \beta_i a_i + \sum_{i=1}^{m} \beta_i b_i \tilde{v}_i \qquad (20b)$$

therefore

$$f(\tilde{v}) - f(\tilde{u}) = \sum_{i=1}^{m} \beta_i b_i (\tilde{v}_i - \ddot{u}_i) \qquad (20c)$$

Thus the differences among the a_i do not affect the sign of $f(\tilde{v}) - f(\tilde{u})$ but different choices of b_i can change it.

If we choose

$$a_i = 0$$
$$b_i = 1/\beta_i$$

then Equation (20a) becomes

$$\tilde{U} = \sum_{i=1}^{m} \tilde{u}_i \qquad (21)$$

Thus, if according to one scaling the utilities of the mother and father are each to be weighted k times that of some child, by another scaling they may be counted equally with the same effect on social choice.

Next let us consider the effect of rescaling the average log rule in Equation (17) or, equivalently, the product rule in the MB translation of GM Theorem 2. The former is perhaps clearer, being a separable (sum-of-functions) expression. If $\tilde{u}_i$ is a nonzero constant times u_i, then also, inversely,

$$u_i = b\tilde{u}_i \; i = 1, \ldots, m \qquad (22a)$$

and we get

$$V = \Sigma \log(\tilde{u}_i)$$
$$= \Sigma \log(b_i u_i)$$
$$= \Sigma \log(b_i) + \Sigma \log(u_i) \qquad \textbf{(22b)}$$

The first term on the right in Equations (22b) does not depend on the u_i, and the second does not depend on the b_i. Therefore multiplying by constants does not affect the comparison between utility vectors.

On the other hand adding constants a_i to the u_i—even adding the *same* constant to each u_i thus—

$$\tilde{u}_i = a + u_i \qquad \textbf{(23)}$$

may have a large effect on the ordering of the u. For example, imagine varying a from zero to some (positive or negative) constant. Thus

$$V = \Sigma \log(a + u_i) \qquad \textbf{(24a)}$$

$$\frac{dV}{da} = \Sigma(a + u_i)^{-1} \qquad \textbf{(24b)}$$

In particular, at $a = 0$,

$$\frac{dV}{da} = \sum u_i^{-1} \qquad \textbf{(24c)}$$

Thus the effect on V of a small change in voter utility u_i is *inversely proportional* to its magnitude.

VOTING BLOCKS

Sometimes it is useful to think of groups of voters as *voting blocks*. We define a voting block to be any set with two or more voters in any partition of voters. Examples include parents versus children, public employees versus taxpayers versus other stakeholders in the choice of a pension plan portfolio, and the voters in the various U.S. states. If a partition distinguishes K voting blocks, then $f(u)$ in MB Theorem 1 may be written as

$$f(u) = \sum_{k=1}^{K} \left(\sum_{i \varepsilon P_k} \beta_i u_i \right)$$
$$= \sum_{k=1}^{K} U_k \tag{25a}$$

where

$$U_k = \sum_{i \varepsilon P_k} \beta_i u_i \tag{25b}$$

Thus in choosing between two candidates u and v, the vote may be among voting blocks rather than individuals, as long as the utilities of the candidates to the voting blocks are defined as in Equations (25).

THE LUCE, RAIFFA, AND NASH (LRN) CHOICE RULE

Luce and Raiffa (1957) review the work of Arrow, Hildreth, and Goodman and Markowitz regarding social choice, and present their own proposal in this area. Theirs is a generalization of the Nash solution to the two-person bargaining problem; hence our designation of it as the Luce, Raiffa, and Nash (LRN) rule. Specifically, its ranking criterion is

$$U = \prod_{i=1}^{m}(u_i - u_i^0) \qquad (26a)$$

where u_i^0 is the utility attached to some minimally acceptable candidate for voter i. In particular,

$$\underline{u}_i \le u_i^0 \le \overline{u}_i \qquad (26b)$$

Luce and Raiffa note that the ordering specified by Equations (26) is not affected by the choice of α_i and β_i in a linear transformation, since

$$\begin{aligned} V &= \prod_{i=1}^{m}\left(\alpha_i + \beta_i u_i - (\alpha_i + \beta_i u_i^0)\right) \\ &= \prod_{i=1}^{m}\beta_i(u_i - u_i^0) \\ &= \left(\prod_{i=1}^{m}\beta_i\right)\left(\prod_{i=1}^{m}(u_i - u_i^0)\right) \end{aligned} \qquad (27)$$

Thus V is a multiple of U, showing that, indeed, a linear transformation does not alter the rankings of the utility vectors. *But* they *do* depend on the choice of u_i^0. In particular, Luce and Raiffa propose their rule only for comparing utility vectors such that

$$u_i > u_i^0 \text{ for } i = 1, \ldots, m \qquad (28)$$

Therefore the LRN rule itself does not meet our minimal requirement that the social ranking rule rank *every* feasible vector, but their idea of basing social choice on the Nash bargaining solution is worth exploring.

NASH SYMMETRY

The LRN criterion in Equation (26a) is based on the Nash solution to the two-person bargaining problem. Nash derives his solution from eight *assumptions*. The first five imply that (1) each of two bargainers seeks to maximize expected utility, and (2) the solution to the two-person bargaining problem is a function of available pairs (u_1, u_2). Social rankings that comply with the MB axioms also comply with this conclusion of Nash's analysis, since it is part of MB Axiom 0. In addition, we will see that Nash's Assumptions 6 and 7 are similar to, but not quite the same as, MB Axioms 0 and 1. These differences are not of significance for the present discussion. What interests us is Nash's eighth assumption—a different symmetry assumption from MB Axiom 2. This alternative symmetry assumption is quite attractive, as we shall see, but it is not compatible with either MB Axiom 2 or Axiom 3. Our main focus in the present section will be social choice functions that are consistent with MB Axioms 0 and 1, plus *Nash's* symmetry condition.

We will show that Nash's conclusion in this matter—given *his* own premises or *ours*—is in error. Specifically he concludes that the "product rule" is necessary as well as sufficient to meet his assumptions. We will show that a large class of functions $f(u_1, u_2)$—and, more generally, $f(u_1, \dots, u_m)$—satisfy these assumptions. Among these there is a simple, easily interpreted subset that we recommend to the consideration of social choice scholars and future game-of-life DSS designers.

Some differences between the Nash formulation and ours are due to differences in the problems being addressed. In particular, in a two-person bargaining situation there is the possibility that no bargain will be struck. In this event the two players retain the utilities of the status quo, $\left(u_1^0, u_2^0 \right)$. Clearly neither player has an incentive to accept an offer in which its $u_i \leq u_i^0$. Nash, quite reasonably, scales the u_i functions so that

$$u_1^0 = u_2^0 = 0$$

The solution (0, 0) is just as good as (0, 1) to Bargainer 1, and is the likely outcome if (0, 1) is Bargainer 2's best offer. In particular, Nash's Assumption 6, his Pareto optimality assumption, is stronger than MB Axiom 1, namely

6. *If α is a point in S such that there exists another point β in S with the property $u_1(β) > u_1(α)$ and $u_2(β) > u_2(α)$, then α ≠ c(S).*

S in Assumption 6 is the set of available (u_1, u_2) vectors. Nash assumes that S "is compact and convex and includes the origin." c(S) is the "choice" that the two bargainers agree to. Comparing Nash's Assumption 6 with MB Axiom 1 we see that a vector v can dominate a vector u as defined in MB Axiom 1 but not as defined in Nash's Assumption 6. Nash's seventh assumption is that

7. *If the set T contains the set S and c(T) is in S, then*
c(T) = c(S).

The Assumption 7 requirement is met as long as choice maximizes a choice function, $f(u)$. Nash's Assumption 8 has an explanatory prelude:

> *We say that a set S is symmetric if there exist utility operators u_1 and u_2 such that when (a, b) is contained in S, (b, a) is also contained in S; that is, such that the graph becomes symmetrical with respect to the line $u_1 = u_2$.*

8. *If S is symmetric and u_1 and u_2 display this, then c(S) is a point of the form (a, a), that is, a point on the line $u_1 = u_2$.*

We refer to this as *Nash symmetry* and consider it a very attractive social choice requirement. For example, suppose that one of the two guests in the GM "tea versus coffee" example assigns utility levels u and v to tea and coffee, respectively, whereas the other (symmetrically) assigns the same levels to coffee and tea, respectively; Nash's answer would be to flip a coin to decide.

Nash then says, "We now show that these conditions *require* that the solution be the point of the set in the first quadrant where $u_1 u_2$ is maximized." (Emphasis added.) This is not correct. It is sufficient but not necessary, as shown in the following:

Lemma Letting $u = (u_1, u_2)$, **IF** $f(u)$ satisfies the following conditions:

a. $f(u)$ is defined for all feasible u.

b. $f(u)$ is strictly increasing. That is, for any feasible u and v, if $u \geq v$ and $u \neq v$, then $f(u) > f(v)$.

c. $f(u)$ is strictly concave, that is, $f(\alpha u + (1 - \alpha)v) >$ $\alpha f(u) + (1 - \alpha)f(v)$ for all feasible $u \neq v$ and $\alpha \in$ $(0, 1)$; and

d. $f(u_1, u_2) = f(u_2, u_1)$ for all feasible (u_1, u_2) vectors

then $f(u)$ satisfies all eight of Nash's assumptions.

It also satisfies an axiom system that is the same as Nash's but with MB Axiom 1 instead of Nash's Assumption 6. Examples of functions satisfying the IF conditions of the lemma include $f(u)$ of the form

$$f(u) = g(u_1) + g(u_2) \qquad (29)$$

where g is strictly increasing and strictly concave.

Proof of Lemma

The first five of Nash's assumptions are satisfied by the assumption that f is a function of the two (or m) voter utilities. Nash's Assumption 6 is satisfied because f is strictly increasing. Assumption 7 is satisfied if the choice is made by any numerical ranking function. We will show that the symmetry and strict concavity of f assure that Assumption 8 is satisfied. This assumption says that **IF** what *we* call S_A is symmetric, **THEN** the choice will be on the diagonal. Nash does *not assume* that S_A **is** symmetric; only that it is compact, convex, and contains the origin. As such, it might *not* contain any diagonal point *other* than the origin. To prove the lemma, assume that S_A is in fact symmetric. In other words, if

$$u = (u_1, u_2)$$

is available then so is

$$v = (u_2, u_1)$$

Condition d of the lemma says that

$$f(u) = f(v)$$

and the strict concavity of f implies that

$$\frac{1}{2}f(u) + \frac{1}{2}f(v) < f\left(\frac{1}{2}u + \frac{1}{2}v\right)$$

$$= f\left(\frac{1}{2}u_1 + \frac{1}{2}u_2, \frac{1}{2}u_2 + \frac{1}{2}u_1\right) \qquad (30)$$

which is on the diagonal. Since Equation (30) holds for any feasible off-diagonal u, the lemma is proved.

QED

Nash's criterion, max $u_1 u_2$, is equivalent to Equation (29) with $g(u_i) = \log(u_i)$. A different choice of a strictly concave, strictly increasing $g(u_i)$ can lead to a different choice $c(S)$ if S is not symmetric.

A PROPOSAL

If u is m-dimensional with $m \geq 2$, Nash symmetry is exhibited by

$$F(u) = \sum_{i=1}^{m} g(u_i) \qquad (31)$$

where g is any strictly concave, strictly monotonic function of one real variable. Our Chapters 2, 3, and 4 illustrated that quadratic approximations to such functions are usually quite robust. We therefore propose for the reader's consideration the use of a quadratic approximation to $F(u)$, namely

$$Q(u) = \sum_{i=1}^{m} q(u_i) \tag{32a}$$

where the concave quadratic q is chosen so that its derivative is positive in the relevant range, namely

$$q'(u_i) > 0 \tag{32b}$$

for

$$0 \leq u_i \leq 1 \qquad \text{for all } i \tag{32c}$$

We will not present axioms or conditions that are necessary and sufficient for the use of $Q(u)$ in Equation (32) as a social ranking function. Such are often informative if they are available, but they are not required. Like shopping for a house or a car, one may have a list of minimal requirements but, beyond that, the decision is based on various attributes, some favoring one choice and others favoring others.

As discussed at length in Chapters 2, 3, and 4, maximum average $Q(u)$ in Equation (32a) is EV efficient, where E *here* represents average utility

$$E(u) = \frac{1}{m}\sum_{i=1}^{m} u_i \qquad\qquad (33a)$$

and V variance of utility

$$V(u) = \frac{1}{m}\sum_{i=1}^{m}(u_i - E(u))^2 \qquad\qquad (33b)$$

Rather than deciding on a social ranking function, a choice could be made from an $E(u)$, $V(u)$ efficient set. GM Theorem 1 would choose the point on this frontier with maximum $E(u)$, whereas GM Theorem 2 would choose a point that approximately maximizes average $\log(u)$. This approach requires explicit utility functions for the participants, but leaves the social choice function implicit.

In the choice of return distributions, the tradeoff between E and V is known as risk aversion. In social choice, it should be thought of as inequality aversion. A graph displaying the average utility versus "inequality" tradeoff curve would naturally use the standard deviation of u

$$\sigma(u) = \sqrt{V(u)} \qquad\qquad (33c)$$

rather than variance. In an interactive system, the viewer should be able to select specific points from this (average u, dispersion of u) tradeoff curve, and be shown histograms or density function graphs of the associated u distributions.

If it is deemed desirable to treat stakeholders asymmetrically (e.g., as in the case of parents versus children versus pets), this can be accomplished by either the scaling of the respective utility functions, or a one-share one-vote arrangement rather than a one-voter one-vote arrangement. It would also be possible for the number of votes, i.e., the n_i in Equation (18), to be different in the calculation of $E(u)$ in Equation (33a) versus the $V(u)$ in (33b), i.e., n_i^E versus n_i^v. In this case, the $E(u)$ that appears in Equation (33b) must be calculated using the n_i^v for Equation (33b) to be correct; and the interpretation of $\sigma(u)$ in Equation (33c) becomes problematic.

LIBERTÉ, ÉGALITÉ, PROSPÉRITÉ

The two criteria in Equations (33a) and (33b) or, equivalently, Equation (33c), may be thought of as a fusion of the fundamental objectives of France and the United States. The United States–declared right to "the pursuit of happiness" is the right to seek maximum expected utility. The French "liberté, égalité, fraternité" shares "liberty" with the U.S. creed; and criterion (33b) adds equality to our own proposed goals. As to fraternité, it seems to us that liberty and the pursuit of happiness require one to have the freedom to choose with whom to be fraternal.[1]

11

JUDGMENT AND APPROXIMATION

INTRODUCTION

A major conclusion of the preceding chapters is that the game-of-life investment context is well beyond our current and foreseeable optimization capabilities. In practice, therefore, formal analysis must frequently resort to approximation, and call upon judgment. The present chapter further explores the division of labor between analysis and judgment, and the use of approximation in analysis. Topics covered include the Markowitz (1959) proposals in this area, the Markowitz and van Dijk (2003) heuristic for approximating an (unknown) derived utility function, the Blay and Markowitz (2016) procedure for tax-cognizant portfolio allocation (TCPA), and "buckets," a.k.a. "mental accounts," as a methodology for approximately maximizing expected utility in situations, or for utility functions that we have excluded from our discussions so far.

EU MAXIMIZATION: EXACT, APPROXIMATE; EXPLICIT, IMPLICIT

In Chapter 2 we distinguished between exact and approximate maximization of single-period expected utility (EU). We further subdivided approximate solutions between those in which the approximation was explicit and those in which it was implicit. In the former, an explicit utility function is given, as well as a procedure to approximately maximize its expected value. In the latter, relevant tradeoffs are offered to the investor and the choice is made "intuitively." We view the latter as the investor implicitly seeking an EU-maximizing action. The same distinction—between exact and approximate EU maximization and explicit versus implicit approximation—applies to the maximization of the EU of the "game-as-a-whole" in dynamic (many-period) choice situations. Among exact solutions we will now also distinguish between those that are "analytic" and those that are "algorithmic." In the former the solution is a formula; in the latter it is a computing procedure that produces the numerically correct solution for any specific case.

Markowitz (1959) Chapter 13 presents proposals for implicitly maximizing EU for dynamic real-world games, to take into account both intertemporal relationships and the relationships between the portfolio selection decision and an investing family's needs and desires. The next section of the present chapter reviews these proposals. Except as otherwise noted, we still consider these as practical proposals for implicit EU maximization.

THE HOUSEHOLD AS INVESTOR

Part IV of Markowitz (1959) presents its fundamental assumptions. The first three chapters of that part present the theory of rational decision making under risk and uncertainty. The final chapter of that part, and of the book itself, is titled "Applications to Portfolio Selection," and is concerned with how to make practical the theory presented in the three preceding chapters. This last chapter, Chapter 13, of Markowitz (1959) begins thus:

> **Assumptions**
>
> *The first sections of this chapter consider portfolio selection when the following three conditions are satisfied:*
>
> (1) *the investor owns only liquid assets;*
>
> (2) *the investor maximizes the expected value of $U(C_1, C_2, \ldots, C_T)$, where C_t is the money value of consumption during the tth period (C_t could, alternatively, represent money expenditure deflated by a cost of living index);*
>
> (3) *the set of available probability distributions of returns from portfolios remains the same through time (if C_t is deflated consumption, then it is a "real return," taking into account changes in price level whose probability distribution is assumed constant).*

Later we consider modifications of these assumptions.

After its initial section on assumptions, Chapter 13 has sections titled

- "The Dynamic Programming Analysis"
- "The Single Time Period Utility Analysis"
- "Associated Utility Functions"
- "The Evaluation of Measures of Risk"

These are topics that we have expanded on in various chapters of Volumes I and II of this book. Finally the next-to-last section of Markowitz (1959) begins by reminding the reader that Assumptions 1, 2, and 3 have been applicable thus far and outlines its intentions as follows:

We shall now discuss cases in which one or more of the above assumptions does not hold. Specifically we shall consider instances involving

(a) consumer durables;

(b) nonportfolio sources of income;

(c) changing probability distributions;

(d) illiquidities; and

(e) taxes.

Thus Markowitz promises to deal with what we have been calling the "context" of portfolio selection. He continues:

> *In each case we shall discuss how the additional consideration changes the single period utility function, and how the efficient set analysis can be accordingly modified.*

> *In the instances considered, our approach leads to one of three general conclusions:*

> i. *No modification is needed. The additional consideration is one which the investor should take into consideration in selecting a portfolio from among those offered by an ordinary* [mean-variance] *efficient set analysis.*
> ii. *Modifications are required and are feasible. Portfolios deemed efficient while ignoring the consideration may be inefficient when the consideration is introduced. The consideration may be introduced into the efficient set analysis without excessive cost.*
> iii. *It is impossible or patently uneconomical to introduce the modification in a theoretically correct manner. Perhaps formal analysis can be valuable, however, if modified to account roughly for the consideration in question.*

If we tried to apply our efficient set technique to the general problem of business uncertainties through time, we would probably come to a fourth conclusion:

iv. The particular mode of analysis is too far removed from the needs of the subject to be bolstered by intuitive modifications. Another approach (such as Monte Carlo analysis . . .) merits consideration.

The subsection on consumer durables explains briefly the difficult utility-maximizing decision that the investor must struggle with deciding how much to save, or dissave perhaps, to purchase *consumer durables*, as well as to support current consumption. The conclusion of the subsection is:

all the investor need know concerning available portfolios is summarized in an E,V efficient analysis. Given one set of non-portfolio decisions, one E,V efficient portfolio maximizes expected utility. For another set of non-portfolio decisions, perhaps another efficient portfolio maximizes utility. Given the whole set of E,V efficient combinations, the rational investor can determine which portfolio is optimum while considering both his portfolio and non-portfolio opportunities.

In other words Markowitz recommends that the portfolio analyst tell the decision makers of the household what their opportunities are with respect to portfolio risk and return. The household decision makers must then decide to what extent they want to take advantage of or forgo those opportunities, as part of a complex utility-maximizing exercise of the sort that human decision makers (HDMs) must face every day.

Following the subsection on consumer durables is a subsection on *exogenous assets*. This supposes that "the portfolio is not the investor's only income," explains why "the probability distribution of returns from other sources is thus assumed given, but is not irrelevant to the selection of a portfolio," and explains how nonportfolio sources of income can be represented as exogenous assets in a general portfolio selection analysis.

Markowitz next considers the case of changing probability return distributions. Specifically he says,

> *Let us consider a particular case of probability distributions changing through time. Specifically, suppose that available distributions depend on some number b which measures the "bullishness" or "bearishness" of the market. For given decisions concerning nonportfolio expenditures, the single stage utility function to be maximized depends on the value of the portfolio Y and the level of b:*
>
> $$U = U(Y, b).$$
>
> *If U is approximately quadratic, that is,*
>
> $$U = Y + \alpha b + \beta Y^2 + \gamma b Y + \delta b^2,$$

then expected utility is

$$EU = E + \alpha Eb + \beta EY^2 + \gamma EbY + \delta EY^2.$$

[The last term should read δEb^2] *The choice of portfolio cannot affect Eb and Eb². The selection of portfolio depends on the mean and variance of Y and the correlation between Y and b. Efficient combinations of E, EY^2, and EbY can be generated by treating b as if it were an exogenous asset. Several ordinary efficient set analyses, with greater or lesser weights on b in the value of the portfolio, are required to survey possible combinations of expected return, variance of return, and correlation with b.*

The *b* variable in this proposal could be the output of some econometric forecasting model such as those surveyed in Guerard, Markowitz, and Xu (2013), or it could be some publicly available statistic such as the current average earnings-to-price ratio of the securities in some index.

The passage just quoted shows how to find a portfolio that is efficient in terms of portfolio expected return, portfolio variance, and correlations with some market predictor. It has no advice as to *which* such portfolio to choose. It cannot, since it does not postulate a utility function.

The next subsection of the next-to-last section of Markowitz (1959) is concerned with illiquidities. Markowitz's advice is to reoptimize periodically, "Moving slowly, on the basis of judgment, in the direction of the desired portfolio." The way this has worked out in practice, especially by quantitative money managers dealing with individual securities, is to include: (1) turnover constraints on the choice of portfolio and (2) liquidity constraints on how much to buy or sell at one time, and how much to accumulate in total of illiquid assets. Simulation analysis is used to select liquidity and turnover constraint levels.

The final subsection of the penultimate section of Markowitz (1959) is on taxes. We will discuss the Markowitz (1959) proposal in this area when we discuss the Blay and Markowitz tax-cognizant portfolio analysis (TCPA).

The last section of Markowitz (1959), titled "The Choice of Analysis," advises that

> In designing a portfolio analysis, two objectives should be kept in mind. First, an attempt should be made to keep the analysis simple; second, an attempt should be made to understand the salient implications of major simplifications.

The next-to-last section of Markowitz (1959) tries to carry out this general advice in various portfolio contexts using what we have called *implicit* approximate EU maximization. We now turn to explicit approximate EU maximization.

THE MARKOWITZ AND VAN DIJK METHODOLOGY

In Chapter 8 we discussed dynamic programming's (DP's) "curse of dimensionality." DP calculations with one or two state-variables in well-confined ranges proceed with ease. Those with three or four state-variables typically become computationally intense. Beyond that, the DP procedure quickly becomes out of the question.

Markowitz and van Dijk (2003) (MvD) and Kritzman, Myrgren, and Page (2009) (KMP) present two versions of a heuristic that has proven quite effective in dealing with DP's curse of dimensionality. Specifically, the MvD experiment applies the method to a problem for which the DP optimum can be computed, and finds that the expected utility provided by the MvD heuristic is almost indistinguishable from that of the optimum strategy, as well as being substantially superior to standard heuristics. The KMP experiment applied the MvD heuristic to both small and large problems—namely ones for which the optimal solution can, versus those for which it cannot, be computed economically. They found that the MvD heuristic gives near-optimum results when the latter can be computed, and substantially outperforms standard heuristics in both small and large problems. The MvD heuristic has been used in fact for large rebalancing applications.[1]

The basic idea behind the MvD heuristic is this: The Markowitz (1959) Chapter 13 proposals, summarized earlier, in effect assume that the derived utility function $U_t(s_t)$ is approximately a quadratic function of the state-variables that comprise s_t. Therefore, the investor can approximately maximize $E(U_{t+1}(s_{t+1}))$ by choosing a "good" combination of $E(R)$, $V(R)$, and the covariance of R with other state-variables. Markowitz (1959) uses this argument to justify displaying these statistics to the investor so that the investor can implicitly maximize EU.

In contrast, MvD is an *explicit* approximation method. MvD also assumes that $U_t(s_t)$ is approximately quadratic, and uses numerical methods to search for the quadratic $Q(s_t)$ that "works best." If s_t contains many state-variables, so that the full quadratic with all its cross-products is complex, MvD starts with a conjecture as to some simple, "good enough" special case of Q. For example, perhaps just a sum of squares and/ or only a subset of the variables that comprise s_t will suffice for a satisfactory approximation. Whether the conjectured Q function is a full nonhomogeneous quadratic including linear and cross-product terms, or a simpler special-case form, it typically has a parameter vector, α, to be chosen for "best" performance. MvD uses numerical methods to choose α.

This all sounds very complicated and computationally intense. In principle it could be, but it has not been in the experiments performed so far.

The MvD Experiment

As we noted in Chapter 8, the effective dimensionality of a dynamic investment situation increases radically when one drops the assumption of perfect liquidity. We presume this to be especially true when an ever-changing forecast of returns would make substantial portfolio revisions desirable if securities were perfectly liquid.

Markowitz and van Dijk developed their heuristic specifically to deal with illiquid investments in a changing world. To test this heuristic, they defined a simple, dynamic investment model for which a DP solution could be computed, and evaluated how well their heuristic worked within this model. The objective of their experiment was to provide a "reading" as to how well the MvD method might work for larger problems for which optimum solutions cannot be computed economically.

The MvD experiment is an investment game with two assets: stock and cash. The investor's portfolio can be in any one of 11 states: 0 percent stock, 10 percent, 20 percent, . . . , 100 percent stock. The investor uses a forecasting model that can be in one of five prediction-states: (1) very optimistic, (2) optimistic, (3) neutral, (4) pessimistic, (5) very pessimistic. Thus the system-as-a-whole can be in any of 55 states, depending on the states of the portfolio and of the forecasting model. Transaction costs are incurred when the investor changes its portfolio-state. MvD assumes an unending game, with a utility function such that the optimum next move is a function of which of the 55 possible states prevails currently—but *not* of simulated time.[2] The optimum strategy therefore may be written as an 11×5 *action matrix, $\tilde{A}$*, that specifies the choice of the next portfolio as a function of the current portfolio and the prediction-state. Associated with action matrix $\tilde{A}$ is an 11×5 expected discounted utility matrix, $\tilde{W}(i, j)$, that is the expected present value of utility if the game starts in the portfolio/prediction-states (i, j) and follows action matrix $\tilde{A}$ henceforth. (We know that a best action matrix exists since there is only a finite number of possible action matrices all told.)

MvD Model Summary

The MvD model is summarized in the Markowitz and van Dijk Exhibit 1, which is also Exhibit 11.1 here. The first two items in Exhibit 11.1 note that the model assumes that $t =$ one month, and has a constant risk-free rate of 0.4 of 1 percent (i.e., 40 bps) per month. The table in Item 3 shows, for example, that if the predictive model is in State 1—most optimistic—the expected return for stock for the forthcoming month is 64 bps with a standard deviation of $\sqrt{0.000592} \approx 0.024$. The next four columns present similar statistics for prediction-states 2 through 5.

EXHIBIT 11.1 Summary of Markowitz and van Dijk Investment Model

1. Interval between portfolio reviews: 1 month
2. Risk-free rate, r_f per month, (assumed constant): 0.004
3. Monthly stock return means, $E^1, \ldots, E^5$, and variances, $V^1, \ldots, V^5$, for various prediction-states:

Variable	State: 1	State 2	State 3	State 4	State 5	Steady State
E:	0.0064	0.0050	0.0042	0.0038	0.0027	0.0044
V:	0.000592	0.000556	0.000538	0.000539	0.000567	0.000559
OptX	4.05	1.80	0.37	−0.37	−2.29	0.72

Note: OptX is the investment that would be optimal in each state if there were no transaction costs.

(*Continued*)

EXHIBIT 11.1 (*Continued*)

4. From-to transition probabilities, *P*, between predictive-states:

Old State:	1	2	3	4	5	Steady State
			New State			
1	0.702	0.298	0	0	0	0.1608
2	0.173	0.643	0.133	0.051	0	0.2771
3	0	0.260	0.370	0.348	0.022	0.1363
4	0	0.065	0.179	0.615	0.141	0.2393
5	0	0	0.033	0.164	0.803	0.1865

5. Total Utility

$$U = \sum_{t=1}^{\infty} d^{t-1}u(D_t)$$

The investor's objective is to maximize EU.

For the cases reported, we used a monthly discount factor of $d = 0.99$.

6. We usually refer to "portfolio-state"

$$i = 1, \ldots, 11$$

representing fraction invested

$$p = 0.0, 0.1, \ldots, 1.0$$

Note that

$$p = \frac{i-1}{10}$$

Thus, for example, $p = 0.2$ in the present discussion corresponds to $i = 3$ elsewhere. In computing utility for a period, we define the "effective fraction" invested in stocks during time p_t^e, interval t, as

$$p_t^e = \theta_p \, p_{t-1} + (1 - \theta_p) p_t$$

(*Continued*)

EXHIBIT 11.1 (*Continued*)

where p_{t-1} and p_t are the fraction invested in stock at, respectively, the beginning and end of the time interval, t. In particular, the conditional expected return and variance of return (at time-point) on the portfolio during time interval t given state j, current stock fraction p_{t-1}, and chosen stock fraction p_t are

$$E_t^p = p_t^e E_{t-1}^j + (1 - p_t^e) r_t$$

and

$$V_t^p = (p_t^e)^2 V_{t-1}^j$$

where E_{t-1}^j and V_{t-1}^j are the mean and variance of stock return for time interval t given the prediction-state at $t-1$. Runs reported use $\theta_p = \frac{1}{2}$.

7. Transaction costs equal $c|p_t - p_{t-1}|$ for $c = 0.005$ and 0.02.

8. We assume that

$$Eu(D_t) = E(D_t) - kV(D_t)$$

where $u(D_t)$ is as in Item 5 and k reflects risk aversion. For the cases reported, $k = 0.5$.

9. We assume that the entire return on the portfolio for the month, net of costs, was distributed. Thus, the conditional expected utility for time interval t at time-point $t-1$ given prediction-state j, current portfolio-state i, and selected portfolio-state g is

$$E(u \mid i, j, g) = E_t^p - c|p_t - p_{t-1}| - kV_t^p$$

where $p_{t-1} = 0.1(i - 1), p_t = 0.1(g - 1)$, and E_t^p and V_t^p are defined in Item 6. Note that E_t^p and V_t^p for time interval t depend on the prediction-state at $t-1$.

10. We assume that the return on equities is bounded by some (very large) number M.

The entries in the table in Item 4 show the assumed probabilities, $P(j, h)$ that the prediction-state h (listed at the top of the table) will occur at time $t + 1$ given that the prediction-state j (listed in the left column of the table) holds at time t. The last column of the table shows the long-run, "ergodic," steady-state probabilities of the various prediction-states in Item 4. The last column of Item 3 shows the mean and variance of a random number generated by first drawing a prediction-state according to the steady-state distribution and then drawing a stock return given that prediction-state.

Item 5 says that the investor seeks to maximize the expected value of the discounted future utility function. The experiment uses a discount factor $d = 0.99$ (or a discount rate of 0.01 per month).

Let p_{t-1} be the fraction of the investor's portfolio held in stocks at time $t - 1$ and p_t be the intended fraction for time t. Item 6 defines the "effective fraction" assumed to be held during the interval as determined by parameter θ_p, set to 0.5 in these experiments. The item also notes the consequent portfolio expected return and variance for the month as a function of the prediction-state j, current stock fraction p_{t-1}, and intended fraction p_t. The fraction invested is related to the integer "portfolio-state" i by $p = (i - 1)/10$. (In retrospect letting P stand for a transition probability and p stand for fraction invested was perhaps not the wisest choice of notation.) Item 6 further notes how the mean and variance of portfolio return for the period depend on the fraction p, as well as on the risk-free rate r_f and the conditional mean and variance of the stock given the forecast model's prediction-state.

Item 7 notes that MvD reports the results of two experiments—one with transaction cost $c = 0.005$ per dollar of transaction, and the other with $c = 0.02$.

Item 8 assumes that the expected value, $EU(D_t)$ in Item 5, can be defined by its mean-variance approximation. MvD used a mean-variance tradeoff, k, equal to 0.5, with EU thus approximately equal to $E \log(1 + \text{return})$. (See our Chapter 3.) The fact that the investor's utility function $U(D_t)$ is assumed to be approximately quadratic does *not* obviously imply that the *derived* utility functions in the two games (with $c = 0.005$ *and* $c = 0.02$) are also approximately quadratic.

Returning to the table in Item 3, note that the last row presents the investment that would be optimal in each prediction-state in the absence of transaction costs, and with negative positions and leverage permitted. This was computed assuming $\theta_p = 0$ in Item 6, and $k = 0.5$ in Item 8.

Item 9 notes that the MvD experiment assumed that all returns, net of cost, are "distributed" each month. In particular, it assumed that losses are collected from the investor as well as gains distributed to it. This assumption is expressed in two ways: first, in the calculation of the contribution to expected utility for the period (as shown in Item 9), and second, implicitly, in the assumption that if at time $t - 1$, the investor targets fraction p_t, then in fact p_t will be the fraction invested in stocks at time t. This assumption—that returns are distributed—keeps the state space from ballooning.

Item 10 assumes that security returns are bounded by some huge number. MvD uses this assumption to show that

$\lim\limits_{T \to \infty} E\left[\sum\limits_{t=1}^{T} d^{t-1} u(D_t) \right]$, the calculation of which a (finite) computer can approach in finite time, equals $E\left[\sum\limits_{t=1}^{\infty} d^{t-1} u(D_t) \right]$ which is the stated investment objective and cannot be computed by a finite computer in finite time.

MvD Results

The utility of the game given a particular state s_t satisfies the Bellman equation

$$U(s_t) = \max_{\alpha} \ \{EU(s_t, \alpha) + dE(U(s_{t+1}|s_t, \alpha)\}$$

where s_t is the state of the system at time-point t, at the beginning of time interval t; the maximization is over the possible actions one can take given states s_t (in our case, a choice of the next p from $p = 0.0, 0.1, 0.2, \ldots, 1.0$); $EU(s_t, \alpha)$ is the expected utility of time interval t (in our case, as given in Item 9); $U(s_t)$ on the left side is the expected utility of the game-as-a-whole if one starts in state s_t; and the final term on the right side is the discount rate times the expected value of this utility over all the states that can occur in the next period, where the distribution depends on the current state and the action taken.

MvD conjectured that the derived utility function $U(s_t)$ for the game in Exhibit 11.1 could be adequately approximated by a linear function of a portfolio's conditional mean and variance:

$$U = E_w E_{pt} + V_w V_{pt} \tag{1}$$

where E_{pt} and V_{pt} are the portfolio's mean and variance for the forthcoming month given the predictive model's current state, whereas E_w and V_w are fixed weights that are not dependent on the predictive-state. This conjecture proved quite successful. Tables 11.1 and 11.2 present the action matrices for the DP solution and for the MvD heuristic, respectively. In each table Panel A shows the result for transaction cost $c = 0.005$, and Panel B shows it for $c = 0.02$. The entries in each panel of the two tables show the new stock-fraction p_t recommended by the strategy as a function of the current portfolio-state p_{t-1} (on the table's left) and the prediction-state (across each table's top). For example, the first column of Panel A of Table 11.1 says that if $c = 0.005$, and the prediction model is very optimistic, then the DP solution prescribes a move of the portfolio-state to 100 percent invested in stock no matter what the current portfolio-state may be; whereas Panel B says that if $c = 0.02$ and the prediction model is very optimistic, the DP solution prescribes a move of the stock-proportion up to 0.6 if it is less than this, and to leave it at its current level if $p_{t-1} \geq 0.6$. On the other hand, Table 11.2 shows that when the predictive model is very optimistic the MvD heuristic calls for the same action as the DP solution for all values of p_{t-1} and for both values of c.

The heading of Table 11.1 states that the action tables in Panel A and Panel B are each the results of 1,200 iterations of the DP algorithm. Panel A further notes that its action table was optimal from iteration 17 onward, whereas that in Panel B was optimal from iteration 211 onward. In other words, the DP calculation showed that the action matrix in Panel A

TABLE 11.1 Optimum Action Matrixes: Fraction of Stock at *t* (1,200 iterations)

Fraction of Stock at *t* – 1	1	2	3	Prediction-State 4	5
A. Cost = 0.005; A* optimum from iteration 17					
0.0	1.0	0.3	0.0	0.0	0.0
0.1	1.0	0.3	0.1	0.1	0.0
0.2	1.0	0.3	0.2	0.2	0.0
0.3	1.0	0.3	0.3	0.3	0.0
0.4	1.0	0.4	0.4	0.4	0.0
0.5	1.0	0.5	0.5	0.5	0.0
0.6	1.0	0.6	0.6	0.6	0.0
0.7	1.0	0.7	0.7	0.7	0.0
0.8	1.0	0.8	0.8	0.8	0.0
0.9	1.0	0.9	0.9	0.9	0.0
1.0	1.0	1.0	1.0	1.0	0.0
B. Cost = 0.02; A* optimum from iteration 211					
0.0	0.6	0.0	0.0	0.0	0.0
0.1	0.6	0.1	0.1	0.1	0.1
0.2	0.6	0.2	0.2	0.2	0.2
0.3	0.6	0.3	0.3	0.3	0.3
0.4	0.6	0.4	0.4	0.4	0.4
0.5	0.6	0.5	0.5	0.5	0.5
0.6	0.6	0.6	0.6	0.6	0.6
0.7	0.7	0.7	0.7	0.7	0.7
0.8	0.8	0.8	0.8	0.8	0.8
0.9	0.9	0.9	0.9	0.9	0.9
1.0	1.0	1.0	1.0	1.0	0.9

TABLE 11.2 Action Matrix for MV Heuristic: Fraction of Stock at t

Fraction of Stock at $t-1$	1	2	3	Prediction-State 4	5
A. $Cost = 0.005$; $E_{wt} = 4.40$; and $V_{wt} = -0.44$[a]					
0.0	1.0	0.3	0.0	0.0	0.0
0.1	1.0	0.2	0.1	0.1	0.0
0.2	1.0	0.2	0.2	0.2	0.0
0.3	1.0	0.3	0.3	0.3	0.0
0.4	1.0	0.4	0.4	0.4	0.0
0.5	1.0	0.5	0.5	0.5	0.0
0.6	1.0	0.6	0.6	0.6	0.0
0.7	1.0	0.7	0.7	0.7	0.0
0.8	1.0	0.8	0.8	0.8	0.0
0.9	1.0	0.9	0.9	0.9	0.0
1.0	1.0	1.0	1.0	1.0	0.0
B. $Cost = 0.02$; $E_{wt} = 10.0$; and $V_{wt} = -1.0$[b]					
0.0	0.6	0.0	0.0	0.0	0.0
0.1	0.6	0.1	0.1	0.1	0.1
0.2	0.6	0.2	0.2	0.2	0.2
0.3	0.6	0.3	0.3	0.3	0.3
0.4	0.6	0.4	0.4	0.4	0.4
0.5	0.6	0.5	0.5	0.5	0.5
0.6	0.6	0.6	0.6	0.6	0.6
0.7	0.7	0.7	0.7	0.7	0.7
0.8	0.8	0.8	0.8	0.8	0.8
0.9	0.9	0.9	0.9	0.9	0.9
1.0	1.0	1.0	1.0	1.0	1.0

[a] $E_{wt} = 4.40$ and any V_{wt} (−0.52, −0.35) produces the same result.

[b] $E_{wt} = 10.0$ and any V_{wt} (−1.06, −0.99) produces the same result.

was optimum for games of length $= 17, 18, 19, \ldots, 1200$. Nevertheless, as MvD illustrate in their Appendix A, one cannot conclude from this that Panel A of Table 11.1 is the optimum action matrix for the unending game with $c = 0.005$. All that one can guarantee is that the expected utility of the unending game provided by the given action table is within some small amount—in the present case, within $(3.53)(10^{-6})$—of the expected utility provided by the optimum action matrix.

For complex models, Monte Carlo analysis is usually required to estimate the expected value of the infinite sum in Item 5 of Exhibit 11.1, for given parameters of the MvD heuristic. But this can be determined analytically in the MvD illustrative model by solving a 55 by 55 system of linear equations. We used this to compute EU for various values of E_w and V_w in Equation (1). In particular, for $c = 0.005$ the best weights found were

$$\varphi_{0.005} = 4.4E_p - 0.44V_p \qquad \text{(2a)}$$

But $E_w = 4.4$ and any V_w from -0.35 through -0.52 also provided equally high EU, whereas varying E_w by 0.1 in either direction reduced EU. The action table in Panel A of Table 11.2 is almost identical to the DP action table in Panel A of Table 11.1, except for having 0.2 rather than 0.3 at $A(2,2)$ and $A(3,2)$.

The same exercise performed for $c = 0.02$ produced a best E_w and V_w of

$$\varphi_{0.02} = 10.0E_p - 1.0V_p \qquad \text{(2b)}$$

Maximum EU was reached at E_w = 10.0 and (again) with a range of V_w, namely, $V_w \in [-1.06, -0.99]$. The actions presented in Panel B of Table 11.2 are the same as those in Table 11.1 except for 1.0 rather than 0.9 in A(11,5).

MvD's Figures 1 and 2 (not reproduced here) show the expected utility of the game as a function of the game's 55 possible states for

- The DP strategy
- The MvD heuristic
- Other heuristics

The plots for the optimum and for the MvD heuristic were indistinguishable, differing by less than the thickness of a line on the graph. In contrast, lines for other heuristics showed them to be substantially suboptimum in many states. The closeness of the EUs of DP and MvD are corollaries of the closeness of their action tables as shown in our Tables 11.1 and 11.2.

The Kritzman, Myrgren, and Page (2009) (KMP) Experiment

KMP applied the MvD quadratic surrogate method to the rebalancing problem. Their experiment considered a portfolio that is reoptimized every two years, with 24 monthly rebalancing opportunities between reoptimizations. A cost is attached to each play of this "rebalancing game" equal to the sum of two parts, namely trading costs plus a cost ascribed to holding a portfolio that deviates from the desired portfolio. A strategy is sought to maximize the expected log utility of end-of-two-year wealth net of the two costs. KMP compared the MvD method with various other heuristics and with the DP solution for small problems.

KMP tried a quite simple quadratic surrogate for the end-of-month derived utility function, namely a constant times the sum of the squares of deviations of portfolio weights from target weights:

$$Q = d \sum_{i=1}^{n} \left(X_i - X_i^{\text{opt}} \right)^2 \tag{3}$$

This quadratic was much simpler for their problem than using portfolio variance, which would have required the use of some kind of covariance matrix. Their results are highly supportive of the MvD methodology.

Our Tables 11.3, 11.4, 11.5, and 11.6 are drawn from their Tables 2, 3, 4, and 5. Our Table 11.3 shows the historical

TABLE 11.3 Volatilities and Transaction Costs

Rebalancing Asset Class	Index	Standard Deviation	Transaction Cost
Domestic Equities	S&P 500	12.74%	0.40%
Domestic Fixed Income	Lehman US Agg	3.96%	0.45%
Foreign Developed Equity	MSCI EAFE + Canada	13.41%	0.50%
Foreign Bonds	CGBI World ex US	8.20%	0.75%
Foreign Emerging Equity	MSCI EM	18.51%	0.75%

TABLE 11.4 Correlations

	Domestic Equities	Domestic Fixed Income	Foreign Dev. Equities	Foreign Fixed Income
Domestic FI	−0.31			
Foreign Dev Eq	0.84	−0.19		
Foreign Bonds	−0.14	.53	0.16	
Foreign Emerging Eq	0.77	−0.17	0.83	−0.05

returns standard deviations and KMP transaction cost assumptions. Our Table 11.4 shows historical correlations for monthly returns from October 2001 through September 2006 for five asset classes. KMP solved for the expected returns that made the allocations in our Table 11.5 optimum, assuming

$$EU = E - \frac{1}{2}V$$
$$\cong E \operatorname{Log}(1 + R)$$

TABLE 11.5 Optimal Portfolios

	Two Assets	Three Assets	Four Assets	Five Assets
Domestic Equities	60.00%	40.00%	40.00%	40.00%
Domestic Fixed Income	40.00%	40.00%	25.00%	25.00%
Foreign Developed Equity		20.00%	20.00%	15.00%
Foreign Bonds			15.00%	15.00%
Foreign Emerging Equity				5.00%

TABLE 11.6 Performance Comparison—Total Costs (bps)*

Rebalancing Strategy	Two Assets	Three Assets	Four Assets	Five Assets	Ten Assets	Twenty-Five Assets	Fifty Assets	Hundred Assets
Dynamic programming	6.31	6.66	7.33	8.76	NA	NA	NA	NA
MvD heuristic	6.90	7.03	7.58	8.61	25.57	20.38	17.92	12.46
0.25%	15.19	17.01	19.81	21.37	41.93	42.96	41.53	26.88
0.50%	14.11	15.75	17.81	18.92	41.73	38.42	31.15	21.82
0.75%	12.80	14.09	15.32	16.27	40.05	32.95	31.46	25.02
1%	11.54	12.52	13.15	14.13	37.71	31.95	36.74	29.47
2%	8.73	9.20	9.79	10.73	41.94	48.59	56.96	39.33
3%	8.51	8.66	10.14	11.43	61.29	73.78	39.03	41.54
4%	9.46	9.52	12.08	13.78	88.49	93.23	38.55	41.96
5%	11.20	11.21	14.80	16.77	120.19	106.38	102.38	42.03
Monthly	15.65	17.25	20.07	21.85	41.92	42.92	43.34	39.75
Quarterly	11.05	11.86	13.51	14.76	45.17	34.32	33.12	26.54
Semiannually	11.13	11.53	12.67	13.95	69.97	40.75	37.33	24.41

*This table shows results for 5,000 Monte Carlo simulations. A dynamic programming solution is unachievable for the 10- through 100-asset cases, which employ equally weighted portfolios of stocks drawn from the S&P 500.

The KMP experiment included 2-, 3-, 4-, 5-, 10-, 25-, 50-, and 100-asset universes. They used various asset classes for their 2- through 5-asset cases and individual securities for their 10-, 25-, and 100-asset cases. Their Monte Carlo analysis draws i.i.d. returns from joint normal distributions with the above-described moments. In addition to estimating the EU supplied by the MvD heuristic and those supplied by the DP solution for small problems, KMP evaluated the performance of commonly used rebalancing heuristics including rebalancing at certain times (calendar heuristics) or upon certain size deviations (tolerance heuristics). For the calendar heuristics, they fully rebalanced at predetermined time intervals. For the tolerance band heuristics, they fully rebalanced when asset weights breached thresholds of 0.25, 0.5, 0.75, 1, 2, 3, 4, and 5 percent.

Our Table 11.6 summarizes the KMP results. In the 2-asset case, DP did much better than MvD (incurring a 6.31 cost for the former versus a 6.90 cost for the latter). (Consolation prize: MvD did substantially better than other heuristics.) The advantage of DP over MvD shrank as KMP increased the number of assets, and is reversed at five assets. Thus for $m = 5$, MvD was "better than optimal." This is because the DP calculation must assume that possible portfolio vectors are points on a grid. Such a grid *necessarily* becomes increasingly coarse as the number of assets increases. KMP did not apply DP beyond five assets, but evaluated heuristics up to the 100-asset case. It found that the MvD heuristic reduced total costs relative to all of the other heuristics by substantial amounts.

Conclusions Regarding the MvD Heuristic

The MvD and KMP examples show the MvD quadratic surrogate method to be a promising but far from mature technology. It is based on the robustness of the quadratic approximation to a concave utility function as proposed in Markowitz (1959) and illustrated in our Chapters 2, 3, and 4. The method may start with a conjecture as to a subset of simple quadratic functions that could serve as a surrogate for DP's single-period derived utility function. This is followed by an exploration of possibly near-optimal parameter settings. In the two cases tried so far, the initial conjecture was to start with the simplest plausible-for-the-problem quadratic before trying more complex forms. In both experiments, the conjecture served well. What is not clear is whether there was something special about the problems posed in the first two experiments that made them especially suited to the MvD approach and, if so, what is the boundary between suitable versus not-suitable applications. A decade or two of practical application of the methodology should clarify this matter.

THE BLAY-MARKOWITZ NPV ANALYSIS

The last subsection of the next-to-last section of Markowitz (1959) discusses the major illiquidity introduced by capital gains being taxed only when realized. The Markowitz (1959) recommendation is to:

> Define the "worth" of a security or portfolio at the end of the year to be (the market value of the portfolio) minus (taxes payable on realized gains and

income) minus (b) times (unrealized capital gains)
plus (c) times (unrealized capital losses), . . .
For fixed b and c, estimated perhaps on the basis
of past realized capital gains and losses, an ordinary
analysis could be performed in terms of the means,
variances, and covariances of worth thus defined.

The preceding proposal does not consider the availability of accounts such as conventional IRAs, Roth IRAs, and 401(k) accounts—many of them created since 1959. These introduce kinds of illiquidity that are not present in taxable accounts. With a taxable account, an investor can realize the gains at *any time* (and pay the applicable short- or long-term tax), or let the whole account ride, perhaps to be passed on to the investor's heirs. With a conventional IRA account, in contrast, except for certain specified emergencies, the investor cannot withdraw deposited funds or their earnings without penalty until the investor is at least 59½ years old, and must start to withdraw after age 70½. Thus, except for certain emergencies, a 30-year-old investor cannot touch this money without penalty for almost another 30 years, and a 60-year-old cannot shelter money indefinitely this way.

Clearly a large-cap stock in a tax-deferred account is a different kind of investment from one in a taxable account, and ideally should be treated as being in a different asset class. Analyses currently used in practice fall into two major groups:

A. Those that *do* distinguish, e.g., large-cap stocks in taxable accounts from those in tax-deferred accounts;

B. Those that *do not*.

Analyses in Category B include:

B1. Those that analyze taxable and tax-advantaged accounts separately;

B2. Those that analyze the portfolio as a whole ignoring taxes, then choose investment locations using informed judgment.

Approach B1—separate analyses, one ignoring the other—is clearly suboptimal. For example, combinations of securities or asset classes in a tax-deferred account that would be efficient if this were the investor's entire portfolio will typically not be found efficient by a portfolio analysis that can allocate income-producing investments to tax-advantaged accounts and capital gains–producing investments to taxable accounts.

One might conjecture that Approach B2—use informed judgment to locate investments after an MV analysis ignoring taxes—might produce about as good a portfolio as Approach A. But this is not so, no matter how skillful the tax expert who locates the investments. Approach A produces both the asset (or asset class) mix *and* their locations *simultaneously*. A *priori* one should expect that the desirability of an asset or asset class would depend on the availability (or not) of favorable tax treatments in some kinds of accounts, the amounts available, and whether or not other assets or asset classes compete for their availability. Thus tax experts should advise beforehand on the availability of various tax-reducing opportunities, rather than locate positions after an MV analysis.

The typical current practice using Approach A, like that proposed in Markowitz (1959), is to postulate a formula for valuing a security or asset class, then estimate the means, variances, and covariances of the percentage change in the asset or asset-class value—thus valued—as inputs to an MV analysis. Blay and Markowitz (2016) survey proposals for such asset and asset class valuation. This was in fact our initial approach in formulating a *tax-cognizant portfolio analysis* (TCPA) product for 1st Global.

But we rejected all such formulas, including those we found in the literature and additional proposals of our own. An example will serve to illustrate the type of difficulty this approach faces. Confining our attention from this point forward to MV analysis at an asset-class level, consider the problem of valuing a large-cap position in a 401(k) account financed by before-tax dollars. Since capital gains and income are taxed equally when withdrawn from such an account, we need not be concerned with investment basis for tax purposes. The question is: What is a dollar in such an account worth as compared to an after-tax dollar that can be spent now? On the one hand, the value of a before-tax dollar in a tax-advantaged account is reduced by the fact that eventually it must be withdrawn and taxed. On the other hand, its value is increased by the fact that—until it is withdrawn—it can grow unencumbered by taxation. But these two values depend on the length of time until the investor's retirement and the rate at which the investor will withdraw from the tax-advantaged account after retirement.

It appeared to us that one needs to do a *present-value* calculation in order to value a dollar today in some illiquid asset-class/location (AC/LOC) for a specific investor. But such a present value of future withdrawals depends on the return scenario that the asset class experiences between "now" and the investor's final withdrawal. Since this is the result of a random process, one cannot compute a single for-sure present value (PV). Rather, for a set of AC/LOCs one could randomly generate many such scenarios and, from these, estimate the means, variances, and covariances of their PVs. These, in turn, can be the inputs to a portfolio analysis that seeks portfolios of AC/LOCs that are efficient in terms of the mean and variance of *portfolio* PV, subject to constraints such as the total value of the investor's tax-deferred account(s), plus perhaps constraints on the liquidity of the portfolio (so that short-run liquidity problems don't trump long-run PV), and perhaps other portfolio constraints.

This, indeed, became the Blay-Markowitz methodology. It could also be applied to portfolios with other illiquid investments, such as limited partnerships or direct real estate investments, or to corporate project selection decisions. In these cases the investment might involve additional payments into, as well as future payments from, the investment. In such cases a "net present value" (NPV) rather than a PV calculation would be needed, but the same principles would apply: namely, estimate the means, variances, and covariances of NPVs, then use these in a portfolio analysis of NPV efficient portfolios.

The following sections will discuss TCPA principles and some implementation details. Our interest here is not particularly with the tax laws as they exist today, but with MV efficient set analysis of NPV distributions generally, including important implementation considerations likely to be encountered in other applications. We begin with a formal statement of the TCPA model, and then consider implementation issues.

THE TCPA PROCESS

Consider a TCPA of a universe of N asset classes that can be held in K "locations," i.e., account-types subject to different tax treatments. The TCPA procedure randomly generates S samples of joint present values

$$(PV_{11s}, PV_{12s}, \ldots, PV_{iks}, \ldots, PV_{NKs}) \; s = 1, \ldots, S$$

where PV_{iks} is the present value at time $t = 0$ of the withdrawal stream (a.k.a. the consumption stream) generated by the ith asset class, in the kth location, during simulation run s. These are used to estimate PV means, variances, and covariances among N times K AC/LOC PVs.

In the currently implemented TCPA, the PVs are calculated using a discount factor D equal to that of long-term government bonds since 1926, according to Ibbotson (2013). This is taken as the long-term risk-free rate-of-substitution between consumption now and consumption later, including inflation as well as impatience.

A TCPA analysis piggybacks on an existing model for generating jointly distributed returns for a group of asset classes:

$$(r_{it}, r_{2t}, \ldots, r_{Nt}) \; t = 1, \ldots, T$$

where r_{it} represents the return to asset class i during time interval t. We assume that the organization undertaking the TCPA already has such a return-generating model. But more is needed for the TCPA application, since different sources of total return may be subject to different tax treatment. Thus the augmented returns model must generate a sequence of returns by tax type:

$$r_{iht} \quad i = 1, \ldots, N; \quad h = 1, \ldots, H; \quad t = 1, \ldots, T$$

for asset class i, tax category h, and time t. Blay and Markowitz touch on current data sources and procedures for this purpose.

The (r_{iht}) time series serve as inputs into the TCPA simulation model—or *TSim* for short. This transforms the (r_{iht}) series for a particular sample, s, into a present value PV_{iks} for an AC/LOC and sample. A basic assumption here is that the after-tax present value of a return stream can be computed without considering similar information for any other return stream. This is inaccurate, since loss carryforward offsets to gains are at a portfolio level rather than an individual AC/LOC level. But it is an essential assumption of the NPV efficient set analysis generally, rather than a limitation of the current TCPA specifically, since the composition of the portfolio has not been determined yet. In addition, the current TCPA assumes that the investor knows for sure his or her number of remaining years, T, as well as the number of years in the *accumulation phase* T_R before retirement. A later section discusses (1) the seriousness of these and other assumptions, (2) what should be kept in mind when using the TCPA process given these assumptions, and (3) what computational breakthroughs (if any) would be required to overcome these limitations.

In the terminology of Chapter 7, TSim is a synchronous, discrete event simulator with t equal to one month. At the top of its loop, TSim determines whether the month-to-be-simulated is before retirement, i.e., still in the investor's accumulation phase, or after retirement, in the investor's *distribution phase*. If it is in the accumulation phase, the wealth increase (or decrease, if the asset class suffers a loss) depends on the tax treatment of the location. If the location is tax-advantaged (that is, if it is a tax-deferred or tax-exempt account), then the new value W_{t+1} of the AC/LOC is

$$W_{t+1} = W_t(1+R) \qquad (4)$$

where R is the return on the AC.

The situation is more complicated for a taxable AC/LOC. In particular, W_t is not sufficient to characterize the account's status at time t. W_t has to be split between W_{tU} and W_{tA}, i.e., unrealized capital gains and after-tax wealth. Status also includes the amount, if any, of prior losses not already used to offset gains. As already noted, this may be used for a loss carry-forward calculation, but only considering losses and gains on this one AC/LOC.

The current TSim assumes that capital gains on securities purchased in year t are short-term if realized in year t and long-term thereafter. Parameters of TSim include short-term and long-term turnover rates, and the tax rates applicable to income and to realized short-term and long-term capital gains in this location. See the appendix of Blay and Markowitz for the exact calculation.

If the test at the top of the loop determines that the distribution phase has started, then the loop starts with a cash distribution to be used for consumption during the year. If the account is tax-exempt, the entire withdrawal is credited to consumption and discounted to the present. If the account is tax-deferred, the entire withdrawal is taxed as ordinary income (except that if an AC/LOC has both after-tax and untaxed wealth, it is assumed that these are withdrawn proportionally). The balance of the account, not withdrawn for consumption, is grown as in Equation (4).

Blay and Markowitz initially decided that for the objectives of TCPA—namely, the preretirement allocation of wealth to various accounts—a simple consumption rule would suffice. Specifically, they assumed that the investor's consumption would equal current wealth divided by years to go:

$$C_t = \frac{W_t}{T - t} \tag{5a}$$

Blay and Markowitz changed the formula in Equation (5a) when a discussant pointed out that this might violate the minimum distribution requirement, C_{min}, for such accounts. The obvious fix would be to withdraw

$$C_t = \max\left(W_t/(T - t), C_{min}\right) \tag{5b}$$

As this is written the TCPA product under development does something more complicated, because it is part of a package whose front-end asks for T_R and T, but not the investor's age. Therefore it does not know when the investor will reach 59½. The formula used assures that *at least* C_{min} will be distributed provided $T_R \geq 60$ and $T \leq 105$. See Blay and Markowitz for details. It is not clear whether it makes much difference for the purposes of TCPA whether one uses Equation (5a), Equation (5b), or the formula in Blay and Markowitz. We take it as axiomatic that any of these solutions is better than ignoring taxes.

ESTIMATING PV MEANS, VARIANCES, AND COVARIANCES

As discussed earlier, the TCPA process uses TSim to transform a sample of before-tax return sequences into a sample of present values:

$$(PV_{11s}, \ldots, PV_{NKs}) \ s = 1, \ldots, S$$

The TCPA process then estimates the PV means, variances, and covariances from this sample. The obvious way to do that is to use the sample's means, variances, and covariances as estimates of the corresponding population moments. This procedure proved to be quite unstable. For example, the first two rows of Table 11.7 present the sample means and standard deviations of five PV simulation analyses, each with sample size $S = 25,000$ (for the Emerging Market asset class in a tax-deferred account, with $T_R = 30$ and $T = 60$, from an i.i.d. joint lognormal return generator using 1st Global's forward-looking estimates of asset-class means, variances, and covariances). Sample means—and especially sample standard deviations—varied considerably from one sample to the next. In particular, Sample 1 had a standard deviation of $51.84 as compared to $27.91 for that of Sample 3. The problem was that PV distributions are highly skewed, and the sample standard deviation (σ) is quite sensitive to outliers: The σ of one sample would be much greater than that of another because it had a few more right-tail outliers. We found the following estimation procedure quite satisfactory:

- Assume that the PV distributions are joint lognormal, and thus the $\log(\text{PV}_{iks})$ are joint normally distributed.
- Use the sample means, variances, and covariances of $\log(\text{PV}_{iks})$ as estimates of those parameters of the underlying normal distribution.
- Infer the means, variances, and covariances of the PVs from the relationships between the two sets of moments. See Endnote 2 to Chapter 3. In particular, if R and S are joint lognormally distributed, then RS is also, since $\log(RS) = \log(R) + \log(S)$. Thus the endnote can be used to estimate $E(RS)$ and hence $\text{cov}(R, S)$.

TABLE 11.7 A Comparison of the Estimated Means and Standard Deviations of Different TCPA Runs Using Two Different Estimation Methods*

Emerging Market Stocks Held in a Tax-Deferred Account		Simulation Run (25,000 iterations per run)				
		1	2	3	4	5
Simulated present values	Arithmetic mean	$7.29	$6.92	$6.67	$6.65	$7.20
	Standard deviation	$51.84	$28.73	$27.91	$32.44	$35.58
Logs of simulated present values	Arithmetic mean	0.27	0.27	0.25	0.26	0.28
	Standard deviation	1.80	1.80	1.80	1.78	1.80
	Skewness	0.06	0.07	0.04	0.04	0.06
	Excess kurtosis	0.00	0.00	0.02	0.05	0.05
Present value estimates based on logs of simulated present values	Arithmetic mean	$6.63	$6.63	$6.51	$6.29	$6.73
	Standard deviation	$32.91	$32.81	$32.31	$29.78	$33.44

*Values have been rounded. Calculations used unrounded values.

The final two rows of Table 11.7 show the much more stable estimates produced by this process. In particular, the estimated standard deviations range from a low of $29.78 to a high of $33.44.

DISPLAYING THE EFFICIENT FRONTIER

The present value of a withdrawal stream is not intuitively meaningful, even to the present authors, much less for a lay investor. More appealing would be the *average* withdrawal for consumption. The average withdrawal for consumption C_{iks} for a given sample s and AC/LOC i, k can be an ordinary (equally weighted) average or a more generally weighted average

$$A_{iks} = \sum_{t>T_R} w_t C_{ikst} \tag{6}$$

where $T_R + 1$ is the first after-retirement (distribution-phase) period, and the w_t are any nonnegative numbers that sum to one. It turns out to be most convenient, as well as defensible theoretically, to weight withdrawals proportionately to the discount factors used in computing PV_{iks}. Thus

$$w_t = D^t / \sum_{t>T_R} D^t \quad \text{for} \quad t = T_R + 1, \ldots, T$$
$$= kD^t \tag{7}$$

where

$$k = \left(\sum_{t>T_R} D^t \right)^{-1}$$

Equations (6) and (7) imply that the weighted average consumption is proportional to the sample's present value, namely

$$A_{iks} = kPV_{iks} \tag{8a}$$

Therefore

$$E(A_p) = kE(PV_p) \tag{8b}$$

$$V(A_p) = k^2 V(PV_p) \tag{8c}$$

$$\sigma(A_p) = k\sigma(PV_p) \tag{8d}$$

We could show the investor an efficient $E(A_p)$, $\sigma(A_p)$ frontier, but this has the problem illustrated in Figure 11.1. This is the output of a TCPA process using the six asset classes and two locations listed in Figure 11.3 for an investor with

FIGURE 11.1 The Mean and Median Average Postretirement Consumption for a TCPA Run

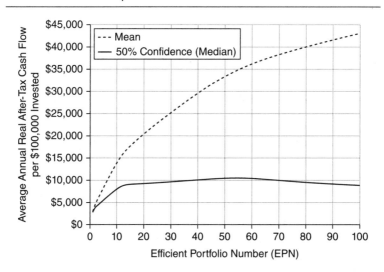

$T_R = 30$ and $T = 60$, and with an equal value of assets in taxable and tax-deferred accounts. The horizontal axis of the figure is an *efficient portfolio number*, EPN, where the efficient portfolio with minimum $V(A_p)$ is assigned EPN = 1 and that with maximum $E(A_p)$ has EPN = 100. The successive efficient portfolios between EPN = 1 and EPN = 100 have equal increments of portfolio standard deviation.

The figure shows each EPN's expected A_p and its median A_p, where the median was computed assuming that the PVs are lognormally distributed. This seemed plausible in light

FIGURE 11.2 Level L Such that the Probability that Average Postretirement Consumption Is Greater than L is 50%, 75%, or 95% in a TCPA Run

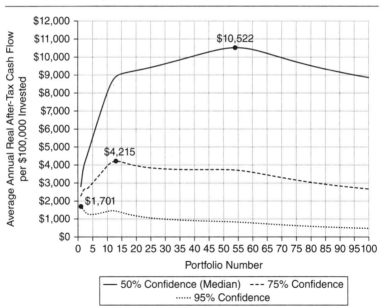

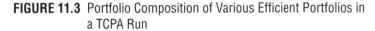

FIGURE 11.3 Portfolio Composition of Various Efficient Portfolios in a TCPA Run

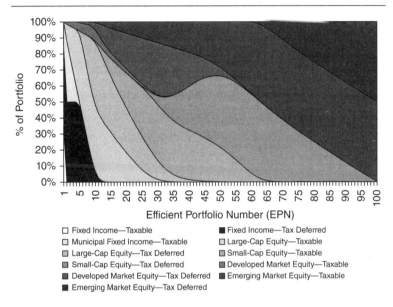

of sampling considerations discussed in the preceding section. The skewness of the A_p distribution is illustrated in the figure by the difference between the $E(A_p)$ curve and the median A_p curve. In particular, the former is highest at EPN = 100, whereas the latter has a maximum at EPN = 54 with the median being fairly flat from EPN $\approx$ 15 and higher. In the region between EPN 50 and 55, the expected value of average consumption is about $34,000 per year for an original $100,000 initial wealth—but there is only a 50-50 chance that it will exceed about $10,500 per annum!

Figure 11.2 shows the median and the 75 percent and 95 percent VaRs for the analysis in Figure 11.1. We see for example that EPN = 1 has the most favorable 95 percent VaR but has a terrible median A_p; whereas by EPN = 13 the median A_p is not too bad and the 75 percent and 95 percent VaRs seem to us acceptable—but the choice is up to the investor of course. We propose Figure 11.2 as an intuitive way to display the available opportunities to an investor.

RESAMPLED AC/LOC PORTFOLIOS

The curves in Figure 11.2 are a variation of what Michaud (1998) refers to as a "resampled frontier," namely, they are "averages" of the frontiers produced by many TCPA analyses using different random seeds. For clarity of presentation, the analysis in our Figure 11.2 has two locations (taxable and tax deferred), as compared to that of Blay and Markowitz, which includes tax-exempt accounts. Resampling seemed desirable in the Blay and Markowitz analysis since, while portfolios were generally stable in terms of AC weights, the allocation of those investments to tax deferred versus tax exempt accounts was quite unstable, even when frontiers were based on sample sizes of 200,000 or more. The implication of this instability seems to be that, given two assets to be located in tax advantaged accounts, it makes little difference which is allocated to a fixed-in-size tax deferred account and which to the tax exempt account.

Figure 11.3 presents the AC/LOC weights of the resampled portfolios for various EPN in Figure 11.2. We see, for example, that the efficient portfolio with EPN = 54 which, according to Figure 11.2, maximizes the median A_p, consists mostly of small-cap and emerging market equities in a taxable account, and fixed income in a tax-deferred account.

TCPA 1.0 ASSUMPTIONS

The assumptions that underlie the current TCPA process can be divided into two groups:

- Assumptions that are fundamental to the NPV efficient set approach generally;
- Assumptions that could be relaxed without giving up this approach.

We will discuss each of these in turn.

Fundamental Assumptions of the NPV MV Efficient Set Approach

We have noted that a fundamental assumption of this approach is that the NPV of an investment can be computed without regard to the performance of the remainder of the portfolio. This is because the remainder of the portfolio is yet to be determined. In particular, in TSim losses sustained in a particular AC/LOC can only be carried forward to gains in the same AC/LOC. Thus TSim will underestimate PV, since it can only take into account a subset of possible opportunities.

Our view is that this underestimate will not be too serious as long as the portfolio consists of asset classes that often win and sometimes lose. Specifically, we assume that a capital loss in one AC/LOC can usually get used by that AC/LOC in the following year, or the year after—thus applying the loss "soon" rather than immediately to another AC/LOC. This error does not seem to us to substantially affect the choice of efficient asset class mix. The error would clearly be more serious if the AC/LOC is not one that often wins and sometimes loses, but is a tax shelter that typically loses so that its losses can be applied to concurrent gains in other AC/LOCs.

In order to overcome this limitation of an NPV analysis, one would have to solve the TCPA process dynamically for the portfolio-as-a-whole. Since this is well beyond the practical limits of exact dynamic programming, the Markowitz-van Dijk approach could be tried. As we saw earlier in this chapter, the MvD approach is still somewhat experimental, but the TCPA problem might well be a fruitful application area for it. This might take some time to make practical. Meanwhile, MV efficient PV analysis appears to work well for the kinds of asset classes most investors use for their retirement accounts.

Special Assumptions of TCPA 1.0

The principal simplifications of the current TCPA are:

1. a known mortality date, and
2. a mechanical consumption rule, as compared to an EU-seeking rule such as that modeled in GuidedChoice's GuidedSpending.

We note, however, that GuidedSpending currently also assumes a known mortality date, and only treats savings in a tax deferred account as opposed to TCPA's multiple LOCs.

The way in which uncertain mortality is reflected in the current use of GuidedSpending and the projected use of the current TCPA is to use a final date T that is well beyond the expected mortality date, so that most participants will die with a larger bequest than the amount they specify. Since the participant is advised to revisit the advice process periodically, T will advance over time for long-lived participants. The asset allocations produced by this process seem plausible, but explicit recognition of random mortality is clearly preferable. This is on the GuidedChoice "to do" list, but it raises a host of issues related, for example, to life insurance and annuities versus financial assets as protection against a family member's dying too early or living too long.

A simulator or DSS that included random mortality, life insurance, annuities, and tax-cognizant investment planning would be a substantial step toward a game-of-life simulator.

BEYOND MARKOWITZ

The Chhabra (2005) paper with this title offers to go "beyond Markowitz" by basing investment policy on considerations in addition to those that Markowitz took into account. It turns out that the "Markowitz" that Chhabra seeks to go beyond is Markowitz (1952a) rather than Markowitz (1959). For example, Chhabra's Section 8.1 says, "In the traditional [Markowitz] approach . . . we consider only market portfolio (investment assets) and ignore the other assets and liabilities from the asset allocation analysis." The "other assets and liabilities" to which Chhabra refers are handled in Markowitz (1959) as "exogenous assets." (An exogenous "asset" can be a liability, as in Sharpe and Tint 1990, or even a benchmark one tries to exceed, as spelled out in Markowitz 1987 and Markowitz and Todd 2000.) On the other hand, Chhabra addresses issues that we have thus far ignored, and should address.

In Volume I we assumed that the investor sought to maximize the expected value of a single-period concave (therefore risk averse) function of return or, equivalently, of end-of-period wealth. We confirmed the Markowitz (1959) observation that if a return distribution is not spread out "too much," EU could be robustly approximated by a function of mean and variance. We found, surprisingly, that one of the two approximations proposed in Markowitz (1959) did moderately well in historical return distributions that included years with losses of 70 percent, 80 percent, and even 90 percent in one out of 101 years.

In the present volume we saw that the single-period utility functions of Volume I are typically *derived* from many-period utility functions via the dynamic programming principle. We have also seen that illiquidities or changing return distributions can introduce state variables other than end-of-period wealth into the derived single-period utility function. But—at least in the two experiments tried to date with the MvD quadratic surrogate approach—the assumption that there exists a good quadratic approximation to the unknown derived utility function works quite well.

Thus to this point the basic Markowitz (1959) proposal—to use the capabilities of the General Portfolio Selection Model to maximize quadratic approximations to derived utility functions, including the use of exogenous assets and the controlling of covariance with other state variables—has been reasonably successful. But along the way we made assumptions. For example the historical real return distribution used in Chapters 3 and 4 to test alternative risk-return approximations to $E \operatorname{Log}(1+R)$ were bounded by roughly a 90 percent loss and a 150 percent gain. But in fact some historical real-return distributions have had a 100 percent loss or near to it. Examples include Imperial Russian bonds bought before the revolution and German fixed income securities bought before the German hyperinflation in the 1920s. Thus there can be downside risks beyond those we have considered that may need to be taken into account.

At the other extreme millions of people buy lottery tickets that offer a chance to win tens of millions of dollars, although they know full well that the issuing body will make a profit. Friedman and Savage (1948) and Markowitz (1952b) show that EU-maximizing agents can buy both insurance and lottery tickets—both at an expected loss—but not if they have concave-everywhere utility functions, as we have assumed thus far.[3]

Merrill Lynch Wealth Management—under Chhabra—handles these considerations by partitioning assets into three sets, usually called "buckets." Imagine three buckets arranged from left to right on a portfolio gain-or-loss axis, with the bucket on the left dedicated to preventing tragically large losses to the investor's total wealth; the bucket on the right dedicated to risky (perhaps lotterylike) investments offering the possibility of lifestyle-changing big wins; and the middle bucket managed using mean-variance analysis. The center bucket is "Markowitz." The buckets on the left and right are "Beyond Markowitz."

Shefrin and Statman (2000) and Das, Markowitz, Scheid, and Statman (2010) (DMSS) refer to "Mental Accounts" (MAs) rather than buckets. As in the Chhabra paper, they divide assets into subsets, each subset being the subject of a different selection process. The separately selected subportfolios are then aggregated into a total portfolio.

Evensky, Horan, and Robinson (2011) (EHR) divide assets into separate accounts (also referred to as "buckets") according to the imminence of need for funds. In particular, they recommend two buckets: one to take care of cash needs for the next five years, including unplanned needs that might occur at the same time that the values of longer-term investments are depressed; and the other "bucket" invested for the longer run.

In the remainder of this chapter we first briefly review this "buckets" literature and then state our own positions on this approach and on the issues it addresses.

"BUCKETS": A BRIEF LITERATURE REVIEW

Both the Shefrin and Statman and the DMSS recommendations allow for $K \geq 1$ MAs and could special-case to $K = 3$ as in the Chhabra treatment. The three analyses differ, however, as to how the aspirations of the three buckets or MAs are to be achieved. The middle bucket in the Chhabra analysis, as we saw, is MV efficient. As far as the present authors can tell from Chhabra (2005), the two outer buckets are determined informally. This may involve relevant calculations that vary from situation to situation, but no general formal analysis is specified.

In the Shefrin and Statman analysis the portfolio in each MA is chosen so as to maximize the probability of exceeding a given aspiration level, α. Thus in the special case of $K = 1$, the portfolio is chosen so as to maximize Prob($R \geq \alpha$). We take a dim view of this criterion, as did Chapter 13 of Markowitz (1959) and as does Chapter 4 of the present book.

The DMSS recommendation also seeks to maximize Prob($R \geq \alpha$), but does so by maximizing the Roy (1952) "Safety First" criterion:

$$SF = \frac{E - \alpha}{\sigma} \qquad (9)$$

In particular, when $K = 1$ the DMSS portfolio is MV efficient. The DMSS conclusion is that even with $K > 1$ the total portfolio is exactly MV efficient in a CAPM world, and approximately so more generally. DMSS argues that its buckets approach is, for many investors, an intuitive way of picking a point on (or close to) the MV efficient frontier. The DMSS buckets and the GuidedChoice scenarios need not be an "either/or" alternative. In particular, DMSS buckets could be part of questions asked prior to a simulation analysis, and a summary of simulated scenarios presented afterwards.

In a section titled "Evensky & Katz Cash Flow Strategy," (page 49) EHR say that

Although we have discussed this concept with our client during the educational session, prior to beginning the risk coaching process we once again emphasize our firm mantra: 'Five years, five years, five years!'

We believe in the concept of time diversification at least in the sense that time provides flexibility for investors to respond to changing market condition. Further, as a general rule, we believe that five years is a good minimum standard to use as a criterion for investment time diversification. It is important to note that this is a rolling, not a fixed, standard. If a client informs us that the investment funds will be needed in exactly five years, the portfolio would not meet our standard one day later when the holding period will have dropped to four years and 364 days.

Is the strategy successful? Unequivocally, yes. The Evensky & Katz strategy has been successful for many years, helping clients weather the 1987 crash, the 2000–2001 tech stock bust, and the 2008–2009 recession.

Thus the Evensky & Katz Cash Flow Strategy was not a hypothesis to be tested in specific contexts, but a universally applicable, hard and fast, categorical rule.

THE "ANSWER GAME"

Player One in the "Answer Game" tells Player Two the answer to some question. Player Two is supposed to guess the question. There is always a plausible question whose proper response would be the given answer. But the question that Player One reveals is a nonsense question involving an unanticipated interpretation of the answer. For example, what is the question whose answer is "Washington Irving"? The obvious "straight" question would be something like, "Who wrote tales about Rip van Winkle and the Headless Horseman?" The comic alternative question is, "Who was the first president, Max?" We now realize that the answer contains a comma: "Washington, Irving." (When the answer is spoken rather than written the existence of the comma can be made ambiguous.)

Here are two more answers. Guess the associated questions:

A. Two buckets

B. Three buckets

Hint: The questions do *not* involve lifting water to the surface of two or three wells. Rather, they involve physically or mentally segregated accounts that provide protection against certain contingencies or exploit certain opportunities. The proponents of these answers in effect pose investment problems for which their proposals are the answer.

FIRST THE QUESTION, THEN THE ANSWER

The bucket approach differs from the view we have taken in this book, particularly with regard to the design of decision support systems (DSSs). Specifically, we seek systems that are robust with respect to innumerable possible scenarios—many more scenarios than anyone would seriously suggest forming physical or mental accounts. In a given situation there are many possibilities that can affect the supply of, and demand for, an investor's wealth. We can perhaps itemize a representative set of these possibilities, but what lies beyond our enumeration capabilities is the myriad of possible combinations with respect to the timing of these. Perhaps some unfavorable event happens early in the investor's trajectory, or almost at retirement time, or during retirement. Or two unfavorable events happen back to back. Or a favorable or unfavorable market event happens in close proximity to some favorable or unfavorable event affecting the need for ready cash. The possible combinations of these—over many years until retirement and/or in retirement—can be astronomical.

Our approach is to

1. Model both
   a. the contingencies the investor faces; and
   b. the investment objectives (in other words, the utility function).
2. Model the strategies the investor can follow—possibly including alternative liquidity constraints on the choice of portfolio.

3. Generate hundreds or thousands of scenarios to evaluate promising strategies.

4. Select the strategy that does best overall for the investor in terms of the criteria in Step 1b.

5. Inform the investor of the result in Step 4, but also try to characterize for the investor what can happen with alternative rules.

6. Let the investor try alternative strategies to find the feasible solution that best suits said investor.

Steps 5 and 6 are important because the investor's actual preferences may be imperfectly reflected in our utility-function characterization of them. Step 3 may be replaced by exact or approximate optimization procedures when available. In fact, the Monte Carlo procedure of Step 3 is itself an approximation procedure standing at the ready for situations in which analytic methods would require an undesirable simplification of the models in Steps 1 and 2.

In this context a proposal involving buckets should be considered a hypothesis to be evaluated by a simulation and feedback process. For example, in the preceding section we noted that the EHR proposal was universal and categorical. On the other hand, Evensky (2006) reports that

> We developed the Evensky & Katz Cash Flow Reserve Strategy (E&K-S) in the mid-1980s. . . .
> At the time, our firm had a long-established five-year philosophy. The mantra "five years, five years,

five years" was frequently repeated to our clients to remind them that we believed the real risk faced by investors was having to sell at the wrong time. . . . Although our mantra had been developed to protect a significant liquidation of corpus, we thought that the same concept might be applicable to our clients' regular, but more modest, cash flow needs. We first considered simply carving out five years' worth of our clients' cash flow needs, similar to the carve-out we would have proposed for a single goal. Unfortunately our calculations indicated that the opportunity cost would exceed the benefit. As we modeled various alternatives, we concluded that a two-year cash flow reserve's carve-out was both economically and behaviorally optimal.

But if five years is correct for one situation and two years for another, perhaps there are situations for which three or four years is correct; or perhaps the client's investment portfolio is sufficiently liquid and sufficiently cautious (i.e., low on the frontier) that all that is needed is one or more cash-equivalent accounts for transactions.

The *question* concerning a particular investor is: What is his, her, or its best strategy given its situation, degrees of freedom, and objectives? The *problem* for the DSS designer is how to design a system to answer this question for a great variety of potential clients. We doubt if any one specific, categorical answer is right for all such questions.

Turning to Chhabra and to Shefrin and Statman, we agree with them that mean-variance analysis may not be appropriate for all portfolio selection situations. Recall that our basic premise is that the RDM seeks to maximize expected utility. Chapters 2, 3, and 4 demonstrated that MV approximations to EU are quite robust for *concave U(R)* if the return distribution is "not too spread out." But what if the return-distribution is "too spread out," as in the case in which $U = \log(1 + R)$ and $R = -1$ is possible. Today's computers and algorithms would have no problem finding an optimum solution to such a situation, even for large-size problems. Some of the intuitive appeal of "risk-return" analysis (discussed in Chapter 2) would be lost by using an explicit utility function. But this would be better than using a one-size-fits-all approximation to an unstated objective.

An example of a utility function that is not everywhere concave is the Markowitz (1952b) proposal described in our Endnote 3. This utility function includes a convex as well as concave segments. A three- (or more-) bucket approach is sometimes defended as a way of approximately maximizing EU for such a not-everywhere-concave $U(R)$. But the state-of-the-art for maximizing nonconcave functions has developed by leaps and bounds in recent years. In particular, the problem of choosing a portfolio to maximize a nonconcave $EU(R)$ can be approximated as a mixed linear-integer programming problem, for which progress is constantly being reported. Perhaps even now—as this is being written—this type of problem is solvable for useful-size portfolio selection problems. The probability of this increases with time.

Thus it can be said in all seriousness that, in the design of DSSs, as technology evolves, "The questions stay the same; the answers change."

12

THE FUTURE

Harry M. Markowitz

INTRODUCTION

MPT is now 62 years old.[1] Sixty-two years from now, in 2076, the United States will be 300 years old and MPT will be 124. Much has happened to the world and financial practice in the *past* 62 years. For example, 1952 saw the birth of MPT, whereas the recent BNY Mellon (2014) survey estimates that the majority of endowments and pension plans—controlling tens of trillions of dollars' worth of assets—use MPT regularly. In 1952, the modern computer was in its infancy. Now the computing capabilities of cell phones are the stuff of 1950s science fiction. Finally, the infrastructure that now makes MPT practical—including financial databases, models of expected returns, models of covariance, the top-down view of investing, and mean-variance approximations to expected utility— were then either embryonic or nonexistent.

A friend of mine (one of the many brilliant people whose help and friendship I acknowledged in the acknowledgments section in Volume I) recently said to me that we older folk had the advantage of being first in the field, and that by now all the important discoveries have been made. My view is quite the contrary. I believe that we have barely scratched the surface with respect to both

- financial decision support systems, and
- market models capable of answering many important policy questions.

Preceding chapters of this book included major proposals for future financial simulators and decision support systems. In particular, Chapter 7

- argued the virtues of detailed market simulators;
- introduced the idea of a game-of-life simulator for family financial planning generally, including portfolio selection among other financial decisions; and
- proposed building decision support systems (DSSs) that would guide a participant toward rational game-of-life decisions; two GuidedChoice products were offered as first steps in this direction.

Chapter 9 compared alternative glide-path philosophies, and ended with a challenge for future utility function development to characterize the objectives that the glide-path strategy is supposed to serve.

Chapter 10 discussed portfolio selection in light of its multiple stakeholders, including old and new proposals for "social choice."

Chapter 11 included proposals:

- to approximate the optimal solution to the large dynamic programming problems that often arise in many-period financial analysis; and
- for tax-cognizant portfolio analysis.

The present chapter offers few, if any, further suggestions concerning the *content* of financial simulators and DSSs. Rather it is concerned with how they can be implemented in a timely manner. The central question of this chapter is: What kind of facilities should be put in place so that a financial analyst or systems design team can:

A. specify unambiguously a stylized or detailed simulator, or a simple or complex DSS;

B. produce an *efficient* implementation of the specified simulator or DSS—ideally without the inevitable slips between specification and implementation that happen when implementation involves reams of coding by a huge team; and

C. modify an ongoing DSS as times and theories change, including the reformatting of extensive existing data without interrupting operations.

"System specification" referred to in Item A may be procedural or nonprocedural. "Procedural" here means programming: the writing out of a set of instructions as to how a simulator or DSS is to proceed. The following discussion of procedural specifications picks up from that in Chapter 7. "Nonprocedural" involves selecting properties of the desired system as inputs to a *program generator* that writes the program for you. The ideas presented here on nonprocedural systems specification evolved from manufacturing applications, especially the building of real-world *job shop simulators*. I begin my story there.

JSSPG

While the terminology of job shop models reflects their origins in the analysis of manufacturing shops, the job shop model type is quite flexible and widely applicable. Restricting ourselves initially to manufacturing applications, simulators that represent these vary endlessly. Ginsberg, Markowitz, and Oldfather (1965) (GMO) sought to place a great variety of these conveniently at a user's disposal. Specifically, Figure 12.1 shows a photo-reduced copy of the GMO Job Shop Simulation Program Generator (JSSPG) questionnaire. JSSPG allowed a user to select among various assertions about job shop simulation models. To do so, the user entered Xs in the spaces for those assertions that were applicable to a desired model. A keypunch operator punched these Xs into punched cards to be read by the card reader of one of the giant computers of the day, housed in an air-conditioned room with raised flooring for under-floor cabling, sporting a little over 32,000 (yes, *thousand*, not million) 36-bit words of main storage with magnetic tapes as its mass storage. Based on these inputs, JSSPG punched out a SIMSCRIPT (I) program

FIGURE 12.1 JSSPG Questionnaire Answer Sheet

A. Resource description				cc
Shift change options	No shifts		x	1
	Every day the same			2
	Every week the same			3
	General			4
Job-resource relationship	One resource			5
	Two resources		x	6
Resource availability per shift	Secondary resource	Input	x	7
		Random		8
	Primary resource	Input	x	9
		Random		10

O. Characteristics for decision rules			cc
Estimated to actual process time	Always the same		1
	Same form/type	x	2
	Different forms/types		3
	Same form/resources		4
	Different forms/resources		5
Due-date increment	Exogenous		6
	Same form	x	7
	Different forms		8
Dollar value	Exogenous		9
	Same form	x	10
	Different forms		11

B. Job characteristics			cc
There are job types		x	1
Job arrivals are exogenous			2
Other exoc inputs	Routing & process time		3
	Type & quantity		4
	Type		5
	Random types		6
	Quantity, no types		7
	Arrival only, no types		8
Inter-arrival times	Same form, random types		9
	Same form	x	10
	Different forms		11
Ending routing	Fixed, not by type		12
	Fixed, by type	x	13
	Random, not by type		14
	Random, by type		15
Process time/lot	Same form	x	16
	Different forms		17
Quantities	Same form		18
	Different forms		19
Set-up time/lot	Same form		20
	Different forms		21
Process time/lot	Same form		22
	Different forms		23
Factor/ resource	Same form		24
	Different forms		25
Primary-secondary efficiency factor			26

D. Decision rules				cc
General priority rules	First come, first served		x	1
	Shortest process time			2
	Longest process time			3
	Earliest arrival			4
	Earliest due-date			5
	Largest value			6
	Random			7
	User's function			8
Fixed routing only	Slack rules	Equal weights		9
		Unequal weights	x	10
	Look-ahead	Number of jobs		11
		Hours of work		12
		Not final stage first	x	13
		Final stage first		14
		Not final final not final		15
Resource assignment — Secondary for primary	First available		x	16
	Most available			17
	Weighted sum			18
Resource assignment — Primary for secondary	First available		x	19
	Most jobs			20
	Most hours of work			21
	Greatest priority			22
	Weighted sum			23
Disposal-job completion	Primary first		x	24
	Secondary first			25
Disposal-shift	Primary first			26
	Secondary first			27

(*Continued*)

FIGURE 12.1 *(Continued)*

E. Analysis		cc
Form of output	Output tape......................	1
	Analysis reports................. ✗	2
Interim reports	Exogenous............................ ✗	3
	Periodic..............................	4
Interim content	Resource utilization............ ✗	5
	Queue statistics ✗	6
	Job statistics...................... ✗	7
Summary content	Resource utilization........... ✗	8
	Queue statistics................. ✗	9
	Job statistics..................... ✗	10

**JSSPG Questionnaire
Answer Sheet**
(Note: cc - Card Column)

F. Probability distribution

Distribution type

Uniform.	Constant.	Random.	Exponential.	Log normal.	User's.	Uniform.	Constant.	Random.	Exponential.	Log normal.	Weibull.	Erlang.	User's.	Uniform.	Constant.	Random.	Poisson.	User's.	Uniform.	Constant.	Random.	Exponential.	Log normal.	Weibull.	Erlang.	User's.	Uniform.	Constant.	Random.	Exponential.	Log normal.	Weibull.	Erlang.	User's.	cc
1	2	3	4	5	6	7	8	9	10	11	12	13	14	15	16	17	18	19	20	21	22	23	24	25	26	27	28	29	30	31	32	33	34	35	cc
		✗						✗																											

Inter-arrival times	Process times/lot	Quantities	Set-up times/lot	Process times/unit

Distribution type

Uniform.	Exponential.	Normal.	User's.	Uniform.	Constant.	Random.	Log normal.	User's.	Uniform.	Constant.	Random.	Exponential.	Log normal.	User's.	Uniform.	Constant.	Random.	Log normal.	Weibull.	Erlang.	Normal.	Poisson.	cc
36	37	38	39	40	41	42	43	44	45	46	47	48	49	50	51	52	53	54	55	56	57	58	59	60	61	62	63	cc
	✗													✗						✗			

Factor/resource	Est.-act. process times	Due-date increment	Dollar value	Utility functions

Name of characteristic

G. Initial input values

Maximum number of

Initial	Job no.	Deck name	Man no.	Shifts/day	Day types	Week types	Primary resources	Secondary resources	Job types	cc
1 2 3 4 5	6 7 8 9 10 11	12 13 14 15 16	17 18 19 20 21	22 23 24 25	26 27 28 29	30 31 32	33 34 35	36 37 38	39 40	cc
2 3 3 6	J S S P G	G 4 4 3 0				3		4		2

with the specified features. It also printed the program in case
the user wanted to modify the generated program. The JSSPG
user used the SIMSCRIPT (I) compiler to compile the generated (and perhaps modified) program. The final result was a
general-purpose simulator with the specified capabilities that
could be run repeatedly with various input data.

As Figure 12.1 shows, the JSSPG questionnaire asked the user to select among job shop features in various areas, including:

A. *Resource Description,* such as whether the shop is to have only one type of resource (often called "servers") or two types (often called "machines" and "workers");

B. *Job Characteristics.* For example, will jobs have "standard types" with type-dependent routings, or will routing specifications be read in as part of the arriving job's description?

. . .

F. *Probability Distributions* to be used in randomly generating job arrival times, process times per lot, etc., as applicable.

Section G, titled "Initial Input Values," did not seek run-time inputs. Its primary purpose was to ascertain the maximum number of individuals of "permanent entity" types, such as shifts per day or days per week. SIMSCRIPT (I) allocated memory at compile-time for the attributes of a maximum number of individuals of each permanent entity type. (SIMSCRIPT II allocates such space at run time.) Section G also includes information to identify the *specific* job shop simulator.

JSSPG was developed at the RAND Corporation (then an Air Force "think tank"), but not primarily for job shop applications. As explained in the Preface on page iii of Oldfather, Ginsberg, and Markowitz (1966) (OGM),

> *The concept allows a user to obtain a computer program by filling out an English language Questionnaire; it was first described in A. S. Ginsberg, H. M. Markowitz, and P. M. Oldfather, <u>Programming by Questionnaire</u>, The RAND Corporation, RM-4460-PR, April 1965. While the concept was developed for job shop simulations, it is general enough to be applied to programming areas other than simulation.*
>
> *This Memorandum is a reference manual for the Questionnaire technique, and is intended for programmers who wish to write Program Generators. The technique is illustrated in terms of the Job Shop Simulation Program Generator (JSSPG), an example developed to test the concept's feasibility and desirability. . . .*
>
> *Programming by Questionnaire should interest all those concerned with developing major computer [application areas].*

In order to build a program generator using the OGM concepts and resources, a development team needed to develop:

1. a questionnaire;
2. a *program source* containing all the lines of code—or fragments of lines of code, in some instances—that might be placed in a generated program; and

3. *decision tables* that specify the Boolean conditions under which certain actions should be taken, including

   a. dropping code from the program source into the generated *source program*;

   b. setting flags for use in later Boolean tests; and

   c. transferring control from a current table to some next table or terminating the generation process.

Thus JSSPG is an example of *data-driven programming*. The program source and the decision tables are JSSPG's *program data*, as distinguished from a modeler's specific responses to the JSSPG questionnaire, which are *application data*.

Today a program generator is called a *wizard* and would use a GUI (graphical user interface). Nevertheless, the OGM "decision table" approach could be of great value in the programming of wizards with capabilities well beyond those of JSSPG. In particular, the decision tables could control the sequence of alternatives offered to the user.

PROPOSALS

I have two principal proposals for the specification and implementation of simulators and decision support systems generally, including financial simulators and DSSs in particular, namely:

1. "SIMSCRIPT M," including SIMSCRIPT II's originally planned Levels 6 and 7, "modernized" in ways discussed in Chapter 7; and

2. the OGM program generator, reprogrammed in SIMSCRIPT M (or a current version of SIMSCRIPT in the meantime), of course generating SIMSCRIPT M (or the current SIMSCRIPT) programs.

Many specific decisions were made in the design of the GuidedChoice DSS that could have been made differently. Examples include the choice of the statistical analysis of returns data, the returns-generating process assumed in the simulator within the GC DSS, and the assumed utility function or glide-path rule. These could be options for a financial DSS generator. Similarly the options available at various points in the design of JLMSim could be alternatives in a market simulator generator.

While writing out and debugging a program source and decision tables is no trivial task, the make-or-break step is that of conceiving the alternative possibilities in a given application area, and how these are programmed. It seems to me that by far the best way to develop a comprehensive program generator for an enormous application area is to grow it incrementally. The OGM process is well suited to such an evolution. One can add program source and decision tables incrementally, either (i) to add new features to an existing area, or (ii) to add a related area. An example of (i) would be adding random machine breakdowns to a fabrication shop. An example of (ii) would be adding assembly lines into which fabricated parts flow from the plant's own shop's or from vendors. In the case of a market simulator such as JLMSim, discussed in Chapter 7, a modification of Type i would be to include additional ways of estimating security means, variances, and covariances. An example of Type ii would be to add aspects of the real economy into the market simulator.

As was noted in Chapter 7, the SIMSCRIPTs may be viewed as *executable modeling languages* (EMLs). Program generators such as JSSPG are also used to specify models that can execute. Thus program generators and the SIMSCRIPT EMLs are examples of *executable model specifiers* (EMSs). In general, one may view the principal objective of *all* SIMSCRIPT development activity as that of placing EMSs of various sorts in the hands of the great variety of users who need to specify models and have them execute as specified.

Ultimately, the building of detailed simulators and DSSs requires programming. In particular, a program generator such as JSSPG includes lines of code in its "program source." It is my observation, based on decades of simulator programming by myself and others, that SIMSCRIPT II reduces simulator programming time manyfold. *A priori,* I would expect the same for the building of DSSs using SIMSCRIPT II through Level 6. Limited experience with IBM EAS-E confirmed this. In particular, Malhotra, Markowitz, and Pazel (1983) illustrates the superiority of IBM EAS-E versus the then newly developed SQL coding. It also reports that

> *EAS-E has been running for some time at Yorktown. It has been subjected to one field test: a rewrite and extension of the Workload Information System of*

Thomas J. Watson's Central Scientific Services (CSS). CSS consists of about 100 craftsmen who do model shop, glass work, electronics, etc., for Thomas J. Watson's scientists and engineers. The old Workload Information System, written in PL/I and assembler, was difficult to modify or extend. The EAS-E version duplicated the function of the old system: it read the same weekly inputs and generated the same outputs. It achieved this with about one-fifth as much source code as the old system. It also showed an even greater, but difficult to quantify, advantage over the old system in terms of ease of modification and extension.

IBM EAS-E also included facilities with which one could browse a database interactively, without any coding. This Browser facility is described in Markowitz, Malhotra, and Pazel (1983).[2]

While the CSS application was of modest size, there is no limit to the size of a specified system (e.g., the number of entities of a given type that could be created, given sufficient space to store them). Also, the structures and procedures implemented for filing, removing, and finding items in ranked sets were designed for enormous (e.g., CA DMV) size sets. We were not confronted with problems of distributed databases, the Internet, the cloud, and hacking, but (as I will note later briefly) these would pose *no greater* problem for a system programmed in a SIMSCRIPT II–based language than for one programmed in any other language.

CURRENT PRACTICE

In fact, complex highly parallel DSSs exist now. Examples include the computerized systems of large retailers such as Walmart, with features such as point-of-sale recording of sales transactions, the automatic ordering of resupply, and management reports. A principal objective of SIMSCRIPT M, and program generators based on SIMSCRIPT M, would be to simplify the production of such enterprisewide systems.

Currently the most widely used enterprisewide DSS generator is SAP. According to von Aspen (2014), the SAP enterprisewide DSS generator (as we would call it) is notoriously hard to learn and use. Surely one could develop an enterprisewide DSS generator in the spirit of JSSPG that would be one or two orders of magnitude easier to use.

As to the *coding* of DSSs, as compared to *generating* them, the reader who is not already familiar with how this is typically done currently using relational databases should ask his or her Internet browser for a description of Enterprise Java Beans (EJBs) and how these mediate between a Java program and a database; then compare this with IBM EAS-E programs and procedures as described here and in the sources cited earlier. The simplicity of the latter as compared to the former should be manifest.

AGENDA

The next few sections continue the Chapter 7 discussion of SIMSCRIPT II features including the proposed Levels 6 and 7. These would also be features of SIMSCRIPT M. I then discuss certain details worked out in the IBM EAS-E implementation of Level 6, including features to facilitate the handling of enormous ranked sets, and to modify an ongoing database without interrupting operations.

Item B in the introduction speaks of an "efficient implementation." To a large extent, the efficiency of an enormous DSS (or market simulator) depends on its ability to exploit the parallel processing opportunities of present and projected computing systems. Except for a brief parting note, the final sections of this chapter discuss parallel processing generally, and its exploitation by event-oriented programs in particular.

LEVEL 6

SIMSCRIPT (I) was intended as a "simulation language." In particular, its manual was titled "SIMSCRIPT: A Simulation Programming Language." As the details of the language took shape, it struck its creators—the authors of Markowitz, Hausner, and Karr (1962)—that its EAS and other capabilities could be of great value for complex programming of various sorts. They therefore allowed the programmer to insert a "nonsimulation" directive at the head of a SIMSCRIPT (I) program. This suppressed the insertion of a timing routine and the requirement for one or more event routines.

It was not until plans for SIMSCRIPT II were on the drawing board, while Bernie Hausner was completing the SIMSCRIPT (I) preprocessor into FORTRAN and Herb Karr was finishing the SIMSCRIPT (I) programming manual, circa 1962, that it struck me that not only could a world to be simulated be described in terms of its entities, attributes, sets, and events, but so could a world represented in a database. In particular, with few, if any, exceptions, the *same* features were essential for DSS as for simulator development, and—except for giving the executing program the option of committing or not committing status changes to a database—there were few, if any, additional programming features that needed to be added to the language.

There are important implementation considerations, not encountered in building simulators, that must be addressed when, for example, two users want to update—or one wants to read and the other to update—the same data at the same time. But these are implementation problems that, insofar as possible, should not burden the application programmer, and are there whatever the specification language.

SIMSCRIPT II Level 6 was the result of an epiphany circa 1962. An updated version of this epiphany would go as follows: SIMSCRIPT II and its supersets, SIMSCRIPTs II.5 and III, have proved capable of evaluating system designs for systems as varied as factories and war plans. To implement a factory thus designed, one has to build buildings, buy equipment, hire labor, etc. To implement a DSS, one has to write programs. Why not use the same programming language to (for example) track the factory's real-time status as to simulate its operation? While one is at it, why not include the factory simulator as a decision support tool in the factory DSS, to forecast possible scenarios starting from the current factory status as reflected in its database? *All the more reason to use the same worldview in the simulator and the DSS.*

SIMSCRIPT FACILITIES

All SIMSCRIPTs (including IBM EAS-E) have two parts:

- Part 1 describes the EAS structure of the simulator, DSS, or other program to be compiled.
- Part 2 describes the actions to be taken by the program's routines, including its Main routine, its event routines if it is a simulator or DSS, and its subroutines and functions.

SIMSCRIPT (I) used a *Definition Form* as its Part 1. The SIMSCRIPT (I) programmer filled in the names of a program's entities, attributes, and sets in appropriately labeled fields, and provided other information such as whether an entity type was permanent or temporary. A keypunch operator punched cards from this form. This made sense in a context in which programmers coded FORTRAN II statements on FORTRAN II programming forms and had them keypunched.

SIMSCRIPT II dropped the Definition Form. Instead, it includes a PREAMBLE section, demarcated by the word "PREAMBLE" at its start and the word "END" at its end. Subsections of the Preamble are headed:

Temporary entities . . .

Permanent entities . . .

Database entities . . .

The contents of these sections include statements such as the following:

> Every Machine-group has a Nr_Free_Machines and owns a Queue
>
> Define Queue a set ranked by Due_date
>
> The System has . . . , owns . . .

A modernized SIMSCRIPT M must permit a PREAMBLE section for compatibility with existing SIMSCRIPT II programs, but should also include a GUI facility for describing the program's EAS structure. Essentially it would allow the user to input an EAS structure in tabular form, similar to Tables 7.1 and 7.3, including optional additional information. (The SIMSCRIPT (I) Definition Form was essentially the GUI interface of its day.) Whether the programmer uses a PREAMBLE section or an EAS GUI, a routine facility of SIMSCRIPT M should be to display the EAS structure in an EAS table. This way a system's EAS table will be updated automatically when the program is amended. Ideally, this documentation, and the Part 2 coding described later, should have version control so that an authorized user can see who made what changes and when.

Part 2 of SIMSCRIPTs (I) and II put a great variety of simulator and (for SIMSCRIPT II as planned) DSS development commands at its user's disposal. These include the basic actions one takes on entities, attributes, and sets including commands that direct the computer, e.g., to create or destroy an entity, compute or read-in the value of an attribute, file an entity into a set, or remove (the first, last, or some specific) entity from a set. We tried to keep the syntax readable with statements such as

CREATE A JOB
FILE JOB IN QUEUE(MG)

where the expression at the end of the second of these is to be read as "Queue of MG." If nothing else, SIMSCRIPT's Englishlike style facilitates checking (perhaps by a team including nonprogrammers) that the system has been implemented as intended.

In addition to commands that specify basic actions, other commands and feature-areas of the SIMSCRIPTs include the generation of random numbers with various probability distributions, WYSIWYG (What You See Is What You Get) report generation, and recursive subroutines and functions.[3] Other programming languages also provide random number generators and report generator facilities, and have recursive subroutines and functions. But none to my knowledge have facilities as convenient as the SIMSCRIPT II ACCUMULATE and TALLY statements for collecting system statistics illustrated in Chapter 7, the COMPUTE and FIND statements illustrated here, or SIMSCRIPT's ability to be both self-documenting and, nevertheless, require significantly less coding than less powerful languages.

An Example

To illustrate SIMSCRIPT's power, the present section describes an algorithm for solving very large sparse linear equation systems such as are encountered in optimization calculations, and the next section shows a fragment of SIMSCRIPT II coding that could be used for this.

We distinguish two varieties of linear equation systems and their associated matrices, namely *dense* and *sparse*. Most of the coefficients of a sparse matrix are zero. The opposite is true of a dense matrix. Among either dense or sparse linear systems, there are those that are "positive definite" and those that are not. For positive definite systems, "Cholesky factorization" is used. Among the remaining sparse matrices, some are characterized by exploitable patterns of their nonzeros and are important enough to have special programs developed to exploit this pattern. Sharpe's (1963) one-factor model is an example. For an arbitrary placement of nonzeros, or when code is not available to exploit an exploitable pattern of nonzeros, a modified version of the sparse matrix techniques of Markowitz (1957) is used.

As an example, suppose a system has 10^6 *variables (columns)* in 10^6 *equations (rows)* with an average of 10 nonzero entries per row or column. Thus the system has a total of 10^7 nonzero entries. Recall from high school algebra how one solved, for example, three equations in three unknowns. In the cases-without-complications that one encounters in high school examples, you would

1. Use the first equation to express X_1 in terms of X_2 and X_3, whose values are yet to be determined.
2. Use the fact that "equals added to equals are equal" to eliminate X_1 from the second and third equations.

You now have two *uneliminated equations* in two *uneliminated unknowns*. You repeat the same process on the two uneliminated equations in the two unknowns, expressing X_2 in terms of X_3, and producing one equation in one unknown, X_3. You solve this for X_3, which allows you to use the second-to-be-eliminated equation to solve for X_2, which, together with the value of X_3, allows you to solve for X_1. Problem solved!

The same *Gaussian elimination* procedure could, in principle, be used to solve 10^6 equations in 10^6 unknowns. Use the first equation to express X_1 in terms of the remaining $10^6 - 1$ variables, and eliminate X_1 from the remaining $10^6 - 1$ equations. Then repeat the process successively until you are left with one equation in one unknown. Solve this one equation. Use the value of the 10^6th variable to find the value of variable number $10^6 - 1$. Then use these two values to solve for the value of the $10^6 - 2^{nd}$, etc.

There are two problems with applying this procedure to large, sparse matrices. First, since the matrix is sparse it may be that a_{11} is zero—or "too close" to zero for numeric stability. In this case, one is not allowed to *pivot* on it; that is, one is not allowed to use the first equation to eliminate X_1, since this would involve dividing by zero or "almost zero." Even if a_{11} is not too close to zero, perhaps some a_{ii} of a later uneliminated equation will be (almost) zero. The second problem with always pivoting on a_{ii}, assuming that it is not zero or almost zero, is that pivot steps can "*fill in*" the uneliminated matrix so that a sparse matrix quickly becomes dense. For example, if a matrix is sparse on average, but the first row happens to have every variable and X_1 appears in every equation, then pivoting on a_{11} will convert a sparse matrix into a dense matrix in one step.

Let m_i and n_j be the number of nonzero elements in the *i*th row and *j*th column, respectively, of the uneliminated set of equations. The *Markowitz rule* chooses as the next pivot *the* (or *a*) nonzero a_{ij} with minimum

$$\text{MR} = (m_i - 1)(n_j - 1) \tag{1}$$

This choice minimizes the maximum possible number of fill-ins. In particular, if either $m_i = 1$ or $n_j = 1$ (a "singleton") no fill-in can occur. If there are two or more singletons then each of these may be taken as the next two (or more) pivots, in any order. The standard procedure currently in use in commercial sparse matrix programs, the *modified Markowitz rule* (MMR), chooses the a_{ij} that minimizes MR in Equation (1) among those a_{ij} whose $|a_{ij}|$ is not "too small."

Example Coding

Figure 12.2 contains SIMSCRIPT II code that one might write to implement the MMR pivot selection rule within a sparse matrix solver. The example assumes that the program's EAS structure includes entity types ROW, COLUMN, and ENTRY; that THE SYSTEM owns a set of UNELIMINATED ROWS; and that each row owns a set of nonzero entries. The ROW_COUNT and COLUMN_COUNT attributes of ROW and COLUMN, respectively, indicate the number of nonzero entries of each.

FIGURE 12.2 SIMSCRIPT II Coding to Select a Pivot

```
FOR EACH I in Uneliminated_Rows,
   FOR EACH Entry In Non_Zero_Entries (I)
   WITH ABS.F(Value(Entry)) > Epsilon
   COMPUTE iStar = Min (I),
      jStar = Min (Column_Nr(entry)) of
      (Row_Count (I) −1)*(Column_Count (Column_Nr(entry)) −1)
```

The code should be almost self-documenting, but here are some points to note while reading the figure, including some already noted in Chapter 7. SIMSCRIPT II is *not* "case-sensitive"; i.e., upper- and lowercase characters are treated identically. Also, line breaks are treated as spaces, and redundant spaces are ignored (except in the "Format Lines" in certain of the SIMSCRIPT II WYSIWYG report generator facilities). SIMSCRIPT II's "FOR phrases," such as

FOR EACH I in UNELIMINATED_ROWS

instruct the SIMSCRIPT II compiler to write code that loops through entities in some set. FOR phrases can also be used to instruct SIMSCRIPT to loop through a sequence of integers, such as

FOR I = 1 to N

A FOR phrase may be qualified by one or more phrases starting with one of the following words: WITH, UNLESS, WHILE, UNTIL followed by a *logical expression.* The latter is either

- an elementary expression—such as one that tests an arithmetic relationship, such as:

  DUE_DATE (JOB) < TODAY; or

- a compound expression involving AND, OR, and/or NOT operators, and perhaps parentheses.

There is *no* limit on how many logical or arithmetic operators can appear in a logical expression. The object of this generality is *not* to encourage the writing of impenetrable layers of arithmetic and logical expressions, but to not have arbitrary boundaries to remember, or to bump into when an extra bit of generality is needed.

A logically meaningful combination of FOR, WITH, WHILE, etc., phrases is referred to as *Control*. Control may be attached to a single statement, such as the COMPUTE statement in Figure 12.2, or to a "DO" statement followed by any number of statements followed by a matching LOOP statement that ends the DO . . . LOOP. A program may have nested loops to any depth. The ALSO DO statement indicates that the DO . . . LOOP in question is to end at the same LOOP statement as the preceding (innermost) DO . . . LOOP. This turned out to be a quite pleasant feature when coding complex decision rules or algorithms.

The COMPUTE statement may stand by itself, as in Figure 12.2, or it (and perhaps other COMPUTE statements) may be within one or more DO . . . LOOPs. In either case, the COMPUTE statement can compute a number of statistics concerning the sequence of entities encountered in the loop, including the mean, variance, standard deviation, minimum or maximum of some expression, and the values that one or more expressions have when the latter minimum or maximum is reached. For example, in Figure 12.2, the specifications

$$iStar = Min (I)$$

$$jStar = Min (Column\_Nr (entry))$$

tell SIMSCRIPT II to store in iStar and jStar the values that I and Column_Nr (entry) have when the expression

$$(Row\_Count (I) - 1) * (Column\_Count (Column\_Nr (entry))-1)$$

takes on its minimum value.[4]

SIMSCRIPT II also has a FIND command that finds a case that meets specified logical conditions, branching depending on whether or not such a case is found. Needless to say—but I will say it again for emphasis—it was the intention of the original SIMSCRIPT II design for all its facilities, including its COMPUTE and FIND commands, to be available for processing both database and/or main-storage entities.

IBM EAS-E FEATURES

IBM EAS-E provided an invaluable opportunity to demonstrate the feasibility and desirability of the concept, and to gain implementation experience. This experience may be of value in designing the implementation of SIMSCRIPT M. See Pazel, Malhotra, and Markowitz (1983) for our implementation approach generally, and Malhotra, Markowitz, and Pazel (1983) for further information, especially on the implementation of ranked sets. The Pazel et al. and Malhotra et al. implementation descriptions are thorough and compact—and defy any further, comprehensive summary here. 'The present section sketches some IBM EAS-E solutions aimed at flexibility and performance, plus some thoughts on further alternatives.

Each IBM EAS-E database—including any number of entity types with their attribute and set relationships—is supervised by its copy of a *Custodian* program. With the VM operating system in use at the T. J. Watson Research Center in Yorktown Heights, NY, simultaneous users—each in their own virtual machine—communicated their requests, including updates, to the Custodian in its virtual machine. IBM EAS-E did not handle distributed databases; but it would not be a particularly great challenge to add intercustodian communication capabilities for distributed databases, or for interdatabase data requests. IBM EAS-E locked information ("READ-WRITE" or "READ-ONLY") at the *individual entity level*, as compared to some database systems that lock at a page or table level. The latter approach locks information that could safely be used by other users. As with other database systems, crash protection assures that in case of a computer crash either *all* changes to the database made by a program or *none* of them would be "official" in the database. For example, if the computer's operating system crashed between the execution of

CREATE A JOB

and

FILE JOB IN QUEUE (MG)

or crashed before all related changes could be properly recorded, then the database would show none of these changes. This is achieved by keeping the old while building the new database status description, then switching the official version from the old to the new by one elemental act (namely recording a new version number). This "all or none" database update applies to changes since the start of a program's execution or since the execution of its last RECORD statement.

The Custodian recognizes "deadlock" situations in which User 1 has Entity A and needs B whereas User 2, who already has Entity B, now announces a *conflicting* need for Entity A. (Two lock requests for a given entity conflict if at least one is a WRITE request.) The Custodian backs out the requests for User 2, who waits for User 1 to finish and release all its locks. IBM EAS-E also provides for backup in case of physical damage to storage.

It seems to me now that, in addition to READ-ONLY and READ-WRITE access, we should also provide *Consistent Copy* access. This would report the status of one or more database entities as of some instant of time with no guarantee that this status is still true when the information is delivered. This could be useful in preparing summary statistics regarding system status as of some point in time. One would have to beat out the implementation details—preferably in dialogue with one or two coworkers—to know whether efficiency considerations might impose limitations on this form of access.

IBM EAS-E allowed changes to the EAS structure of one or more entity types without immediately transforming all existing entities of the modified types to the new format. If an individual in old format was read into main storage, it would be maintained in main storage in "dual form," with both the old version and the new version represented, and then written back to the database in the new format. While in main storage in dual form, the executing program could refer to old-format attributes versus new-format attributes as, e.g., O.<attribute name> versus N.<attribute name>, and similarly for sets. If not specifically modified, the values of attributes and set contents would be rewritten unchanged in the new format. The routine to transform a database entity from old format to new format would be invoked either when called—as in a batch run that transformed all existent entities of the type—or when an entity in old format was encountered by a routine that needed the as-yet-untransformed individual.

IBM EAS-E was designed to efficiently handle enormous ranked sets—much larger ones than those we encountered in our one live application. This was done by having sufficiently large sets broken into subsets that, for even larger sets, could be further broken into subsets of the subsets to any level. Fast access storage and retrieval was achieved by storing this structure as balanced trees (see Malhotra et al. for details). The purpose of this structure was fast storage and retrieval but, as we will see, this same structure could facilitate the use of parallel processing in very large SIMSCRIPT M applications. In compiling code that specified that some action should be taken for all members of a set satisfying some "WITH <logical expression>" condition, the compiled program in the user's VM needed to coordinate with the Custodian program to make efficient use of available ranked sets rather than mechanically fetching each member of a possibly enormous set to test the condition. (See Pazel et al. for details.)

The users of the CSS application were employees of IBM Research using its VM system. The Internet did not exist at the time. Custodian to Custodian communication among trusted Custodians presents no extraordinary challenge, as compared to user to Custodian communication. When the Internet is added, the extraordinary challenge concerns protection from hacking, either on a grand or an isolated scale. This challenge is there whatever the programming language used.

LIKE THE PHOENIX

SIMSCRIPT II through Level 6 existed briefly as IBM EAS-E—but exists no longer.[5] I am optimistic, however, that someone will build it again, if not in the next decade then in the one following or the one after that. It makes good business sense for two reasons. First, with features tailored to the building of detailed simulators and DSSs, it would be a breakthrough in a competitive software market. In particular, I previously contrasted the ease of use of an EAS-based DSS program generator as compared to the difficulty of using SAP. Second, SIMSCRIPT II through Level 6 was built with a relatively trivial number of man-hours as compared to an IBM or MICROSOFT language implementation. The RAND version through Level 5 used one or two programmers at a time over a course of about four years plus a manual writer. The IBM EAS-E version, which added Level 6, took a few more man-years. If the large software developers ignore it, some start-up will make it their big move. Based on a recent luncheon conversation I had with Ana Marjanski (head of the Technical Department at CACI, Advanced Simulation Lab), CACI itself may undertake the development of Level 6. But, as this is written, it is not certain. Essential to the economical production of SIMSCRIPT II was the use of SIMSCRIPT II's Language Writing Language sketched in the next section.

LEVEL 7

The objective of Level 7 was to make SIMSCRIPT II's Language Writing Language (LWL) available to application programmers, perhaps to develop commands or data types for special libraries (similar to C's libraries). For example, a program that made use of a matrix algebra library might be permitted arithmetic and logical expressions involving matrices such as

$$\text{IF } AX > 0$$

where A is a matrix, X is a vector, and 0 here would be understood from context to be the zero vector.

Speaking of SIMSCRIPT II's LWL generally, perhaps my LWL solution—to the implementation problems posed by what I wanted from SIMSCRIPT II—duplicated computer science solutions available in the early 1960s. But my background was OR, not computer science, and I was located then in the Economics Department of RAND Corporation, not in the Computer Science Department of IBM Research (as I would be two decades later). In 1962 it was easier for me to solve my implementation problems than to research whether they had been solved already.

The building of a compiler for SIMSCRIPT II was more demanding than building one for a language such as C, for at least two reasons: One is SIMSCRIPT II's higher-order commands such as its COMPUTE, FIND, ACCUMULATE, and TALLY statements. The other concerns language design choices involving readability rules that need to be remembered.

For example, C keywords are reserved words. Specifically C89 has 32 keywords, including "auto," "break," "case," "char," "const," etc. The programmer may not use any of these for any purpose other than as keywords. Thus the programmer must remember not to have a variable named "case" or a function named "float," or 30 other reserved words. This would be especially onerous in the case of the SIMSCRIPT language because of the richness of the language. For example SIMSCRIPT II report generation facilities include a phrase PAGE IS FIRST. (Not the Queen's English, but the meaning should be clear.) It is in a general format that includes phrases such as for example,

<set.name> IS EMPTY or

<set.name> IS NOT EMPTY.

Thus the SIMSCRIPT II programmer would have to remember to not use "page" as a variable, subroutine, function, or location name, and perhaps "is," "not," "empty," and dozens of others as well. SIMSCRIPT II does however have a large number of variable and function names (such as TIME.V or N. <set name>) that the programmer must avoid. This is easy, since all such names are of the form letter.name or name.letter (or occasionally both).

A second type of rule that is for the compiler writer's convenience, and is not required by SIMSCRIPT II, is parentheses that are required where they are not needed and would typically not appear in English text. For example, a specification such as

$$IF \ y > 0$$

requires parentheses around the logical expression (y > 0) in C that are optional in SIMSCRIPT II.

A third example of a C-language specification designed to make life easy for the compiler writer rather than the programmer, and certainly of no benefit for a nonprogrammer reading a program, is the following: The statement

$$X = 5$$

instructs the computer to set X to 5 whereas

$$X = = 5$$

instructs the executing program to test whether or not X equals 5. SIMSCRIPT II uses X = 5 in either case, as is the practice in written English. It is always clear from context whether an assignment or a test is intended.

In SIMSCRIPT II the assignment statement started with a keyword, as in

$$LET \ X = 5$$

SIMSCRIPT II.5 also allows

$$X = 5$$

to accommodate programmers who are accustomed to such an assignment statement. SIMSCRIPT II.5 (using the SIMSCRIPT II LWL) has no problem recognizing either form.

All this flexibility slows down the compilation process. But even by 1962, modeling costs outweighed compilation costs by so much that there was never a question (in my mind, at least) as to whether the benefits of flexibility and clarity were worth the greater compilation time.

SIMSCRIPT II is written in SIMSCRIPT II. In the first instance, a basic "kernel" of the language had to be written in a different language, SIMSCRIPT (I), but once this kernel worked in SIMSCRIPT (I), the kernel itself, as well as the remainder of the language, could be programmed and compiled in SIMSCRIPT II.

Many aspects of the SIMSCRIPT II compilers are data-driven. In particular, data tables contain the "code" to be written out by the SIMSCRIPT II compiler. Originally assembly language code for specific computers was used. Now SIMSCRIPT II.5 and III generate C code, relying on the C compiler for a particular machine to write assembly language for that machine.

The SIMSCRIPT II Language Writing Language is described in some detail in Markowitz (1979) and briefly summarized in an endnote here.[6]

SIMSCRIPT M ENHANCEMENTS

The SIMSCRIPTs are no exception to the rule that a living programming language must evolve based on experience with the language, the insights of rival product developers, and a changing environment. For example, the Accumulate and Tally statements in SIMSCRIPT (I) were "executable" (Part 2) commands rather than (Part 1) global specifications. Examination of the first "for real" SIMSCRIPT (I) programs written by members of RAND's Logistics Department showed that much of their Part 2 programming consisted of these Accumulate and Tally statements. In particular these "for real" programs could be reduced substantially by "automating" the Accumulate and Tally, that is by specifying them in the program's PREAMBLE (Part 1). I told my colleagues, Bernie Hausner and Herb Karr, to "stop the presses"; it was essential that SIMSCRIPT have an "automatic" Accumulate and Tally. My colleagues argued that the manual and preprocessor were too far along. Bernie Hausner settled the matter with the directive that the automatic Accumulate should be "the first new feature of SIMSCRIPT II."

As noted in the section "The SIMSCRIPTs" in Chapter 7, Herb Karr, with 47½ percent of CACI stock, and Jim Berkson, with 5 percent of the stock, fired me, with 47½ percent of the stock. After a few years, our relationships healed, including between Herb and me, and especially with the technical staff. From time to time I would serve as a consultant to CACI, where I would be brought up to date on features that CACI had added to its proprietary SIMSCRIPT II.5 product, and on unanticipated challenges that the language faced. As discussed at the end of Chapter 7, the most important features that CACI added to SIMSCRIPT II as originally designed were (1) processes, (2) graphics, and (3) in SIMSCRIPT III, subsystems, polymorphism, and strong data typing. While CACI's implementation of these features is proprietary, the features themselves are in the public domain, and should be part of a SIMSCRIPT M.

SIMSCRIPT III introduced "inheritance," but only for "objects" and not for "entities." "Entity" and "object" should be synonymous and inheritance allowed for both (or neither).

Two ideas that arose during the IBM EAS-E project were that of subsidiary entities discussed in Chapter 7, and "consistent copy" discussed earlier in this chapter.

Finally, looking forward a living language needs to incorporate new input/output devices such as

- 3D printers;
- holographic output, so that the progress of selected parts of, e.g., a shop or a war game can be viewed in 3D rather than on a flat screen;
- the sight, sound, touch, and eventually the odor inputs of an automaton; and
- the motor responses of such an automaton.

Concerning the last two items, the EAS-E view is good at representing "worlds," e.g., a simulated world as developed for SIMSCRIPT (I), a world represented in a database as visualized for SIMSCRIPT II Level 6, and the world as represented inside an automaton. In this connection SIMSCRIPT M needs to incorporate continuous as well as discrete simulation as SIMSCRIPT II.5 does (but not necessarily with the same smoothing rules that SIMSCRIPT II.5 uses). Synchronous and asynchronous *discrete event* simulation are ideal for financial simulations, such as the half-dozen financial simulation applications discussed in this volume, as listed in the first section of Chapter 7. In particular, synchronous discrete event simulation is fine for forecasting the probability distributions of retirement wealth. Jacobs, Levy, and Markowitz (2004) argues that asynchronous discrete event simulation is more likely to predict the consequences of investment, trading, or regulatory policies than continuous-time models. But if the purpose of a simulation analysis is to help an automaton land a plane on a carrier deck—or just pick up a misoriented part in an assembly line—continuous simulation is needed.

COMPUTING: PAST, PRESENT, AND FUTURE

Moore (1965) made the following wild prediction:

> *There is a minimum cost at any given time in the evolution of the [semiconductor] technology. At present, it is reached when 50 components are used per circuit. . . .*
>
> *If we look ahead five years, a plot of costs suggests that the minimum cost per component might be expected in circuits with about 1000 components per circuit. . . .*

Over the longer term, the rate of increase is a bit more uncertain, although there is no reason to believe it will not remain nearly constant for at least ten years. That means by 1975, the number of components per integrated circuit for minimum cost will be 65000.

This bold prediction morphed into Moore's Law, which states, roughly, that measures of computer performance (such as clock speed) will double about every two years. (The "two-year" estimate is from the Moore 2006 retrospective revision of an earlier estimate.) Moore's Law has had a remarkably long life. Decade after decade saw debates concerning the ultimate physical barriers that would finally slow the rate of growth of computer performance and when these would kick in.

Fast forward to Fuller and Millett (2011). This is the report of a committee formed by the National Research Council of the National Academies, "Advisers to the Nation on Science, Engineering, and Medicine," consisting of the National Academy of Sciences, the National Academy of Engineering, and the Institute of Medicine. The committee's task was to investigate *The Future of Computing Performance: Game Over or Next Level?* The committee members consisted of about a dozen representatives from academia and industry, including from Advanced Micro Devices, Analog Devices Inc., Google Inc., NVIDIA Corporation, Intel Corp., University of Wisconsin-Madison, Stanford University, University of Texas at Austin, and the University of California, Berkeley. Additional experts who briefed the committee came from, e.g., Carnegie Mellon University, Google Inc. (again), National Science Foundation, Texas Instruments, University of Illinois at Urbana-Champaign, University of Maryland, Microsoft, MIT, University of Michigan, and the University of Virginia. About a dozen more experts with similar affiliations were reviewers. The purpose of this third layer of expertise was "To provide candid and critical comments that will assist the institution in making its published report as sound as possible and to ensure that the report meets institutional standards for objectivity, evidence, and responsiveness to the study charge." The conclusions and recommendations of the committee, presented in a substantial abstract on pages 1 through 3 of its report, include:

> *The only foreseeable way to continue advancing performance is to match parallel hardware with parallel software and ensure that the new software is portable across generations of parallel hardware. There has been genuine progress on the software front in specific fields, such as some scientific applications and commercial searching and transactional applications. Heroic programmers can exploit vast amounts of parallelism, domain-specific languages flourish, and powerful abstractions hide complexity. However, none of those developments comes close to the ubiquitous support for programming parallel hardware that is required to ensure that its effect on society over the next two decades will be as stunning as it has been over the last half-century.*

My view, as argued in part earlier and further argued later, is that—at least as far as simulators or decision support systems are concerned—the "ubiquitous support for programming parallel hardware" that the committee seeks can be supplied by

- SIMSCRIPT M;
- related nonprocedural executable model specifiers;
- a growing set of libraries of special data structures such as trees, networks, and sparse matrices, plus routines and commands to process them; and
- the dependency analysis of modern optimizing program compilers.

Before supplying details as to *how* these means are to achieve the desired ends, I review some features of the world's most successful parallel computer.

VON NEUMANN (1958): *THE COMPUTER AND THE BRAIN*

Von Neumann published this book shortly after the dawn of the computer age. Among his many seminal creations—in addition for example to being the principal author of the previously cited *Theory of Games and Economic Behavior*—von Neumann invented the modern computer. Specifically, in the foreword to the book's third edition (von Neumann, 2012),

Kurzweil explains earlier computer theory and practice and then says,

> It was on these foundations that John von Neumann created the architecture of the modern computer, the von Neumann machine, which has remained the core structure of essentially every computer for the past sixty years, from the microcontroller in your washing machine to the largest supercomputers. . . . In a paper dated June 30, 1945, titled "First Draft of a Report on the EDVAC," von Neumann presented the concepts that have dominated computation ever since. The von Neumann model includes a central processing unit where arithmetical and logical operations are carried out, a memory unit where the program and data are stored, mass storage, a program counter, and input/ output channels. . . . Although von Neumann's paper was intended as an internal project document, it became the Bible for computer designers in the 1940s and 1950s and, indeed, has influenced the building of every computer since that time.

In one sense everything about von Neumann (1958) is obsolete. In another sense its observations are timeless. In particular, von Neumann describes the brain insofar as it was understood then. But neuroscience has advanced greatly since 1956–1957 (e.g., see Kandel, Schwartz, and Jessell 2000 for a detailed survey). Von Neumann describes both the digital computer and the analog computer which were serious competitors in the 1950s. Since then, decades of Moore's Law have caused the practical disappearance of analog computers including the once-ubiquitous slide rule. They have yielded to the present-day descendants of an ancient portable digital computer, the abacus.

Based on the computer as it was then, and the brain as far as it was understood then, von Neumann concluded:

> *Summing up all of this, it appears that the relevant comparison-factor with regard to size is about 10^8 to 10^9 in favor of the natural componentry versus the artificial one. . . . Against this there is a factor of about 10^4 to 10^5 on speed in favor of the artificial componentry versus the natural one.*
>
> *On these quantitative evaluations certain conclusions can be based. . . . First: in terms of the number of actions that can be performed by active organs of the same total size (defined by volume or by energy dissipation) in the same interval, the natural componentry is a factor 10^4 ahead of the artificial one. . . . Second: the same factors show that the natural componentry favors automata with more, but slower, organs, while the artificial one favors the reverse arrangement of fewer, but faster, organs. Hence it is to be expected that an efficiently organized large natural automaton (like the human nervous system) will tend to pick up as many logical (or informational) items as possible simultaneously, and process*

them simultaneously, while an efficiently organized large artificial automaton (like a large modern computing machine) will be more likely to do things successively—one thing at a time—or at any rate not so many things at a time. . . .

Third: it should be noted, however, that parallel and serial operation are not unrestrictedly substitutable for each other.

The principal difference between then and now is that decades of Moore's Law have made it impossible for further speed-ups of single-thread computing to keep up with Man's projections and desires, and the demand for computing services (by the Internet alone, plus more) makes it imperative to reduce watts per computation.

THE COMPUTER AND THE BRAIN, REVISITED

Given all that has happened since the 1950s in computers, finance, and operations research, and given that I have my own "fish to fry," I will be so bold as to present my own observations on "the Computer and the Brain." I will not try to summarize the last half-century's advances in neuroscience, nor try to further summarize the past, present, and future of computers, as did Fuller and Millett. Rather I will note some everyday examples of the amazing parallelism achieved by the human nervous system and ask how our simulators and DSSs could emulate these.

I enjoy having lunch with friends, clients, current or former students, and other interesting people. We eat at one of several nearby restaurants about a mile or so from my office. We walk and talk, eat and talk, walk back and talk, and then I get back to my work, e.g., writing this book. Simple enough. But let us consider what my and my visitor's nervous systems accomplish while walking from my office to a restaurant.

I said we "walk and talk." Walking is a very complex activity. It is a process of continually falling and catching oneself. Even standing is a nontrivial balancing act. But we do it "without thinking," except in my case: when I come to a nontrivial curb, I carefully consider its depth, and decide whether I should just step down or should use my sport-seat/cane to help me.

Talking is no simple task either. They have tried to train various great apes to talk, but they do not have adequate vocal chords. They must express themselves with "sign language" insofar as their mental processes permit. So far, not a single one of them has a literary output comparable to that of Helen Keller.

Children learn language from their parents, including both vocabulary and grammar. Think about it! Small children in Rome two thousand years ago spoke Latin including its impossible grammar. I speak English. So do people from England, Scotland, Wales, South Africa, Australia, Jamaica, and "down south," as does everyone who wants to travel the world or engage in some international business that uses English as its universal language. They all speak with accents—except people born and raised in the Midwest like me. I understand that if one's first language does not distinguish "R" from "L," one may not hear the difference between them. Conversely, R-L-aware speakers cannot distinguish certain phonemes in R-L-deficient languages. This clearly is "nurture" rather than "nature," since all third-generation "Valley Girls" sound the same, no matter which language their grandparents spoke.

Walking and talking seem rather ordinary to me, even when done at the same time. What seems extraordinary to me is to watch and hear Itzhak Perlman play J. S. Bach's "Chaconne." This is a piece for unaccompanied violin that many (including me) believe to be one of the most extraordinary pieces of music ever written. As Brahms wrote Clara Schumann (in a letter dated June 1877, reproduced in Avins 1997, page 166):

> *The Chaconne is for me one of the most wonderful, incomprehensible pieces of music. On a single staff, for a small instrument, the man writes a whole world of the deepest thoughts and the most powerful feelings. If I were to imagine how I might have made, conceived the piece, I know for certain that the overwhelming excitement and awe would have driven me mad.*

Through complex bow work and incredible fingering, Bach achieves (or suggests) two-, three-, and sometimes four-part counterpoint on an unaccompanied violin. But what fascinates me most is when I *see* Itzhak Perlman play this piece. He has the piece memorized and well practiced, of course, since there is no time to sight-read it in concert. But his face looks like the fingers on his left hand, and his right (bow) arm are on their own. He is just listening—very tranquilly—to what *they* are doing.

While I walk and talk my nervous system accomplishes tasks of which I am not even aware. Sometimes when I've walked on country roads I've gotten a pebble in my shoe. I soon become aware of it. I am sure that if I were stung by a bee during a walk it would come to my attention immediately. Somehow the status of pain sensors all over my body—on my skin, in my muscles, in my stomach, wherever I could feel pain—are being monitored continuously, and my consciousness is alerted to their state only when some destructive or threatening event occurs.

A more complex automatic process of mine was called to my attention by a lunchtime visitor. He asked why I looked to my right whenever we came to an alley on my right, but did not look to my left when the alley was on my left. I had not realized that I was doing that, and that I had just done it. The explanation is simple: I am blind in my right eye. If an alley is to my left my peripheral vision or a quick glance to the left provides an instantaneous view of the relevant status of the alley. If I glance to my right my left eye sees only a bit of the rim of my glasses frame and the tip of my nose. I have to turn my head to the right to see if a bicycle or a Prius is about to hit me. Apparently this happens as routinely as a footstep at every alley on my right.

It might seem that all nonconscious nervous system processes are lower-order than conscious ones—like walking as compared to thinking. But this is not true. Routinely, people who solve problems—such as trying to find a proof or counterexample for a conjectured theorem, or trying to find a vexing bug in a computer program—report going to bed with the problem unsolved and waking up with the solution neatly worked out. It is as if some mental process worked like an elf through the night, presenting the solution to the conscious level when the conscious level was ready to receive it.

Not only is the conscious level *not* the brain's only cerebral process, it is *not even* the highest one. For example, when I sit quietly by myself or walk to lunch without a guest, topics pop into my head. The sequence of topics typically reflects a perfectly plausible prioritization of topics that need attention. Who is setting this agenda?

In a recent conversation with a luncheon guest I needed an example to support the hypothesis I present shortly. The following example popped into my head immediately: I was playing baseball with other teenagers in an empty lot near my folks' grocery store. When it was my turn to serve as catcher, my head got in the way of a swinging bat. The other kids helped me, with my bleeding head, get to my folks' store.

One might ascribe the instant popping up of this example to a super-efficient mental storage and retrieval system. But if my mind includes such a super-efficient storage and retrieval system, why can't I remember the names of colleagues at Baruch College with whom I spoke frequently two or three decades ago?

While editing this section, my secretary got me a sandwich from a nearby deli, so that I could get to an imminent medical appointment on time. I asked her to get me a turkey sandwich with extra meat. The label on the wrapped sandwich said "*double* turkey." Immediately, with my focus on editing these passages—and with Shakespeare's *Macbeth* the furthest possible topic from "my mind"—up popped the phrase "*Double, double, toil and trouble.*" I have heard the word "double" countless times over the decades since I first read or saw *Macbeth*—including expressions involving a double play, "double or nothing," and Doublemint gum—but this is the first time my mind associated "double" with "trouble." Before I state my hypothesis about all these goings-on, let me remind you of a salient feature of human memory: Its primary storage mechanism is not static. You can unplug a computer, depriving it of any energy flow, and when you turn it back on, your files are still there. If the human body shuts down, it has no restart button. The basic unit of the nervous system is a specialized cell called a *neuron* with input units called *dendrites* and a relatively long extension called the neuron's *axon*. This ends in several axon terminals that communicate with the dendrites of other neurons across minuscule gaps using chemicals called neurotransmitters. The axon either fires or rests. It is an either/or proposition.

This description of neural activity has the following corollary. The memory of the baseball accident must involve the repeated firing of neurons in some kind of cycle. This does not necessarily mean that any neurons are completely dedicated to this purpose. The situation may be like a VM computing system in which many users have "virtual machines" supported by common physical computing resources. (*Question*: A VM computing system has dispatch and priority rules to dynamically allocate resources among simultaneous users. What process does this for mental resources?)

The baseball accident event set up a mental process that literally keeps that memory alive. I propose that it did one more thing: In effect, it created a "representative" (or "rep") for the memory, or it assigned the memory as one of the "clients" of an existing rep. One of the rep's jobs is to monitor what is going on at the conscious level. As in a large bingo game, general information is "broadcast" to all participants. If the rep hears something (and/or sees, smells, or feels something) relevant to one of the memories it represents, it speaks up. Unlike the bingo game, however, the rep's voice does not automatically get heard at the conscious level. Since many such voices may be competing for attention, there must be a local committee that decides what is worth passing up to higher processes, and a "higher committee" (or committees) that decides what to pass into the conscious process. Thus all levels of my mind's mental management had to concur with the proposal by the rep in charge of the memory of the witches' scene in *Macbeth*.

EMULATION, NOT REPLICATION

It seems to me that parallel computing systems that can process large detailed simulators and DSSs should try to emulate the functionality of the brain, but not necessarily try to replicate the physical mechanisms by which the brain achieves this functionality. For example, static memory—which will not disappear in case of a power failure that defeats backup plans— is obviously safer than replicating nature's memory solution. Also, often there is information that needs to be broadcast widely to many reps. For example, a future JLMSim-style simulator with millions of simulated investors and their traders assigned to hundreds or thousands of reps, would need to continuously "broadcast" security prices. Why not literally broadcast by radio, literally at the speed of light (someday, when nanoradio technology permits, if not already)? The fact that this is not the way the brain works does not imply that this—or other departures from the brain's physical methods—is not a superior solution for our needs.

EVENT INVOCATION OF A THIRD KIND

As reviewed in Chapter 7, SIMSCRIPTs (I) and II offered two types of event invocation: exogenous and endogenous. In particular, an endogenous event is *scheduled* (before the start of a simulation, or in a prior event occurrence) to occur at a *specified time*. But we have just seen that thought processes are triggered by some status change, as when a phrase from a song just happens in a conversation, or a familiar scent wafts by. Analogously, I propose a third type of event invocation, namely "conditional." This would be a form of endogenous event whose occurrence would be specified by a CAUSE or SCHEDULE statement—as it would be now—but rather than have the event happen at a specified time, it would happen if and when a logical condition became true. Specifically, a CAUSE or SCHEDULE statement would end with one of two alternative phrases, either

AT<real valued expression>

or

WHEN<logical expression>

Since the logical expression could be of the form

$$\text{TIME.V} > = <\text{real valued expression}>$$

the WHEN phrase could do what the AT phrase does. But the AT phrase would be retained, both for backward compatibility and because it reads more naturally if a known time delay is the only condition for the invocation of the event. An example of the use of the WHEN phrase in a JLMSim-like context could be

$$\text{SCHEDULE order.review (order.slip)}$$

$$\text{WHEN TIME.V} = \text{TIME.V} + 1 \text{ HOUR or}$$

$$\text{price (stock (order.slip))} < = \text{limit (order.slip)}$$

The JLMSim-like context in which this statement appeared could be a simulated or real-time trading system. Performance considerations may make it desirable to restrict the generality of the logical expression permitted in the WHEN phrase.[7]

PROCESSES THAT PROCESS PROCESSES

A potential source of confusion in discussing the implementation of event-oriented programs in parallel computing systems is the fact that the discussion involves several categories of processes, including

1. a *computer's processes*, such as its arithmetic operations or its fetching and storage of data;

2. *algorithmic processes*, such as solving a system of equations or performing a statistical analysis;

3. *process routines*, as introduced in SIMSCRIPT II.5 and described in Chapter 7; and

4. the manufacturing processes, stock-trading processes, or other *end-user processes* that are represented or controlled by our simulators and DSSs.

In terms of this terminology, the function of the timing routine of an asynchronous simulator has been to represent parallel user processes on computers that perform computer processes sequentially. SIMSCRIPT M would need to compile code that efficiently represented parallel *user* processes on parallel *computer* processors.

EASILY PARALLELIZED PROCESSES (Epps)

A computing system is a task resource system (TRS)—essentially a big job shop—wherein the executing programs generate tasks, and the computing system supplies the resources to fulfill them. As traditionally represented by PERT networks, some tasks can be performed in parallel whereas some must be done in series. A major challenge of computer science is to determine which is which.

EPPs are commonly referred to as embarrassingly parallel processes (see the title of Chapter 3 of Wilkerson and Allen 2005, for example). I see no reason why one should be embarrassed by exploiting the natural parallelism of one's subject; hence my interpretation of the EPP acronym. In terms of the terminology and viewpoint established in the last section, the EPPs discussed here are sets of *computer tasks*—generated by programs that represent, track, or control status changes in real or simulated entities—for which it is easy to design parallel implementation. For example, in a Monte Carlo analysis multiple runs starting with different random seeds can proceed in parallel. The exogenous events of a DSS, such as participants dialing in to view their accounts in the GC DSS, invoke processes that may proceed in parallel.

As already noted, asynchronous simulated events represent parallel user processes. For example, in JLMSim, investor reoptimizations are treated asynchronously, since the actions of the multitude of JLMSim investors and their traders interact with other investors and their traders only in the marketplace. Each investor's reoptimization calculations and portfolio choice can proceed independently of those of other investors.

Synchronized events also include much parallel user processing. During a job shop shift change, for example, work at many machines must be either handed over to the next shift or wrapped up until a later shift. These processes for different machines can proceed in parallel. In JLMSim, similar parallelism occurs in the end-of-day event wherein, for example, each margined account must be checked for a possible margin call. This parallelism can occur in the DSS of a real brokerage back office as well as a simulated one.

In manufacturing, a particular shop may be part of a factory that includes other fabrication shops, along with subassembly, assembly, and paint facilities. The simulation or

real-time tracking of events at each of these shops can proceed in parallel with limited communication between them.
The factory at one location may be part of a many-factory
enterprise with warehousing and transportation processes all
going on in parallel. The manufacturing, transportation, and
warehousing system may be part of an enterprise that includes
subsystems for purchasing (with its supply chain), marketing,
engineering, accounting, and finance (including corporate
budgeting). Each subsystem must coordinate with the others,
but to a large extent they proceed independently.

LOCAL RESOURCE GROUPS

The items just discussed are examples of user processes that are
already largely parallelized. There are also user processes that
do not come parallelized already, but are easily parallelizable.

Suppose that one wished to compute various statistics—
such as the minimum, maximum, sum, average, and standard
deviation—of roughly 10^9 numbers. An example might be a
long series of tick-by-tick transaction data for some security.
(Clearly if the computing of statistics for one security can be
parallelized, the parallelizability of that of any number of securities follows as a corollary.) Suppose further that the computing system involved is like the brain in being able to organize
its resources into a large number of what I will refer to as *local
resource groups* (LRGs). In the case of the brain, an example
would be the neural resources that somehow remember the
teenage baseball game event and assign a "rep" to speak up for
it when relevant. For a flexibly parallelizable computing system,

one may envision an enormous (in capacity, not necessarily in space) array of memory, computing, and communication components; and that a local group of these can be (logically) partitioned off for some purpose. This LRG would have substantial computing, storage, and communication capabilities, perhaps comparable to those of an inexpensive present-day personal computer. An enormous number of LRGs would be available.

The optimal solution to the problem of how many such LRGs to assign to some major task depends on various costs, but by way of example, suppose that a reasonable solution is to have 10^4 LRGs that serve as reps, each of which is in charge of 10^5 numbers. To compute a *sum*, each rep would be asked to sum its 10^5 numbers and pass these subtotals up to a higher level that computes the grand sum. An *average* (arithmetic mean) is computed by computing a sum and a count of the number of numbers involved. A *geometric mean* is produced by computing an average log and then taking an antilog; a *variance* is computed by computing an average square, and then using the formula that

$$\text{Variance} = (\text{Avg. square}) - (\text{Squared avg.})$$

Standard deviation is the square root of variance.

In general this procedure is applicable to any "associative operation." For example, a total is the sum of its subtotals. Similarly the maximum of a whole set is a maximum of maxima. The product of a large set of *matrices* is the product of its subsets. The last example differs from the prior ones in that matrix multiplication is *associative* but not necessarily *commutative*. Thus the rep at the higher level must know where a reported matrix product fits into the sequence of matrix multiplications.

It is typically expeditious to organize data by ranked sets. IBM EAS-E made storage and retrieval efficient for huge ranked sets by breaking them into subsets, possibly made up of subsets of subsets, etc. Various parts of this set/subset structure would naturally be assigned to various LRGs. This would facilitate the computing of statistics as illustrated earlier, as well as fast storage and retrieval.

MICRO VERSUS MACRO PARALLELIZATION

An LRG, as I visualize it, would typically include two or more cooperating processors and their local (fast) storage, plus communication facilities and mass storage for which the LRG would serve as custodian—like the IBM EAS-E custodian, but with intercustodian communication.

The distinction between micro and macro parallelization that I wish to make is the distinction between tasks that can be parceled out to *different* LRGs and those that are best done *within* an LRG. The tasks and subtasks discussed in the section on EPPs can be handled by *macro* parallelization. For example, the discussion of how to quickly compute statistics for 10^9 numbers assumed that this major task was broken into subtasks that were parceled out to many LRGs—and was thus an example of macro parallelization.

A basic computer action, such as that of adding two numbers, involves a number of steps: Each of the two operands must be moved from memory to registers upon which the add instruction operates. They could be first moved into a "cache" of operands in a queue to be operated on. The addition is executed and the result stored in a register. Then this result must be moved to storage. However, it may be that one or both of the operands is already in a register that can be directly accessed by an ALU (arithmetic local unit) that will perform the operation. Also, the result may not need to be stored, since it is a partial sum that will be added to again immediately.

Consider the case in which the operands are fetched from memory and the result is stored back into memory. If this is all that were going on in some serial machine, then the ALU would sit idle while data were accessed and stored. One of the functions of modern high-performance parallel computers is to overlap the data fetching for a forthcoming operation, or the data storage of a prior operation, with the execution of a current arithmetic operation.

This raises the question of whom or what is to decide what is to be done in parallel with what at the micro level. Allen and Kennedy (2002) describe six different ways in which current computers offer parallelism to their users, and present coding tailored to each of these types of hardware. They conclude from this exercise that

> *Explicit representation of parallelism in a source language is not sufficient to guarantee optimal use of parallel hardware. Each of the six machine types presented required a different representation of parallelism— radically different in some cases. Furthermore, getting*

the best form for a specific machine required detailed knowledge of the machine's architecture. This observation suggests that explicitly parallel programs need to be tailored for individual architectures; they lose efficiency when ported from one machine to another.

. . .

Given the increasing lifetime of software and the decreasing lifetime of hardware, these lessons suggest that tailoring code to the specific machine architecture is best left to the compiler.

Thus the assignment of computer resources to computing tasks at a micro level should be left to optimizing compilers tailored to a specific computer architecture. The executing SIMSCRIPT M program, on the other hand, would handle the dispatching of major computing tasks to available LRGs. Such macro parallelization is a classical job shop problem and could call upon a vast tradition of job shop research.

Some LRGs may specialize. For example, perhaps one or more LRGs may have as their specialty the retrieval of archival information. They might therefore have little or no facility to communicate with end users, since their main function is to respond to intercustodian requests for massive little-used data. If all LRGs are the same, then the task-dispatching process is that of a job shop with many servers of one kind. If LRGs differ, macro parallelism would be accomplished as a classical multiserver job shop.

Currently SIMSCRIPT III, like SIMSCRIPT II.5 before it, compiles C code and lets C do the (micro) code optimization.

Ideally, eventually, it might be better if the code optimization process started with SIMSCRIPT (e.g., SIMSCRIPT M). For example, we saw that the SIMSCRIPT II COMPUTE statement specifies a collection of entities over which statistics are to be calculated. If a SIMSCRIPT compiler writes linear code to accomplish this, the C compiler may or may not figure out that certain intermediate results need not be stored.

From the programmer's point of view, a COMPUTE statement is still a COMPUTE statement. Depending on the sizes of the sets from which the subject entities are drawn, and the details of computer hardware, the SIMSCRIPT compiler and run-time operating system will, it is to be hoped, employ good "state-of-the-art" macro and micro parallelism. In general, it should be no harder for an optimizing compiler to figure out what can be done in parallel and what must be done in series based on SIMSCRIPT II–style specifications of the simulator or DSS modeler's intent, than it is to decide this based on linear code that implements this intent.[8]

EPILOGUE

A principal purpose of the *present* chapter has been to show how detailed financial simulators and DSSs could be specified and then automatically generated or compiled so as to take advantage of the massive parallelism of present and future computing systems. The *preceding* chapters considered what these financial simulators and DSSs should contain since, as in all things computer, the rule is: Garbage In, Garbage Out.

NOTES

Chapter 6

1. Before Markowitz (1959) distinguished between what we refer to as HDMs and RDMs, Simon (1947) made essentially the same distinction, characterizing the former as having "bounded rationality." A hypothetical dialogue between Simon (1947) and Markowitz (1959), Plato-style, might have Markowitz (1959) saying,

   > I agree that humans are of bounded rationality. But some seek improvement in one area or another, as attested by the existence of a large number of "how to" books and magazines. I hope to help those who seek better ways to invest. My hypothesis is that practical approximations to rational decisions may serve this purpose.

   We would hope that Simon (1947)'s response would have been supportive.

2. This note illustrates how far beyond the prerequisites of this book is the math required for a rigorous understanding of continuous-time financial models. See Halmos (1974) or Kolmogorov and Fomin (1957) for an as-user-friendly-as-possible rigorous introduction to

such math. Specifically, we will give two examples of how the typical reader's intuition of concepts such as that of a "continuous function" is not prepared for the strange and wondrous things that can occur in the world of continuous mathematics. In both examples, we consider a function

$$y = f(x)$$

defined on the unit interval $0 \leq x \leq 1$ with

$$f(0) = 0 \quad f(1) = 1$$

Both examples exhibit counterintuitive properties.

Example 1. The length L of a continuous path that the point $(x, f(x))$ traces out as x goes from 0 to 1 can usually be approximated by (1) subdividing the "X axis" unit interval $[0,1]$ into n subintervals of length $1/n$; (2) measuring the distance between successive points on the curve at these n points; and (3) summing these distances, thus approximating L. Usually, if n is fairly large, this finite sum will be close to the length of the continuous path traced out as x goes from zero to one. But it is possible that as $n \to \infty$, the sum of these segments increases without limit. In particular, this is true almost certainly for the path traced out by a log of price that follows a Brownian motion as assumed by Black and Scholes (1973), including paths that happen to have $f(1) = 1$ as well as starting at $f(0) = 0$. We daresay that few if any nonmathematical readers have any intuitive notion of how a continuous curve can cover an infinite distance as it travels from (0, 0) to (1, 1).

Example 2, Cantor's Function. Our second example uses the concept of a "set of measure zero." By way of illustration, recall that there is zero probability that a random variable r, uniformly distributed between zero and one, will equal precisely 0.5, since this probability must be less than the probability that the random variable will fall somewhere between $0.5 - 1/n$ and $0.5 + 1/n$. The latter can be made less than any positive number by choosing n sufficiently large. One says that in the interval [0, 1] the single point {0.5} is a "set of measure zero." Similarly, there is a zero probability that r will equal any one of a finite number of prespecified values, such as {0.01, 0.02, ... , 0.99, 1.00}. This too is a set of measure zero. Less obvious, but a standard result in mathematical probability theory (as shown in Kolmogorov and Fomin), is that there is zero probability that r will be a rational number. On the unit interval the rational numbers are a set of measure zero; therefore the irrational numbers are a set of measure one.

The Cantor function

$$y = f(x)$$

is defined for $0 \leq x \leq 1$. It has a derivative "almost everywhere" on this interval.

Specifically,

$$\frac{dy}{dx} = 0$$

except on a set of measure zero. Nevertheless, the Cantor function is a continuous function from $f(0) = 0$ to $f(1) = 1$, with $f(x)$ therefore equal to every value in $[0, 1]$ somewhere along the way as x goes from 0 to 1. (See Halmos for a description of the Cantor function.)

3. It may seem that, with modern high-frequency stock trading, the distinction between "high-frequency" and "continuous" trading could be ignored. To the contrary, this distinction remains at least as important as ever. For example, the following item appeared in the *Wall Street Journal* while this chapter was being drafted:

> *High-speed traders are using a hidden facet of the Chicago Mercantile Exchange's computer system to trade on the direction of the futures market before other investors get the same information. . . . The advantage often is just one to 10 milliseconds, according to people familiar with the matter and trading records reviewed by The Wall Street Journal. But that is plenty of time for computer-driven traders, who say they can structure their orders so that the confirmations tip which direction prices for crude oil, corn and other commodities are moving.*

> May 1, 2013, C1

On a more leisurely time scale, on the front page of the June 13, 2013 issue, under the headline "Traders Pay for an Early Peek at Key Data," the *Wall Street Journal* reported that

> *On the morning of March 15, stocks stumbled on news that a key reading of consumer confidence was unexpectedly low. One group of investors already knew that. They got the University of Michigan's consumer report two seconds before everyone else.*

In the real world, a few milliseconds is clearly a lot longer than instantaneous.

Continuous-time models frequently assume (1) continuous price movement, (2) continuous trading, and (3) perfectly liquid markets. This combination of assumptions is not only highly unrealistic, but can even be destructive. For example, in mid-1987 $90 billion worth of institutional funds were being managed using "portfolio insurance" (not to be confused with *portfolio theory*). Portfolio insurance was a mathematical formula that replicated a call on the S&P 500. According to the Black-Scholes option pricing model, calls are redundant since one can achieve the same effect by shifting one's cash-to-stock ratio back and forth continuously in time. Portfolio insurance specified daily portfolio shifts that approximated the Black-Scholes continuous-time shifts. The advantage of using a mathematical procedure equivalent to a call on the S&P 500, rather than actual calls themselves, was that investing institutions could not in fact buy $90 billion worth of calls on the S&P 500. On the other hand, it seemed to the sellers and buyers of portfolio insurance that this much, and more, could be managed following a Black-Scholes-based formula.

The formula guaranteed that if the market went up an investor would make about as much as it would have made if the investor had bought that many dollars' worth of calls at their Black-Scholes price; whereas if the market went down the investor would only lose roughly the price of the replicated calls. This was achieved by buying when the market went up and selling when the market went down. In particular, the portfolio insurance formula prescribed sales fast enough so that if the market declined a great deal, the investor would be out of equities soon enough to ensure that the investor would not lose more than the price of the replicated call.

But many large funds buying as the market went up tended to drive the market up further and, conversely, many large funds selling as the market fell tended to drive the market downward even faster. The market fell substantially on the Friday before "Black Monday," October 19, 1987. That meant that portfolio insurers had to sell. Large brokerage firms knew this, and sold first. Portfolio insurers usually used S&P 500 *futures* rather than the actual (*spot*) market because of the former's greater liquidity. But in the tumult of Black Monday, the futures market became disconnected from the spot market, at which time sales of S&P 500 baskets of stocks had to be executed through the spot market. According to the report of the Presidential Task Force on Market Mechanisms (Brady, Cotting, Kirby, Opel, and Stein, 1988), page 41:

> *The formulas used by portfolio insurers dictated the sale of $20 to $30 billion of equities over this short time span. Under such pressure, prices must fall dramatically. Transaction systems, such as DOT, or market stabilizing mechanisms, such as the NYSE specialists, are bound to be crushed by such selling pressure, however they are designed or capitalized.*

This is as compared to "specialist buying power estimated to be no more than $3 billion at the start of Monday," according to note 5, page 36.

The problem was that portfolio insurance was based on the Black-Scholes model, which assumes continuous trading in a perfectly liquid market. The model itself is neither right nor wrong. It is a set of premises with interesting mathematical implications. The hypothesis that the model was applicable when its prescriptions were applied by institutional investors with $90 billion under management, was worse than wrong. It was disastrous.

At a roundtable at Baruch College held shortly after Black Monday, Markowitz spoke first and asserted that the severity of the crash was due to the widespread use of portfolio insurance. Fischer Black spoke second, and asserted that as long as the assets under management (AUM) of investors who rebalance their portfolios equals or exceeds the AUM of portfolio insurers, the existence of portfolio insurers is benign, since rebalancers sell when prices rise and buy when prices fall, thereby always being on the other side of the market from portfolio insurers.

A simulator, reported in Kim and Markowitz (1989) (KM), was programmed specifically to test Black's assertion. The KM simulator uses the constant proportion portfolio insurance (CPPI) version of portfolio insurance proposed in Black and Jones (1987). This simplifies the computation of the requisite portfolio insurance purchases and sales, but has general properties very much like those of synthetic option portfolio insurance. The KM model (programmed in SIMSCRIPT II.5) is like JLMSim, described in Chapter 7, in that prices and volumes are endogenous, the result of the crossing of supply and demand due to orders generated by investors following mechanical rules. The principal difference between JLMSim and the KM model is that the investors in the former are MV optimizers whereas those in the latter are either rebalancers or portfolio insurers. The number of investors of each type are parameters of the KM simulator. The general conclusion of Kim and Markowitz was that "Thus in this test tube world with one-third CPPI investors and two-thirds rebalancers, crashes of the magnitude of October 19, 1987, happen almost every quarter."

Chapter 7

1. We ignore here, and throughout this volume, "simultaneous equation" models in which the values of two or more state variables are determined as the solution to a set of simultaneously applicable equations.

2. Robinson (1974) provided a rigorous treatment of "infinitesimals." Leibnitz tried to use such in his version of the calculus, but did not have a well-developed enough formal logic at his disposal to carry it off. In Robinson's "nonstandard analysis" an infinitesimal, ε, is a "hyper-real number" greater than zero but smaller than any positive real number. It combines with real numbers and powers of epsilon as Leibnitz would have expected. For example,

$$4.000 < 5.0 - 1000\varepsilon < 5.0 < 5 + 1000\varepsilon^2$$
$$< 5.0 + 0.001\varepsilon < 1/\varepsilon < 1/\varepsilon^2 \qquad \textbf{(N1)}$$

SIMSCRIPT II includes predefined constants, such as PI.C, which approximates pi (π). It also has a constant RINF. C that represents infinity. In particular, the phrase "RINF. C > R" is true for any real variable R. SIMSCRIPT II could also have included a constant EPSILON.C such that

$$0 < EPSILON.C < R \qquad \textbf{(N2)}$$

would always be TRUE for any $R > 0$. More general expressions such as (N1) would also be TRUE.

EPSILON.C could prove very useful in asynchronous simulation programming. We note in the text that in both synchronous and asynchronous simulations, a single event may in fact be a sequence of infinitesimally separated successive events. Currently, in asynchronous simulations, if two events are scheduled for the same simulated time, there is no way that the two events can interleave their actions. One event routine gains control first and executes all its actions before the other. The possibility of interleaving actions could be introduced, neatly and generally, by the introduction of EPSILON.C. For example, a process could schedule actions to occur at a time equal to the current time plus time increments equal to any of the *positive* hyperreal values in (N1). These would be performed in the sequence indicated and could interleave actions with other processes with the "real" clock stopped. Also, various analysis routines, to be executed after all simulated events, could be scheduled at

$$\text{SimTime.V} = i/\varepsilon \text{ for } i = 1 \text{ to } n$$

3. The difference between the Markowitz "game of life" and Gary Becker's "Economics of Life" is a matter of where attention is primarily focused. The game of life focuses on financial planning under uncertainty, whereas Becker's work tends to emphasize major lifestyle decisions such as whether to embark on a life of crime. See Becker and Becker (1997).

Chapter 8

1. In this connection we think of a strategy as being like a retractable tape measure. Its *normal* form is retracted. When it is in use, it is *extended.* Such tape measures are used *extensively.*

2. The dynamic programming methodology presented here appears in the vNM solution to games with complete information. Bellman (1957) extends this methodology, with much attention to the existence and uniqueness of long-run solutions to various discrete and continuous games.

3. As compared to a situation such that, for any action α, there is a still better one, β, because EU is unbounded or the constraint set is not "compact."

4. *Stochastic linear programming* (SLP) is an alternative to dynamic programming for the optimization of dynamic models. In general, any linear programming (LP) problem (Dantzig 1951, 1963) seeks the minimum or the maximum of a linear function

$$f(X) = \sum_{j=1}^{n} c_j X_j$$

subject to linear equality constraints

$$\sum_{j=1}^{n} a_{ij} X_j = b_i \ i = 1, \ldots, m$$

in nonnegative variables

$$X_j \geq 0 \ j = 1, \ldots, n$$

In a many-period nonstochastic LP (Dantzig 1955b) the constraint equations may be partitioned into sets $P_1, \ldots, P_T$ of constraints that concern resources available, or product produced, in time periods $t = 1, \ldots, T$. A given "activity" X_j may have "inputs" and "outputs" ($a_{ij} \neq 0$) confined to one period or spread over many periods. If we add randomness (Dantzig 1955a), then constraint equations may be partitioned by time $t = 1, \ldots, T$ and scenarios $s = 1, \ldots, S$. A given activity may have its nonzero a_{ij} confined to one (scenario, period) combination or spread over many. SLP consists of techniques to facilitate the solution of such LP problems. This approach excels in models in which the dimensionality, n, of the state space is much too large for exact DP optimization but T is small. Thus neither DP nor SLP is practical when both n and T are large.

Wets and Ziemba (1999) is an issue of the *Annals of Operations Research* devoted to stochastic programming including an enormous bibliography. Some applications are reproduced in the Ziemba and Mulvey (1998) collection of articles on *Worldwide Asset and Liability Modeling*. In their introductory chapter, Ziemba and Mulvey summarize the state of the art at the time as

> *Computational difficulties arise due to the nature of the scenario tree within the stochastic programming framework. The number of decision variables grows exponentially. In most cases, we can prune the tree by reducing the number of branches emanating out*

of the nodes, especially for nodes that lie towards the end of the planning horizon. Also, we can apply variance reduction procedures and other statistical procedures, such as importance sampling (Infanger 1994), and the expected value of perfect information (Dempster 1997).

The primary algorithms for solving stochastic programs fall into three categories: direct solvers, especially interior point methods . . . decomposition methods based on Bender's decomposition . . . and decomposition methods based on augmented Lagrangians . . . . These algorithms are highly effective in taking advantage of the scenario tree structure. We are now able to solve nonlinear stochastic programs with over 10,000 scenarios. Thus, as computers become 40–50% faster per year, we can grow the size of the stochastic program in a similar fashion.

Our focus on DP rather than SLP is not due to their relative abilities to solve large dynamic problems. Rather, it is due to our use of the DP principle for explicit and implicit MV approximations to optimal dynamic strategies such as those explained in Chapter 11. For example, the Markowitz and van Dijk heuristic, described in Chapter 11, addresses this case based on a quadratic approximation to the (unknown) derived utility function.

Ziemba (2015) reviews alternative approaches to many-period portfolio selection. In particular, Ziemba says of:

Simulation: There is usually too much output to understand, but it is very useful as a check.

Mean variance: This is okay for one period but hard to use in multi-period problems and with liabilities. It assumes means and variances are known.

Expected log: . . .

Stochastic control: . . .

Stochastic programming/stochastic control: . . .

Stochastic programming: This is my approach.

Continuous time modeling, though popular in the academic world, seems to be impractical in the real world.

Not surprisingly our own views differ on certain points, such as Ziemba's characterization of mean-variance analysis as "single-period," as compared to Markowitz (1959) Chapter 11—and the whole of the present volume. As to "knowing" means and variances, one of the benefits of mean-variance analysis is that *only* means, variances, and covariances need be estimated, *not* whole joint distributions.

Chapter 9

1. See Endnote 3 of Chapter 8.
2. We speak here of the "cautious" investor rather than the "risk-averse" investor, since established terminology calls an investor "risk-averse" as long as it has a strictly concave utility function. Thus, in terms of the terminology used

here, there could be risk-averse investors who are not cautious.

3. On January 6, 2014, Markowitz sent the following email to Roger Ibbotson and others:

> *Dear All,*
>
> *On Page 176 of Ibbotson SBBI Classic Yearbook for 2013, it says that Overall, Ibbotson estimates that the typical investor's human capital is more bond-like than stock-like. Ibbotson models average human capital as 30% equities and 70% bonds. This decision was reached in June 1998 amongst members of Ibbotson's Advisory Board at the time. Members included Harry Markowitz, Daniel Kahneman, Jeff Jaffe, Shlomo Benartzi, John Carroll, and Richard Thaler.*
>
> *I do not recall such a meeting. My memory is not great, but I usually remember whose advisory boards I have served on. For example, I recall serving on an advisory board for a unit of TCW under Sherrie Grabot, together with some or all of the above named individuals, but I don't recall (in that context or any other) voting on the bond-versus-stock characteristics of human capital.*
>
> *Does anyone remember this meeting or can otherwise clarify this reference?*
>
> *Best wishes, Harry*

The only reply was from Roger Ibbotson on January 8, 2014, as follows:

Dear Harry,

On June 11, 2008 there was a meeting of the Ibbotson Advisory Board held at the TCW office in LA in regards to the TCW Guided Choice Program. According to the minutes, all of the aforementioned participants were present, in addition to Ibbotson Associates employees. I was not present, since I was in Chicago at an IA Conference at the time. I was present at a subsequent meeting of the Advisory Board at the Ibbotson office in Chicago in which you were also present, along with several other participants. You may have been present at these meetings on behalf of TCW. IA was at the time involved in joint activities with TCW.

I will advise Morningstar/IA to revise the wording on the new 2014 SBBI Yearbook to carefully reflect what happened. The new 2014 SBBI is currently in process.

Roger

Page 188 of the 2014 SBBI says that

Ibbotson's Advisory Board in 1998 included Harry Markowitz, Daniel Kahneman, Jeff Jaffe, Shlomo Benartzi, John Carroll, and Richard Thaler. The

Advisory Board provided guidance on a variety of lifetime advice topics. One item that stemmed from these meetings is the idea that a typical investor's human capital is similar to a junk bond. During "normal" times junk bonds trade more like bonds, but during times of economic turmoil junk bonds trade more like equities. Ultimately, Ibbotson decided to model the typical investor's human capital as 30% equities and 70% bonds.

This is in accord with Markowitz's memory, with Markowitz serving as a TCW representative at these joint meetings. Subsequently TCW spun off GuidedChoice with Sherrie Grabot as its CEO. A while after that, Grabot asked Markowitz to form the GuidedChoice R&D team as recounted in Chapter 7.

4. It can be shown using either the analyses in Arrow or Pratt or the quadratic approximation in Equation (2) of our Chapter 2 that the mean-variance approximation to the utility function in Equation (1c) of the present chapter will pick a portfolio lower on the efficient frontier than that of log-utility if $a < 0$ and higher on the frontier if $a > 0$. Samuelson wrote $U(W_T)$ in Equation (1c) as

$$U = W^\alpha/\alpha \quad \alpha \neq 0 \tag{N1}$$

Mossin used yet another equivalent formula. Since choice is unaffected by multiplying a utility function by a *positive* constant, Equation (N1) implies the same choices as Equation (1c) with its Equation (1d) and (1e) special cases. But so would

$$U = \alpha W^\alpha \qquad \text{(N2)}$$

The reason Equation (N1), or equivalent, is used in the literature is because the choices implied by Equation (1b) are the limiting case of (N1) as $\alpha \to 0$. The text use of Equation (1c) avoids this discussion.

The breakpoint, $\tilde{W}$, could be determined in various ways, such as

a. Ask the investor for a target level.

b. Choose a target wealth sufficient to virtually guarantee an income stream that is a given percentage of current income.

c. Let $\tilde{W}$ be the retirement wealth level that the investor would have had if it had left its money in cash equivalents.

The utility function in Equation (16) of Chapter 9 is piecewise CRRA, with two pieces. One could have a similar function with three or more CRRA pieces, such as one with two breakpoints depending on information such as GuidedSpending's C_L and C_U consumption levels.

5. Let

$$s = \sqrt{T} \qquad \text{(N1)}$$

then

$$\hat{w} - \tilde{w} = k\sigma s - ms^2$$
$$= s(k\sigma - ms) \qquad \text{(N2)}$$

We see immediately that $\hat{w} = \tilde{w}$ at $s = 0$ and at

$$s = \frac{k\sigma}{m} = K \qquad \text{(N3)}$$

Setting its first derivative to zero, we see that $\hat{w} - \tilde{w}$ is greatest at

$$\hat{s} = \frac{k\sigma}{2m}$$
$$= K/2 \qquad \text{(N4)}$$

At this point, the difference equals

$$\hat{w} - \tilde{w} = \frac{k^2\sigma^2}{2m} - \frac{mk^2\sigma^2}{4m^2}$$
$$= \frac{k^2\sigma^2}{4m} \qquad \text{(N5)}$$

Since $T = s^2$, we have $\hat{w} - \tilde{w} = 0$ at $T = 0$ and $T = K^2$. The difference is greatest at

$$T = \frac{k^2\sigma^2}{4m^2} = K^2/4 \qquad \text{(N6)}$$

The maximum difference is still as in Equation (N5), since s and T do not enter the latter result.

6. "Archaeology of Computers: Reminiscences, 1945–1947," *Communications of the ACM* 15(7):694, July 1972, special issue: "Twenty-Fifth Anniversary of the Association for Computing Machinery."

Chapter 10

1. The Iancu and Trichakis (2014) article, "Fairness and Efficiency in Multiportfolio Optimization," appeared after this chapter was complete except for minor editing. Iancu and Trichakis alerted us to the venerable "fairness" literature. According to Atkinson (1970),

> *As . . . was pointed out by Dalton . . . in his pioneering article* [Dalton (1920)], *underlying any such measure* [of income inequality] *is some concept of social welfare and it is with this concept that we should be concerned. He argued that we should approach the question by considering directly the form of the social welfare function to be employed. If we follow him in assuming that this would be an additively separable and symmetric function of individual incomes, then we would rank distributions according to*
>
> $$W \equiv \int_0^{\bar{y}} U(y)f(y)dy.$$
>
> *My main concern in this paper is to explore the implications of adopting this approach and its relationship to the conventional summary measures of inequality.*

According to Bertsimas, Farias, and Trichakis (2012), "Samuelson (1947) provided the first formulation in which the relevant constraint set for the planner was the set of achievable utility allocations, . . . , an idea which became central in this area." As to current practice, Bertsimas et al. tell us that

> *Fortunately, we have available to us an axiomatic treatment of attitudes toward inequity. This axiomatic treatment has deep roots in early philosophy and has quantitatively culminated over the last 50 years in a family of social welfare functions parameterized by a single parameter that measures the attitude of the system designer toward inequities. This family is given by*

$$\sum_{j=1}^{n} \frac{u_j^{1-\alpha}}{1-\alpha}.$$

The parameter $\alpha \geq 0$ measures an aversion to inequality. (Emphasis in original.)

More generally, in their article "An Axiomatic Theory of Fairness in Network Resource Allocation," Lan, Kao, Chiang, and Sabharwal (2010) tell us that current practice consists of *either* (a) the α-fairness measure described earlier or (b) one or another statistical measures, of which "Jain's index," proposed in Jain, Chiu, and Hawe (1984), is among the more widely used. Jain's measure is

$$J = \frac{(E(u))^2}{Eu^2}$$

where E represents arithmetic mean or expected value depending on whether one is characterizing a given set of u_i or a probability distribution of u. Since

$$V(u) = Eu^2 - (Eu)^2$$

an allocation that maximizes J for a given E also minimizes V for that E. It seems to us that

$$\sigma(u) = \sqrt{V(u)}$$

is the more intuitive measure (of *inequality* rather than *fairness*). The Jain et al. objection to V (and therefore σ) is that it is not bounded or independent of choice of scale. That objection seems inapplicable in the case in the text, since the utilities themselves are normalized to lie in the $[0, 1]$ interval.

A recent alternative proposal, as opposed to α fairness or the Jain measure, is that in the Jagabathula and Shah (2011) article, "Fair Scheduling in Networks Through Packet Election," as summarized in their abstract, they

> *describe a notion of packet based fairness by establishing an analogy with the ranked election problem: packets are voters, schedules are candidates and each packet ranks the schedules based on its priorities. We then obtain a scheduling algorithm that achieves*

*the described notion of fairness by drawing upon the
seminal work of Goodman and Markowitz (1952).*

Chapter 11

1. The following statement was kindly supplied by Will
   Kinlaw, CFA, Senior Managing Director, Head of Portfolio
   and Risk Management Group, State Street Global
   Exchange, State Street Associates.

   *Mark [Kritzman] just reminded me that you are
   looking for an email confirmation that it is okay to
   mention in your book that State Street used the MvD
   approach. That would be absolutely fine. Our advisory
   business, which is housed within State Street Global
   Exchange, has used the MvD method extensively on
   behalf of dozens of clients. In particular, we have used
   it as an approximation for "sub-optimality" costs in
   our optimal rebalancing solution. It is an excellent
   approximation.*

2. Bellman (1957) speaks of *time-independent* dynamic
   situations as opposed to *time-dependent* situations. In a
   time-dependent situation time-until-the-end is a state
   variable. In a time-independent situation, it is not. For
   example, suppose that at each time point t an investor
   divides his or her wealth between consumption C_t and
   investment I_t in the forthcoming period, i.e.,

$$W_t = C_t + I_t \tag{N1}$$

Wealth in the next period depends on return on investment:

$$W_{t+1} = I_t(1+R_t) \qquad \text{(N2)}$$

Assume in this example that returns R_t are i.i.d. The objective is to maximize the expected value of discounted utility of consumption:

$$U = \sum_{t=1}^{\infty} u(C_t)/(1+d)^t \qquad \text{(N3)}$$

At any particular point in time, t, the score so far is

$$U_t = \sum_{i=1}^{t} u(C_i)/(1+d)^i \qquad \text{(N4)}$$

The total score will be the sum of two parts:

$$U = U_t + \sum_{i=t+1}^{\infty} u(C_i)/(1+d)^i$$

$$= U_t + (1+d)^{-t} \sum_{i=1}^{\infty} u(C_{t+i})/(1+d)^i \qquad \text{(N5)}$$

Since U_t is already determined by time-point t, and returns are i.i.d., the remaining game is identical to the original game except for inconsequential constants in the game's utility function. Therefore, the optimal decision is independent of t and U_t. Thus the situation is "time-independent."

On the other hand, in the cases such as those analyzed in Chapter 9, where utility depended on wealth W_T at retirement time, the optimal choice of portfolio generally depends on the length of time until retirement. Thus the decision there is time-dependent. Time-independent situations are sometimes called "recursive," since essentially the same game can "recur" repeatedly.

3. As an item in an implicit or explicit household budget, the purchase of lottery tickets seems to us more likely to be considered a form of entertainment than an investment. This suggests a basically different view of gambling than in Friedman and Savage (1948), or in Markowitz (1952b). We start by reviewing the latter and then presenting our alternative.

    Friedman and Savage (FS) hypothesize that households maximize the expected value of a utility-of-wealth function, $EU(W_t)$, where U has a convex region, as well as two concave regions. Markowitz demonstrates that the behavior of FS agents depends on which of three regions its wealth W falls into:

    a. $W \leq W_L$

    b. $W \geq W_H$

    c. $W \in (W_L, W_H)$

    for some $W_L < W_H$

    Markowitz considers two agents with wealth halfway between W_L and W_H, i.e., $W = (W_L + W_H)/2$, and shows that there is no fair bet that they would each prefer to one with a 50-50 chance of one agent moving up to W_H and the other falling to W_L. Thus, with a flip of a coin, one would become rich and the other poor. The two agents would prefer to engage in this bet rather than stay with the status quo. Furthermore, an agent who is almost rich (with wealth just short of W_H) would not insure against a loss that would bring its wealth down to W_L. To the contrary, its most preferred fair bet would be one that would have a high probability of bringing its wealth up to the magic level of W_H, with a very small probability of having its wealth fall to the low W_L level. Finally, the FS hypothesis implies that poor people (with wealth below W_L) do not buy lottery tickets.

Markowitz (1952b) argues that these major implications of the FS hypothesis contradict common experience. The Markowitz (1952b) hypothesis is that utility is a function of change in wealth ΔW, where ΔW is the change from "customary" wealth. The latter equals current wealth except in the case of recent windfall gains or losses. $\Delta W = 0$ ("no change") is located at one of the inflection points of a curve like that of FS, namely the inflection point with a concave portion to its left and a convex portion to its right. Thus the Markowitz (1952b) agent is cautious on the downside (buying insurance against losses) and risk-seeking on the upside (buying lottery tickets). However, both the downside caution and the upside risk-seeking are limited in extent, because Markowitz assumes that $U(\Delta W)$ is bounded above and below. In particular, on the upside the agent would prefer to keep a large (life-altering) gain with certainty than accept a double-or-nothing offer. On the downside if the agent is already hopelessly in debt, a double-or-nothing offer might be a life saver. Markowitz (1952b) thus explains the existence of both gambling and insurance without the questionable implications of FS.

The idea that the buying of lottery tickets may be an entertainment item in a budget throws a new light on the matter. Insurance is bought to avoid large losses whose impact is made more severe because a household might have to liquidate illiquid assets (such as its house in an extreme case) to cover such a loss. In any case it would probably have to adjust expenditures to a radically new level.

The purchase of lottery tickets is different. The tickets are purchased by participants who are fully aware that this is a zero-sum game, with the state taking its cut off the top. But someone will win, and "if you don't play, it won't be you." The date of the drawing is noted; the individual thinks about, or the family discusses, what it will do if it wins the BIG prize; after the drawing takes place, the individual or family checks its numbers, perhaps sees that it has one of the minor prizes and must go through the process of collecting it, or notes how close it came to winning something big, and considers whether the budget allows it to plunge back into the next week's drawing or to wait a while before trying again.

We have not explored what, if any, are the verifiable implications of this hypothesis versus that of Markowitz (1952b).

Chapter 12

1. When this chapter was first drafted in 2014.

2. I am much indebted to John Gilvey—now deceased, then head of the Center's Central Scientific Services—for the opportunity to test an implementation of SIMSCRIPT II Level 6 "for real."

3. A function or subroutine is called *recursive* if it can call upon itself directly or indirectly. The SIMSCRIPT II compiler, itself written in SIMSCRIPT II, uses the fact that its subroutines are recursive when it compiles an arithmetic expression. The subroutine that writes code to evaluate an arithmetic expression typically calls on a routine that compiles code to evaluate a variable. But if the variable is subscripted, its one or more subscripts may be arithmetic expressions. In this case, the routine to evaluate an expression calls on the routine to evaluate a variable which, in turn, calls on the routine that evaluates an expression, which may again, in turn, call upon the routine that evaluates an expression etc., to any depth. Thus the variable and expression routines can recur any number of times.

4. One could code a more efficient MMR pivot selection algorithm, making good use of SIMSCRIPT II facilities; but this would take more explanation. For example, one

could order the set of uneliminated rows—and columns—
by the number of nonzero entries, looping from least to
greatest, using the minimum m_i or n_j not yet processed
to compute a smallest possible remaining MMR score,
terminating the search if the MR score of the proposed
next pivot equals this minimum possible next MR value.
Having entries in sets owned by both ROW and COLUMN
can also facilitate the Gaussian elimination step.

5. I removed Level 5 with its simulation capabilities from
the RAND version of SIMSCRIPT II lest CACI, feeling
threatened, sued IBM. While the suit would have had no
merit, I feared that IBM top management would elect the
"easy way out" and drop the project.

While what we named "EAS-E," and I here call IBM
EAS-E, was sufficient to demonstrate the feasibility of
SIMSCRIPT II Level 6, it was less than ideal even for
programming DSSs that do not use simulation analysis
to forecast status; since SIMSCRIPT II as planned would
have allowed database entities and real-time events to
make use of (clearly desirable) Level 5 facilities such as
the scheduling of (endogenous) real-time events and the
accumulation of system performance.

6. The first task of the SIMSCRIPT II LWL is to break an
incoming sequence of characters into *tokens*, namely,
either:

- a "word," such as "A" or "Machine_Group" or "B47";
- an integer or decimal number, such as 12 or 12.345;

- an arithmetic operator, such as +, −, *, /, or **, where a pair of asterisks specifies exponentiation; or
- another special character such as a parenthesis or a comma.

The same methodology for doing so, as described in the next paragraph, could be used to process distinctly different alphabets, such as the strokes of a Chinese typewriter, mathematical symbols such as $\forall \; \exists \; \in \; \neg$, or perhaps spoken phonemes.

The SIMSCRIPT II LWL procedure for breaking a character sequence into a sequence of tokens uses a table whose rows represent one or another possible token that is currently "working." Examples include "integer" (e.g., 47), "real" (e.g., 47.8), "word" (e.g., CREA, so far), or "nothing" (after a blank or at the start of a new line). The columns of the table represent different possible character types (e.g., letter, number, blank or line break, etc.) of the next character in the incoming sequence. The contents of the table specify what will be "working" next. For example, if an integer like "3" is working and the next character is a letter, such as "S," then a "word" (i.e., "3S") is the next value of working. What *was* working and what is working *next* indicate whether or not a token is complete and can be moved to a token stream.

As described in Markowitz (1979), one of the EAS-oriented, data-driven aspects of the SIMSCRIPT II LWL is the transformation of tokens into commands. Here again we must distinguish between the compiler's data and application data. The compiler's data consist of patterns describing the syntax of each SIMSCRIPT II command. The application data, originally a stream of characters, are now a stream of tokens. The compiler's pattern for a particular statement (either a command or a definition) views the statement as owning a set of parts, with each part owning a set of alternatives. An alternative may specify:

- a literal character string such as C R E A T E;
- a primitive such as an integer or a "word"; or
- another pattern, such as one called "variable."

This other pattern in turn could own parts with alternatives that could in turn refer to other patterns, etc. (This is an EAS description comparable to a Backus Naur Form description. See Knuth 1964.) The STRUCT routine attempts to fit a pattern to the incoming stream of tokens, tracing out in turn any patterns referred to by the statement pattern.

If it succeeds, STRUCT returns control to a higher routine, indicating that structuring has been successful. The compiler next calls on the routine that knows how to process the particular command, such as a structured CREATE statement. More complex commands, such as COMPUTE, can often be coded in terms of more basic commands. SCRIPT data tables describe how the complex commands can be SCRIPTed out as more primitive commands. This scripting process has much in common with the OGM program generation process. See Markowitz (1979) for further details about SIMSCRIPT's LWL.

7. The implementation to be avoided if possible involves checking all outstanding WHEN conditions *after* the execution of every event (endogenous or exogenous) and *before* calling upon a routine to process the next event. Ideally, one would like to check only those WHEN conditions—*if any*—that could possibly have been triggered because of a status change. SIMSCRIPT II's existing monitoring features may help in this regard. Any attribute (of THE SYSTEM or another entity) can be defined as a VARIABLE MONITORED ON THE LEFT (or RIGHT). It is the possibility of monitoring on the left that is relevant in the present context. For an attribute to be monitored on the left, the SIMSCRIPT II programmer provides a routine that receives the value to be stored in the attribute, takes whatever actions it is programmed to do, and then stores some value (perhaps, but not necessarily, the value it received) in the space used to store the attribute in question. A SIMSCRIPT M compiler could define as monitored on the left any attribute used in a WHEN phrase. The requisite monitoring routine for this variable could create a note with the relevant information concerning what attribute of which individual has been changed, file this note in a suitable set, and flag

that at least one relevant status change has occurred. After the completion of one event occurrence and before invoking the next one, the timing routine of a simulator, or the controller routine of a DSS, could check whether a relevant event has occurred, and act accordingly.

A logical expression can include a "<set> IS EMPTY" (or NOT EMPTY) phrase. In this connection, SIMSCRIPT II's facility for allowing the programmer to specify a routine to be called BEFORE FILING or AFTER REMOVING a member of a specified set can serve the same function for changes in set status as variable monitoring serves for changes in attribute status.

8. Kahneman (2011) analyzes human thought in terms of two systems: System 1 is the first responder; lazy System 2 will override or supplement the System 1 response if it deems it necessary. Some comparison at this point between the cognitive model presented here and that in Kahneman seems mandatory.

It is possible for two alternative theories to explain the same observations. An example is Newton's theory of gravity versus the general theory of relativity. These have indistinguishable implications for many practical problems. The same may be true for Kahneman's dual-cognitive model and the polycognitive model presented here. That said, I still am obliged to sketch how my model incorporates the phenomena focused on by Kahneman.

I view the nervous system as a task/resource system (TRS). Countless tasks are being accomplished simultaneously: one (or a few) consciously; most nonconsciously. Tasks include the monitoring of sensory inputs, including one's visual field, plus sounds, odors, tactile (skin) sensations, and internal states such as stomach acidity. Another type of task (in addition to sensation monitoring) is the remembering of recent and less recent "memories" of all sorts, such as current plans that may not be the immediate focus of attention; past episodes, such as the day (or night) you proposed to your wife; and skills like tying shoes and the multiplication tables. Since the brain has no static store, these must be actively remembered and be at the ready to respond when relevant.

All of the above, and more, must consume mental resources. There must also be some kind of process (or processes) that assigns resources to tasks. In particular, there must be a process that decides on the area of current conscious focus. For example, if you are driving and all is going smoothly, the driving process can be put on automatic, mostly, and your mind can wander to a current plan, like calling someone for a particular purpose, and considering when and how this is to be done. Then a thought intrudes: "That is the sound of a distant siren." With the driving process still on automatic, mostly, your current conscious focuses on questions as to the distance and direction of the siren, and will you have to pull over.

Kahneman ascribes the performance of some of the consciously performed tasks to System 1 and others to

System 2. I assume that recognition of a sound pattern as a siren is a System 1 accomplishment, and that mulling over the day's forthcoming activities is a System 2 task. It seems to me that the task of estimating the distance and direction of a sound is sometimes a System 1 task and sometimes a System 2 task, depending on whether the answer "is obvious" or takes however much thought-time distinguishes System 1 from System 2 tasks. Kahneman says that

> *Whenever you are conscious, and perhaps even when you are not, multiple computations are going on in your brain, which maintain and update current answers to some key questions: Is anything new going on? Is there a threat? Are things going well? Should my attention be redirected? Is more effort needed for this task? You can think of a cockpit, with a set of dials that indicate the current values of each of these essential variables. The assessments are carried out automatically by System 1, and one of their functions is to determine whether extra effort is required from System 2. (Page 59)*

I would add that, whether you are conscious or not, your brain is also doing "multiple computations" to help it accomplish deferred or suspended System 2–type tasks.

REFERENCES

Allen, R., and K. Kennedy. 2002. *Optimizing Compilers for Modern Architectures: A Dependence-based Approach.* San Diego, CA: Academic Press.

Arrow, K. 1951. *Social Choice and Individual Values.* 3rd ed. (2012). New York: John Wiley & Sons.

———. 1965. "Aspects of the Theory of Risk Bearing." Yrjo Jahnsson Saatio, Lecture 2, Helsinki. Reprinted in *Collected Papers of Kenneth J. Arrow*, Vol. 3 (1984).

Atkinson, A. B. 1970. "On the Measurement of Inequality." *Journal of Economic Theory* 2(3): 244–263.

Avins, S. 1997. *Johannes Brahms: Life and Letters.* New York: Oxford University Press.

The Bank of New York. 2005. New Frontiers of Risk: The 360° Risk Manager for Pensions and Nonprofits. New York.

The Bank of New York Mellon Corporation. 2014. New Frontiers of Risk: Revisiting the 360° Manager. New York.

Becker, G. S., and G. N. Becker. 1997. *The Economics of Life: From Baseball to Affirmative Action to Immigration, How Real-World Issues Affect Our Everyday Life.* New York: McGraw-Hill.

Bellman, R. E. 1957. *Dynamic Programming.* Princeton, NJ: Princeton University Press.

Bernoulli, D. 1954. Translated from the Latin as "Exposition of a New Theory on the Measurement of Risk." *Econometrica* 22: 23–36. (First published in 1738.)

Bertsimas, D., V. F. Farias, and N. Trichakis. 2012. "On the Efficiency-Fairness Trade-Off." *Management Science* 58(12): 2234–2250.

351

Bierman, H., Jr., and S. Smidt. 2007. *The Capital Budgeting Decision: Economic Analysis of Investment Projects*. 9th ed. New York: Routledge.

Black, F., and R. W. Jones. 1987. "Simplifying Portfolio Insurance." *Journal of Portfolio Management* 14(1): 48–51.

Black, F., and M. Scholes. 1973. "The Pricing of Options and Corporate Liabilities." *Journal of Political Economy* 81(3): 637–654.

Blay, K. A., and H. M. Markowitz. 2016. "Tax-Cognizant Portfolio Analysis: A Methodology for Maximizing After-Tax Wealth." *Journal of Investment Management*. 14(1): 26–64.

Brady, N. F., J. C. Cotting, R. G. Kirby, J. R. Opel, and H. M. Stein. 1988. The Presidential Task Force on Market Mechanisms. Washington, DC: U.S. Government.

Brealey, R. A., S. C. Myers, and F. Allen. 2008. *Principles of Corporate Finance*. 9th ed. New York: McGraw-Hill.

Breiman, L. 1961. "Optimal Gambling Systems for Favorable Games." Fourth Berkeley Symposium on Probability and Statistics.

Campbell, J. Y., and L. M. Viceira. 2002. *Strategic Asset Allocation: Portfolio Choice for Long-Term Investors*. New York: Oxford University Press.

Censor, Y., and S. Zenios. 1997. *Parallel Optimization: Theory, Algorithms, and Applications*. New York: Oxford University Press.

Chhabra, A. B. 2005. "Beyond Markowitz: A Comprehensive Wealth Allocation Framework for Individual Investors." *Journal of Wealth Management* 7(4): 8–34.

Cramér, H. 1946. *Mathematical Methods of Statistics*. Princeton, NJ: Princeton University Press.

Dahl, O. J., and K. Nygaard. 1966. "SIMULA: An ALGOL-Based Simulation Language." *Communications of the ACM* 9(9): 671–678.

Dalton, H. 1920. "The Measurement of the Inequality of Incomes." *The Economic Journal* 30 (119): 348–361.

Dantzig, G. B. 1951. "Maximization of a Linear Function of Variables Subject to Linear Inequalities." In *Activity Analysis of*

Production and Allocation, ed. T. C. Koopmans, 339–347. New York: John Wiley & Sons.

———. 1955a. "Linear Programming Under Uncertainty." *Management Science* 1(3 and 4): 197–206.

———. 1955b. "Notes on Linear Programming: Part VIII, IX, X— Upper Bounds, Secondary Constraints, and Block Triangularity in Linear Programming." *Econometrica* 23(2): 174–183.

———. 1963. *Linear Programming and Extensions*. Princeton, NJ: Princeton University Press.

Das, S., H. M. Markowitz, J. Scheid, and M. Statman. 2010. "Portfolio Optimization with Mental Accounts." *Journal of Financial and Quantitative Analysis* 45(2): 311–334.

Dempster, M. A. H. 1997. Parallel Solution of Large Scale Dynamic Stochastic Programmers. University of Cambridge Report.

Dimson, E., P. Marsh, and M. Staunton. 2002. *Triumph of the Optimists*. Princeton, NJ: Princeton University Press.

Evensky, H. 2006. "Withdrawal Strategies: A Cash Flow Solution." In *Retirement Income Redesigned: Master Plans for Distribution*, ed. H. Evensky and D. B. Katz, 185–201. New York: Bloomberg Press.

Evensky, H., S. M. Horan, and T. R. Robinson. 2011. *The New Wealth Management: The Financial Advisor's Guide to Managing and Investing Client Assets*. Hoboken, NJ: John Wiley & Sons.

Evensky, H., and D. B. Katz. 2006. *Retirement Income Redesigned: Master Plans for Distribution*. New York: Bloomberg Press.

Fisher, L., and R. L. Weil. 1971. "Coping with the Risk of Interest-Rate Fluctuations: Returns to Bondholders from Naive and Optimal Strategies." *Journal of Business* 44(4): 403–431.

Friedman, M., and L. J. Savage. 1948. "The Utility Analysis of Choices Involving Risk." *Journal of Political Economy* 56: 279–304.

Fuller, S. H., and L. I. Millett. 2011. *The Future of Computing Performance: Game Over or Next Level?* Washington, DC: National Academies Press.

Ginsberg, A. S., H. M. Markowitz, and P. M. Oldfather. 1965. Programming by Questionnaire. Santa Monica, CA: The RAND Corporation Memorandum RM-4460-PR.

Goodman, L. A., and H. M. Markowitz. 1952. "Social Welfare Functions Based on Individual Rankings." *American Journal of Sociology* 58(3): 257–262.

Guerard, J. B., H. M. Markowitz, and G. L. Xu. 2013. "Global Stock Selection Modeling and Efficient Portfolio Construction and Management." *Journal of Investing* 22: 121–128.

Hakansson, N. H. 1971. "On Optimal Myopic Portfolio Policies, With and Without Serial Correlation of Yields." *Journal of Business* 44(3): 324–334.

Halmos, P. R. 1974. *Measure Theory*. New York: Springer-Verlag.

Hildreth, C. 1953. "Alternative Conditions for Social Orderings." *Econometrica* 21(1): 81–94.

Hume, D. 1962. *A Treatise of Human Nature Book I: Of the Understanding*. Cleveland, OH: World Publishing Company. (First published in 1739.)

Iancu, D. A., and N. Trichakis. 2014. "Fairness and Efficiency in Multiportfolio Optimization." *Operations Research* 62(6): 1283–1301.

Ibbotson, R. G. 2013. *Ibbotson SBBI Classic Yearbook 2013: Market Results for Stocks, Bonds, Bills, and Inflation 1926–2012*. Chicago: Morningstar.

———. 2014. *Ibbotson SBBI 2014 Classic Yearbook: Market Results for Stocks, Bonds, Bills, and Inflation 1926–2013*. Chicago: Morningstar.

Infanger, G. 1994. *Planning Under Uncertainty: Solving Large-Scale Stochastic Linear Programs*. Danvers, MA: Scientific Press.

Jacobs, B., K. Levy, and H. M. Markowitz. 2004. "Financial Market Simulation." *Journal of Portfolio Management* 30(5): 142–152. Reproduced in Markowitz (2010b).

Jagabathula, S., and D. Shah. 2011. "Fair Scheduling in Networks Through Packet Election." *IEEE Transactions on Information Theory* 57(3): 1368–1381.

Jagpal, S. 1999. *Marketing Strategy and Uncertainty*. New York: Oxford University Press.

Jain, R., D. W. Chiu, and W. Hawe. 1984. A Quantitative Measure of Fairness and Discrimination for Resource Allocation in Shared Computer Systems. Digital Equipment Corporation. Technical Report TR-301.

Kahneman, D. 2011. *Thinking, Fast and Slow*. New York: Farrar, Straus and Giroux.

Kandel, E. R., J. H. Schwartz, and T. M. Jessell. 2000. *Principles of Neural Science*. 4th ed. New York: McGraw-Hill.

Kelly, J. L., Jr. 1956. "A New Interpretation of Information Rate." *Bell System Technical Journal* 35: 917–926.

Kim, G., and H. M. Markowitz. 1989. "Investment Rules, Margin, and Market Volatility." *Journal of Portfolio Management* 16(1): 45–52. Reproduced in Markowitz (2010b).

Kiviat, P. J., R. Villanueva, and H. M. Markowitz. 1968. The SIMSCRIPT II Programming Language. Santa Monica, CA: The RAND Corporation Memorandum R-460-PR.

Kleene, S. C. 1971. *Introduction to Metamathematics*. Groningen, Netherlands: Wolters-Noordhoff Publishing.

Knuth, D. E. 1964. "Backus Normal Form vs. Backus Naur Form." *Communications of the ACM* 7(12): 735–736.

Kolmogorov, A. N., and S. V. Fomin. 1957. *Elements of the Theory of Functions and Functional Analysis*. Rochester, NY: Graylock Press.

Kritzman, M., S. Myrgren, and S. Page. 2009. "Optimal Rebalancing: A Scalable Solution." *Journal of Investment Management* 7(1): 9–19.

Kuhn, H. W., and S. Nasar, eds. 2002. *The Essential John Nash*. Princeton, NJ: Princeton University Press.

Lan, T., D. Kao, M. Chiang, and A. Sabharwal. 2010. "An Axiomatic Theory of Fairness in Network Resource Allocation." 2010 Proceedings IEEE INFOCOM, San Diego, CA.

Latané, H. A. 1957. "Rational Decision Making in Portfolio Management." PhD Dissertation, University of North Carolina.

———. 1959. "Criteria for Choice Among Risky Ventures." *Journal of Political Economy* 67(2): 144–155.

Levy, H. "Aging Population, Retirement and Risk Taking." *Management Science:* (forthcoming).

Levy, M., H. Levy, and S. Solomon. 2000. *Microscopic Simulation of Financial Markets: From Investor Behavior to Market Phenomena.* San Diego, CA: Academic Press.

Luce, R. D., and H. Raiffa. 1957. *Games and Decisions: Introduction and Critical Survey.* New York: Dover Publications.

Macaulay, F. R. 1938. *Some Theoretical Problems Suggested by the Movements of Interest Rates, Bond Yields and Stock Prices in the United States Since 1856.* New York: Columbia University Press.

MacLean, L. C., E. O. Thorp, and W. T. Ziemba, eds. 2011. *The Kelly Capital Growth Investment Criterion: Theory and Practice.* Hackensack, NJ: World Scientific Publishing Co.

Malhotra, A., H. M. Markowitz, and D. P. Pazel. 1983. "EAS-E: An Integrated Approach to Application Development." *ACM Transactions on Database Systems (TODS)* 8(4): 515–542. Reproduced in Markowitz (2010b).

Markowitz, H. M. 1952a. "Portfolio Selection." *Journal of Finance* 7(1): 77–91. Reproduced in Markowitz (2010b).

———. 1952b. "The Utility of Wealth." *Journal of Political Economy* 7(1): 151. Reproduced in Markowitz (2010b).

———. 1957. "The Elimination Form of the Inverse and Its Application to Linear Programming." *Management Science* 3(3): 255–269.

———. 1959. *Portfolio Selection: Efficient Diversification of Investments.* 2nd ed. (1991). New York: John Wiley & Sons.

———. 1976. "Investments for the Long Run: New Evidence for an Old Rule." *Journal of Finance* 31(3): 1273–1286. Reproduced in Markowitz (2010b).

———. 1979. SIMSCRIPT. In *Encyclopedia of Computer Science and Technology*, ed. J. Belzer, A. G. Holzman, and A. Kent. New York: Marcel Dekker. Reproduced in Markowitz (2010b).

———. 1987. *Mean-Variance Analysis in Portfolio Choice and Capital Markets*. Cambridge, MA: Basil Blackwell.

———. 1991. "Individual Versus Institutional Investing." *Financial Services Review* 1(1): 1–8. Reproduced in Markowitz (2010b).

———. 2006. "Samuelson and Investment for the Long Run." In *Samuelsonian Economics and the Twenty-First Century*, ed. M. Szenberg, L. Ramrattan, and A. A. Gottesman, 252–261. Oxford: Oxford University Press.

———. 2010a. "Portfolio Theory: As I Still See It." In *Annual Review of Financial Economics*, ed. A. W. Lo and R. C. Merton, 1–23. Palo Alto, CA: Annual Reviews.

———. 2010b. *Selected Works*. Hackensack, NJ: World Scientific Publishing Co.

———. 2015. "Consumption, Investment and Insurance in the Game of Life." *Journal of Investment Management* 13(1): 1–19.

Markowitz, H. M., B. Hausner, and H. W. Karr. 1962. SIMSCRIPT: A Simulation Programming Language. Santa Monica, CA: The RAND Corporation Memorandum 3310-PR.

———. 1963. *SIMSCRIPT: A Simulation Programming Language*. New Jersey: Prentice-Hall.

Markowitz, H. M., A. Malhotra, and D. P. Pazel. 1983. "The ER and EAS Formalisms for System Modeling, and the EAS-E Language." In *Entity-Relationship Approach to Information Modeling and Analysis*, ed. P. P. Chen, 29–47. (North Holland) ER Institute: Elsevier Science Publishers B. V. Reproduced in Markowitz (2010b).

Markowitz, H. M., and G. P. Todd. 2000. *Mean-Variance Analysis in Portfolio Choice and Capital Markets*. Hoboken, NJ: Wiley.

Markowitz, H. M., and N. Usmen. 1996a. "The Likelihood of Various Stock Market Return Distributions, Part 1: Principles of Inference." *Journal of Risk and Uncertainty* 13: 207–219. Reproduced in Markowitz (2010b).

———. 1996b. "The Likelihood of Various Stock Market Return Distributions, Part 2: Empirical Results." *Journal of Risk and Uncertainty* 13: 221–247. Reproduced in Markowitz (2010b).

Markowitz, H. M., and E. L. van Dijk. 2003. "Single-Period Mean-Variance Analysis in a Changing World." *Financial Analysts Journal* 59(2): 30–44. Reproduced in Markowitz (2010b).

Merton, R. C. 1990. *Continuous-Time Finance.* Cambridge, MA: Blackwell Publishers. Reprint, 1993.

Michaud, R. O. 1998. *Efficient Asset Management: A Practical Guide to Stock Portfolio Optimization and Asset Allocation.* Boston: Harvard Business School Press.

Moore, G. E. 1965. "Cramming More Components onto Integrated Circuits." *Electronics Magazine,* 114–117.

———. 2006. "Moore's Law at 40." In *Understanding Moore's Law: Four Decades of Innovation,* ed. D. Brock. Philadelphia: Chemical Heritage Foundation.

Mossin, J. 1968. "Optimal Multiperiod Portfolio Policies." *Journal of Business* 41(2): 215–229.

Nash, J. 1950a. "The Bargaining Problem." *Econometrica* 18(2): 155–162.

———. 1950b. "Equilibrium Points in n-Person Games." *Proceedings of the National Academy of Sciences* 36(1): 48–49.

———. 1951. "Non-Cooperative Games." *Annals of Mathematics* 54(2): 286–295. Reproduced in Kuhn and Nasar (2002).

Oldfather, P. M., A. S. Ginsberg, and H. M. Markowitz. 1966. Programming by Questionnaire: How to Construct a Program Generator. Santa Monica, CA: The RAND Corporation Memorandum RM-5129-PR.

Pazel, D. P., A. Malhotra, and H. M. Markowitz. 1983. "The System Architecture of EAS-E: An Integrated Programming and Data Base Language." *IBM Systems Journal* 22(3): 188–198. Reproduced in Markowitz (2010b).

Pratt, J. W. 1964. "Risk Aversion in the Small and in the Large." *Econometrica* 32(1–2): 122–136.

Reid, D. W., and B. V. Tew. 1987. "An Evaluation of Expected Value and Expected Value-Variance Criteria in Achieving Risk Efficiency in Crop Selection." *Northeustern Journal of Agricultural and Resource Economics* 16(2).

Rice, S. V., H. M. Markowitz, A. Marjanski, and S. M. Bailey. 2005. "The SIMSCRIPT III Programming Language for Modular Object-Oriented Simulation." Proceedings of the 37th Conference on Winter Simulation.

Robinson, A. 1974. *Non-Standard Analysis.* New York: American Elsevier Publishing Co.

Roy, A. D. 1952. "Safety First and the Holding of Assets." *Econometrica* 20(3): 431–449.

Russell, E. C. 1975. *Simulating with Processes and Resources in SIMSCRIPT II.5.* Los Angeles: CACI, Inc.

Samuelson, P. A. 1969. "Lifetime Portfolio Selection by Dynamic Stochastic Programming." *Review of Economics and Statistics* 51(3).

———. 1979. "Why We Should Not Make Mean Log of Wealth Big Though Years to Act Are Long." *Journal of Banking & Finance* 3(4): 305–307.

Savage, L. J. 1954. *The Foundations of Statistics.* 2nd revised ed. (1972). Dover, NY: John Wiley & Sons.

Savage, S. L. 2009. *The Flaw of Averages: Why We Underestimate Risk in the Face of Uncertainty.* Hoboken, NJ: John Wiley & Sons.

Sharpe, W. F. 1963. "A Simplified Model for Portfolio Analysis." *Management Science* 9(2): 277–293.

Sharpe, W. F., and L. G. Tint. 1990. "Liabilities—A New Approach." *Journal of Portfolio Management* 16(2): 5–10.

Shefrin, H., and M. Statman. 2000. "Behavioral Portfolio Theory." *Journal of Financial and Quantitative Analysis* 35(2): 127–151.

Simon, H. A. 1947. *Administrative Behavior: A Study of Decision-Making Processes in Administrative Organizations.* 4th ed. (1997). New York: Free Press.

Sun, W., A. Fan, L. W. Chen, T. Schouwenaars, and M. A. Albota. 2006a. "Optimal Rebalancing for Institutional Portfolios." *Journal of Portfolio Management* 32(2): 33–43.

———. 2006b. "Using Dynamic Programming to Optimally Rebalance Portfolios." *Journal of Trading* 1(2): 16–27.

Towler, G., and R. Sinnott. 2013. *Chemical Engineering Design: Principles, Practice and Economics of Plant and Process Design*: Amsterdam: Elsevier.

Turing, A. M. 1936–1937. "On Computable Numbers, with an Application to the Entscheidungs Problem." *Proceedings of the London Mathematical Society* 42: 230–265. *A correction*, ibid., Vol. 43 (1937), pp. 544–546.

Valentas, K., L. Levine, and J. P. Clark. 1991. *Food Processing Operations and Scale-Up*. New York: Marcel Dekker.

von Aspen, J. 2014. *Getting Started in SAP: How to Transform Your Career and Become a Highly Paid SAP Expert*. CreateSpace Independent Publishing Platform.

von Neumann, J. 1958. *The Computer and the Brain*. 3rd ed. (2012). New Haven, CT: Yale University Press.

von Neumann, J., and O. Morgenstern. 1944. *Theory of Games and Economic Behavior*. 3rd ed. (1953). Princeton, NJ: Princeton University Press.

Wets, R. J.-B., and W. T. Ziemba, eds. 1999. *Annals of Operations Research*. Vol. 85. Amsterdam: Baltzer Science Publishers.

Wilkerson, B., and M. Allen. 2005. *Parallel Programming: Techniques and Applications Using Networked Workstations and Parallel Computers*. 2nd ed. Upper Saddle River, NJ: Pearson Education.

Ziemba, W. T. 2015. "Portfolio Optimization: Theory and Practice." In *Quantitative Financial Risk Management: Theory and Practice*, ed. C. Zopounidis and E. Galariotis, 155–211. Hoboken, NJ: Wiley.

Ziemba, W. T., and J. M. Mulvey, eds. 1998. *Worldwide Asset and Liability Modeling*. Cambridge, UK: Cambridge University Press.

INDEX

ABOUT THE AUTHOR

Harry M. Markowitz is a Nobel Laureate and the father of Modern Portfolio Theory. Named "Man of the Century" by *Pensions & Investments* magazine, he is a recipient of the Prestigious John von Neumann Theory Prize for his work in portfolio theory, sparse matrix techniques, and the SIMSCRIPT programming language.